1962

This book may be ker

A REVIEW OF GERMAN

A
REVIEW OF GERMAN

GRAMMAR PRACTICE
BASED ON SELECTED TEXTS

BY

STEN G. FLYGT
VANDERBILT UNIVERSITY

W · W · NORTON & COMPANY · INC · New York

The use of material from *Das Tropenaquarium* and
Der große Krieg in Deutschland has been authorized
by Dr. Thure von Uexküll and Frau Marietta Bohm.

Contents

Foreword

Probably most students of a foreign language, no matter what the method or book used to introduce them to it, feel their knowledge of the grammatical structure of that language is inadequate. Even though the instruction may be excellent and the achievement of the student satisfactory, he is haunted by the sense that he isn't really "getting" it. Hence the continuing demand for skeleton grammars, outline grammars, and tricky devices of various sorts which the student most frequently is unable to use properly. Hence, too, the practice, once almost universal, of using a review grammar, a practice which has come to have fewer and fewer adherents for a number of reasons, two especially: the study of grammar for grammar's sake has grown increasingly repugnant and foreign to students in the United States and the time used in learning the abstract structure of a language has come to seem time stolen from the more urgent task of reading material of literary or cultural significance.

The last-mentioned objection might vanish, however, if study material of literary and cultural significance could be combined with a synoptic review of the grammatical structure of the language by means of stimulating exercises. For exercises need not be the tedious repetition of empty paradigms but instead can be addressed both to the meaningful manipulation of intellectually respectable material and to rigid semantic scrutiny of grammatical forms. A textbook of this sort might satisfy the student's and the teacher's craving for system without sacrifice of other more important values.

This book is an attempt to effect such a combination. It has been tested in a number of situations and found adaptable to various purposes. It has been used where the review grammar has traditionally been used, at the beginning of the second year. But it has also been used successfully in the last twelve weeks or so of the first year, after the students have finished the introductory grammar and supplementary readings. Thus it holds out the very exciting prospect of enabling a first-year student to come to grips with the actual words of such illustrious figures as Mozart, Schopenhauer, and Alexander von Humboldt.

This kind of reading is made possible by the use of parallel German and English texts. Although this method of teaching has gained increasing acceptance in the last fifteen years or so, a word or two about the advantages of the method may be in order.

The most striking advantage has already been stated by implication: it eliminates the necessity of using simple-minded texts written in painful "Baby German" or "Grammar Dutch" and permits the early use of authentic material. But the other advantages are great also. For one thing, it cuts to a minimum the time lost in the relatively unprofitable task of thumbing through the pages of a glossary and in the frustrating uncertainty whether a given combination of words really means what it seems to mean. The time thus gained can be used to great advantage in building up a large vocabulary and in practicing difficulties of syntax until they are mastered. For another thing, the parallel-text plan makes possible the standard of complete understanding of the text being studied and the standard of a fully acceptable normal English version. Indeed, it gives the student some notion of the art of translation and makes him aware, perhaps for the first time in his experience, that the normal modes of English idiom are not the inevitable embodiment of the universal laws of thought.* It is, of course, not to be inferred that the translations here supplied are deemed the perfect or the best possible translations. Rather, much can be gained in the way of sharpening the student's sense of style and idiom by encouraging him to improve upon the English

* For a discussion of the pre-eminent importance of language study in general liberal education see S. G. Flygt, "Ends vs. Goals in Foreign Language Study," *Journal of General Education,* April 1951.

versions both in the basic texts and in the exercises. Finally, perhaps it should be pointed out that the use of a translation, while it simplifies the student's task in the sense that it eliminates much unprofitable effort, does not make the study of language easy and does not in any sense cheapen it, but indeed, for all the reasons mentioned, makes possible a deepening and enrichment of it, by enabling the student to focus his attention sharply upon matters of form, syntax, idiom, and style.

SUGGESTIONS FOR USING THE TEXT

Perhaps the first thing to be said about using this book is that it is thoroughly integrated. The German texts are basic to each lesson, the Grammatical Comment discusses grammatical features which are prominent in the text, and the Exercises exemplify and afford practice in the material of the immediate Unit and also of preceding Units. As the instructor works his way through the book he will find that the practice material is cumulative in its arrangement and effect. Those points of grammar which require the most practice—verb forms, use of tenses, word order—come earliest in the book, and those matters which cause least impediment to understanding—substantives and adjectives—come last. Every one of the ten Units is designed to afford practice in verb forms; every one of the last nine Units affords practice in the use of tenses; every one of the last eight, practice in peculiarities of word order; and so on. The principle of cumulative effect applies also to the matters of idiom which are explained in the footnotes of the German text. The principle of cumulative effect, however, does not apply to the subject matter and intrinsic difficulty of the texts themselves. Since the texts have not been composed for the purpose of this book and have not been "doctored" in any way save by occasional omissions, they are of somewhat varying and not regularly increasing degrees of difficulty. This arrangement simulates the natural experience of reading a fairly wide selection of books or essays as interest dictates and may help to prepare the student for the sometimes rather rude shock of disillusionment which he is likely to experience after he has learned the material in his courses well and sets out to read something on his own.

After this general observation it may be in order to give a specific account of how this book has been used successfully.

In the first class meeting the instructor goes through the basic text of the first Unit, reading it aloud very slowly, discussing the translation, looking up the notes, and explaining whatever difficulties may arise. The first assignment is to master the German text, and here it may be emphasized that nothing less than full understanding of the meaning of every word and phrase, *out of context,* should be the aim and standard in this part of the work.

In the second meeting the students are checked on their mastery of the text and the remaining time is devoted to a discussion of the Grammatical Comment, that is, to as much of the Comment as the instructor feels will need further explanation and clarification. The out-of-class assignment is to work out with the aid of the Grammatical Comment the first section of the Exercises, which requires the student to underline the correct word or words. These first Exercises for all Units are grouped at the end of the text as pages 179-210, which can be torn out of the book and handed in at the beginning of the third meeting, to be corrected by the instructor and returned at his convenience.

The third meeting can then be devoted to working out in class the remaining Exercises or as much of this material as time and the purpose of the instructor make it expedient to do. In some Units the remaining Exercises can be done very handily in the class hour, in other Units they will take more time. If the instructor has no more than ten or eleven weeks to devote to this text he can keep within his allotted time by omitting certain portions of the Exercises. Or, if he has more time, he can spend as many additional meetings on the Exercises as he deems desirable.

In other words, it is expected that the average number of class meetings required to complete a Unit will be three. Some, like the second and the tenth, can be done in two days, whereas others may require four days. The fourth and the seventh Units, incidentally, have been found to require more time than the others.

Perhaps a word might be in order as to the nature of the Exercises. A glance at them will show that they employ a number of rather novel techniques, all based upon the conviction that the student's growing but uncertain *Sprachgefühl* should not be confused by his being confronted by a multitude of truncated forms and by incorrect grammar, nor should he be required to juggle empty paradigms and construct meaningless sentences. But he is required to focus his attention sharply upon sentences of respectable intellectual content in order to ascertain the precise meaning of the correct forms he has before him. The exercises require the student to perform certain tasks which should interest him because of the purposiveness which is derived from their subject matter. The task is ostensibly of semantic import, but the correct performance of it is dependent upon accurate and precise grammatical knowledge. In this connection it cannot be overemphasized that the important thing is not the solutions of the problems as such, but *rather the process of arriving at the solutions.* For this reason the student must translate accurately every German sentence in the Exercises and understand why one sentence or one solution is either the only correct one or the best one.

A word about examinations. Experience has shown that frequent hour examinations on the material of this book are helpful. They can perhaps best be given at the end of the third, the sixth, and the tenth Units. They can be taken directly from the texts and Exercises or, preferably, they can be based upon a reworking of the material studied. In order to facilitate the task of constructing new sentences for such examinations, each word entered in the vocabulary is followed by an Arabic numeral which indicates in which Unit the word was first used. This will enable the instructor to make up new sentences at any stage and be sure that he is not using words which the student has not yet encountered.

I wish to express my indebtedness to my colleague, Professor Paul Guenther, of Vanderbilt University, for giving me the benefit of his experience with this book, and to Professor Thomas E. Colby, of Columbia University, who used a preliminary form of it in one of his classes and made many and useful specific suggestions. I am especially pleased to acknowledge my indebtedness to Professor Jack M. Stein, of Harvard University, the editor of German texts for W. W. Norton & Company, with whom I have exchanged ideas about techniques, methods, and aims of language teaching for a good many years. Indeed, it is likely that this book would never have been written, had not Professor Stein persuaded me that it or something like it might make a useful contribution to the craft of our profession.

STEN G. FLYGT

Vanderbilt University

A REVIEW OF GERMAN

To the Student

In each of the following Units you will find a short passage in German, by a well-known or even illustrious writer, and a translation of that passage into normal English. You will be expected to master the German text with the help of the translation. Work over the German as often as you need to in order to be able to read it through rapidly and understand it completely as you read. Do not be content with partial mastery.

In some instances, English idiom requires that a German clause or phrase be translated freely. In such cases, the Notes to the English Text will supply a literal translation so that you can analyze and understand the German construction. The Notes to the German Text, however, direct your attention to certain expressions which occur so frequently and are so important that you will be required to memorize and practice them.

Following the German Text, its translation, and the Notes, you will find a systematic discussion of some points of grammar with illustrations drawn from the German text you will have mastered. Study this discussion of the grammar and refer to it when you work out the exercises which illustrate what has been explained and which are based upon the German text of the chapter.

You are also urged to read the Foreword so as to gain a better understanding of the aims of this book and of the techniques which it employs. You are apt to profit more from using it if you have a good idea of the theory of language teaching and learning which underlies it.

FIRST UNIT

A SELECTION FROM

Peter Schlemihls
wundersame Geschichte

BY ADELBERT VON CHAMISSO

(1781-1838)

It is usually an occasion for admiring amazement when anyone attains literary success in a language which is not native to him. And to achieve the stature of a minor classic in the literature of one's adopted country, although not unique, is indeed a noteworthy accomplishment. For examples of this kind of distinction one thinks at once, in English literature, of Joseph Conrad, and in German literature, of Adelbert von Chamisso.

Chamisso was born in 1781 of wealthy and titled parents at the chateau of Boncourt in the province of Champagne in France. His father, the Count de Chamisso de Boncourt, had risen to a position of influence in the service of Louis XVI and thus found it necessary to emigrate together with his family as the revolutionary forces became unbridled. For some years the family was dispersed throughout German territories, eking out a precarious living. Finally young Adelbert gained a foothold in the Prussian court and embarked upon a military career, which he abandoned for literary and scientific studies as soon as possible, for unlike most of the *émigrés,* he had been fired with enthusiasm for the literature and culture of the land which had sheltered him. He was never able, however, to make a complete break with the past and his own

4

origins: he spoke German with an accent to the end of his life and was always haunted by a sense of divided loyalty.

Something of this sense of not belonging can be detected in the novella *Peter Schlemihls wundersame Geschichte,* from which the first reading selection is taken. *Peter Schlemihl* is one of those truly popular stories which become best sellers all over the globe. The fantastic realism of the story about the man who traded his shadow for immense wealth and thereby made himself unhappy for life has the universal fascination of the fairy tale combined with the challenge to interpretation of self-conscious modern symbolism, a symbolism which is announced in the very name of the hero. For *Schlemihl* is a word taken from Yiddish argot which signifies a clumsy person who through no real fault of his own fails at everything, a ne'er do well, a lout. But Schlemihl is more than merely a vehicle to communicate Chamisso's sense of personal frustration, for Schlemihl must engage in a desperate struggle against the temptation to compromise with evil in order to gain acceptance by his fellow human beings—a struggle which is not limited to any particular time or place or person.

AUS PETER SCHLEMIHLS
WUNDERSAME GESCHICHTE
VON ADELBERT VON CHAMISSO

Wie erschrak ich, als ich den Mann im grauen Rock hinter mir
her[1] * und auf mich zu[2] kommen sah. Er nahm sogleich den Hut
vor mir ab und verneigte sich so tief, als noch niemand vor mir
getan hatte. Es war kein Zweifel, er wollte mich anreden, und ich
5 konnte, ohne grob zu sein, es nicht vermeiden. Ich nahm den Hut
auch ab, verneigte mich wieder und stand da in der Sonne mit
bloßem Haupt wie angewurzelt. Ich sah ihn voller Furcht stier an
und war wie ein Vogel, den eine Schlange gebannt hat. Er selber
schien sehr verlegen zu sein; er hob den Blick nicht auf, verbeugte
10 sich zu verschiedenen Malen, trat näher und redete mich an mit
leiser, unsicherer Stimme, ungefähr im Tone eines Bettelnden.

„Möge der Herr meine Zudringlichkeit entschuldigen, wenn ich
es wage ihn so unbekannter Weise aufzusuchen; ich habe eine
Bitte an ihn.[3] Während der kurzen Zeit, wo ich das Glück genoss
15 mich in Ihrer Nähe zu befinden, hab' ich einigemal — erlauben
Sie, daß ich es Ihnen sage — mit unaussprechlicher Bewunderung
den schönen Schatten betrachten können, den Sie in der Sonne,
und gleichsam[4] mit einer gewissen edlen Verachtung ohne selbst
darauf zu merken, von sich werfen, den herrlichen Schatten da zu
20 Ihren Füßen. Verzeihen Sie mir die freilich kühne Zumutung.
Sollten Sie sich wohl nicht abgeneigt finden mir diesen Ihren
Schatten zu überlassen?" Er schwieg, und mir ging's wie ein
Mühlrad im Kopfe herum.[5] Was sollt' ich aus dem seltsamen
Antrag machen mir meinen Schatten abzukaufen? Er muß verrückt

* Notes to the German Text are on page 8 of this Unit and in corresponding positions in other Units.

PETER SCHLEMIHLS

WUNDERSAME GESCHICHTE

ADELBERT VON CHAMISSO

How startled I was when I saw the man in the gray coat coming
along behind and [right]*ᵃ* * up to me. He immediately doffed his
hat and bowed lower than anybody had ever bowed to me before.*ᵇ*
There was no doubt that he wanted to speak to me and I could not
avoid it without being rude. I doffed my hat and bowed, too, and **5**
stood there bareheaded in the sun as though rooted to the spot.
I stared at him fearfully,*ᶜ* like a bird charmed by a snake. He
seemed to be very embarrassed himself; he did not look up, bowed
a good many times, came closer and addressed me in a soft and
unsure voice, something like that of a beggar.*ᵈ*   **10**
 "Please excuse my forwardness in venturing to approach you
thus, Sir, even though you do not know me.*ᵉ* I have a request [to
make] of you. During the short time that I had the good fortune
to be near you—[if] you will permit me to say so—I was occasionally able to observe with inexpressible admiration that lovely **15**
shadow, which you, so to speak, cast away in the sun with a certain
aristocratic disdain and without paying any attention to it, that
wonderful shadow there at your feet.*ᶠ* Pardon my, to be sure,
[rather] daring presumption. Perhaps you might feel inclined to
dispose of it to me?"*ᵍ* He said no more and things went around in **20**
my head like a mill wheel. What was I to make of this strange pro-
posal to buy my shadow? "He must be crazy," I thought, and in an
altered tone which was better suited to the obsequiousness of his
own I replied: "Come, come, my friend, aren't you satisfied with

* Notes to the English Text are on page 9 of this Unit and in corresponding positions in other Units.

25 sein, dacht' ich; und mit verändertem Tone, der zu der Demut des seinigen besser paßte, erwiderte ich also: „Ei ei, guter Freund, habt Ihr denn[6] nicht an Eurem eigenen Schatten genug? Ich verstehe wohl Ihre Meinung nicht ganz gut; wie könnt' ich nur meinen Schatten . . ." Er unterbrach mich: „Ich erbitte mir nur Erlaubnis, 30 hier auf der Stelle diesen edlen Schatten aufheben zu dürfen und zu mir zu stecken; wie ich das mache, sei meine Sorge. Dagegen als Beweis meiner Erkenntlichkeit gegen den Herrn überlasse ich ihm die Wahl unter allen Kleinodien, die ich in der Tasche bei mir führe: die echte Springwurzel, Wechselpfennige, Raubtaler, 35 das Tellertuch von Rolands Knappen, ein Galgenmännlein zu beliebigem Preis; doch, das wird wohl[7] nichts für Sie sein; besser Fortunati Wünschhütlein, neu und haltbar restauriert; auch ein Glückssäckel, wie der seine." „Fortunati Glückssäckel," fiel ich ihm in die Rede, und wie groß meine Angst auch[8] war, hatte er 40 mit dem einen Wort meinen ganzen Sinn gefangen. Ich bekam einen Schwindel, und es flimmerte mir wie doppelte Dukaten vor den Augen.

„Belieben gnädigst der Herr diesen Säckel zu besichtigen und zu erproben." Er steckte die Hand in die Tasche und zog einen 45 mäßig großen, festgenähten Beutel von starkem Leder an zwei tüchtigen ledernen Schnüren heraus und händigte mir selbigen ein. Ich griff hinein und zog zehn Goldstücke daraus, und wieder zehn, und wieder zehn, und wieder zehn; ich hielt ihm schnell die Hand hin: „Topp! der Handel gilt,[9] für den Beutel haben Sie 50 meinen Schatten." Er schlug ein, kniete vor mir nieder, und mit einer bewundernswürdigen Geschicklichkeit sah ich ihn meinen Schatten, vom Kopf bis zu meinen Füßen, leise von dem Grase lösen, aufheben, zusammenrollen und falten und zuletzt einstecken.

NOTES TO THE GERMAN TEXT

1. **hinter mir her** *along behind me.*
2. **auf mich zu** *up to me.*
3. **eine Bitte an ihn** *a request of him.*
4. **gleichsam** (an adverb) *so to speak, as it were.*
5. **mir ging's im Kopfe herum** *it went around in my head, my head swam.*

your own shadow?*ʰ* I probably don't really understand what you 25
mean; how could I possibly . . ."*ⁱ* He interrupted me: "I am only
requesting permission to pick up and pocket this magnificent
shadow right now. Let it be my concern how I do it. In return, as
proof of my gratitude to you, Sir, I will give you the choice of all
the treasures which I have with me in my pocket: a genuine pick- 30
lock, gold-bearing pennies, homing Taler, the tablecloth [that once
belonged to] Roland's page boy, a gallows mannikin at a suitable
price. Still, this is probably not for you. Fortunatus' wishing-cap
[would be] better, durably made over not long ago; also a purse
just like his."*ʲ* "Fortunatus' purse," I interrupted him,*ᵏ* and how- 35
ever great my uneasiness was, with that one word he had caught
all my attention. I grew faint and there was a flickering before my
eyes like double ducats.

"If you will be so good, Sir, as to examine this purse and try it
out."*ˡ* He put his hand in his pocket and pulled out a moderately 40
large well-stitched purse of strong leather with*ᵐ* two stout leather
thongs and handed it to me. I put my hand in and pulled out ten
gold pieces, and another ten and another ten and another ten;
I quickly held out my hand to him: "Agreed! The deal stands. For
that purse you [may] have my shadow." He shook my hand, knelt 45
down before me, and I saw him with admirable adroitness gently
pry my shadow loose from the grass from head to toe, raise it, roll
it up, fold it, and finally put it in his pocket.

NOTES TO THE ENGLISH TEXT

a.   Words in brackets have been supplied by the translator for
the sake of smoother English.

b.   **verneigte sich so tief, als noch niemand vor mir getan hatte**
bowed as low as nobody had yet done before me.

c.   **Ich sah ihn voller Furcht stier an**   *I looked at him staringly
full of fear.*

d.   **ungefähr im Tone eines Bettelnden**   *approximately in the
tone of one begging.*

e.   **„Möge der Herr meine Zudringlichkeit entschuldigen, wenn
ich es wage ihn so unbekannter Weise aufzusuchen."**   *May
the gentleman excuse my forwardness, if I venture to seek
him out in such an unacquainted way.* The man in the gray
coat addresses Peter Schlemihl with exaggerated respect.

6. **denn:** in a question this word indicates interest on the part of the speaker; do not translate.

7. **wohl** *probably, no doubt.* When used thus with **wohl** the future tense may be translated by the English present; similarly, the future perfect with **wohl** may be translated by the English past. See the Second Unit, Grammatical Comment I B 4.

8. **wie groß auch** *however great, no matter how great.* This is one of the important uses of **auch:** to express concession. Cf. **wenn meine Angst auch groß war** *even though my fear was great.*

9. **gilt** *is valid.* The verb **gelten (galt, gegolten, gilt)** is frequently very hard to translate. It has such meanings as: *be worth, have value, be valid, be accepted, apply to.*

f. hab' ich einigemal mit unaussprechlicher Bewunderung den schönen Schatten betrachten können, den Sie in der Sonne und gleichsam mit einer gewissen edlen Verachtung ohne selbst darauf zu merken, von sich werfen. *I have a few times been able to observe with inexpressible admiration the beautiful shadow which you cast from yourself in the sun and, so to speak, with a certain aristocratic disdain, without paying attention to it yourself.*

g. „Sollten Sie sich wohl nicht abgeneigt finden?" *Should you perhaps feel not disinclined?*

h. habt Ihr denn nicht an Eurem eigenen Schatten genug? *haven't you enough with your own shadow?* (What is the function of **denn**?)

i. wie könnt' ich nur meinen Schatten [verkaufen]?

j. The **Springwurzel** can open any lock; a **Wechselpfennig** produces a gold coin every time it is turned; a **Raubtaler**, a coin, always returns to its owner and brings with it all the other coins which it has touched; the tablecloth produces all sorts of fine food and drink upon command; a **Galgenmännlein** may be dug up under a gallows and will help its owner find hidden treasure; Fortunatus had a wishing-cap and purse with magic powers.

k. fiel ich ihm in die Rede   *I fell into his speech.*

l. Belieben gnädigst der Herr etc.: The subject, **der Herr**, has a plural verb for extreme courtesy: *Will the gentleman most graciously deign etc.*

m. **an:** here, *by means of.*

GRAMMATICAL COMMENT—
VERBS: THE BASIC FORMS

I. Principal Parts

  A. As you know, English and German are sister languages and therefore have strong family resemblances. Some of the most striking resemblances occur in the verb systems of the two languages and can readily be seen when we compare the principal parts of corresponding English and German verbs:

	INFINITIVE	SIMPLE PAST	PAST PARTICIPLE
WEAK	*fold*	*folded*	*folded*
	falten	**faltete**	**gefaltet**
STRONG	*fall*	*fell*	*fallen*
	fallen	**fiel**	**gefallen**

  B. The principal parts of a verb are so called because they are the forms which tell us what all the other forms are and help us to grasp the entire system to which any particular verb form may belong. (It is therefore very important to learn the principal parts of unfamiliar verbs as you look them up.) In German, as in English, there are two main types of verb systems which have been given the fanciful but time-honored names "weak" and "strong." There is also in German a class of verbs called "mixed," and a very small group of irregulars.

II. Weak Verbs

  A. The weak verb system, as you can see from the example **falten,** in the first paragraph, is very simple: the vowel of the stem (falt-) never changes, and "pastness," both in the simple past and the past participle, is indicated by an added *t:* **faltete, gefaltet.** This *t* is so important in indicating pastness that, if, for example, the verb stem ends in *d* or *t* as does **falt-,** it is set off from the stem by an inserted *e,* so that it can be heard distinctly. In such verbs as **stecken**, however, no such *e* is needed and the principal parts of this verb are: **stecken, steckte, gesteckt.** The stem of **stecken**, of course, is **steck-**.

B. As you have already discovered, word endings are very important in German, just as important as they are in English, but there are many more of them. Thus, whereas English has only one regular present tense ending, namely *s* for the third person singular, German has four different endings, but two of them do double duty, so to speak. Observe the present tenses of the two weak verbs we have considered, which are to be taken as patterns for all weak German verbs:

SINGULAR		PLURAL	
ich steck -e	*I stick*	wir steck -en	*we stick*
du steck -st	*you stick*	ihr steck -t	*you stick*
er steck -t	*he sticks*	sie steck -en	*they stick*
	Sie steck -en (SING. and PL.)	*you stick*	
ich falt -e	*I fold*	wir falt -en	*we fold*
du falt -est	*you fold*	ihr falt -et	*you fold*
er falt -et	*he folds*	sie falt -en	*they fold*
	Sie falt -en	*you fold*	

Notice particularly that the *ending t* added to the stem as in **er** (**sie, es**) **steckt, er** (**sie, es**) **faltet** unmistakably identifies the form as present in tense, just as the *s* in *sticks* and *folds* identifies these two as present-tense forms.

C. The simple past tense of a verb is its second principal part with the endings appropriate to the person and number. The past forms **steckte** and **faltete**, therefore, may be analyzed as follows: present stem (**steck-, falt-**) plus tense-sign *t* (**steck-t-, falt-et-**) plus personal ending (**steck-t-e, falt-et-e**). Thus, *I stuck, was sticking, I folded, was folding*, etc.:

ich steckte	wir steckten	ich faltete	wir falteten
du stecktest	ihr stecktet	du faltetest	ihr faltetet
er steckte	sie steckten	er faltete	sie falteten
	Sie steckten		Sie falteten

Notice the one great difference between these endings and the present-tense endings, namely, that the third person singular does *not* end in *t*.

D. The future tense in German, as in English, is a compound tense made up of the present tense of the future auxiliary and the infinitive of the verb in question. Thus, *I will fold, you will fold,* etc.:

ich werde falten	wir werden falten
du wirst falten	ihr werdet falten
er wird falten	sie werden falten
Sie werden falten	

E. The perfect tenses of a German verb and an English verb resemble each other greatly in that they are both made up of a tense auxiliary and the past participle of the verb in question. Thus, the present perfect tense, *I have folded, you have folded,* etc.:

ich habe gefaltet	wir haben gefaltet
du hast gefaltet	ihr habt gefaltet
er hat gefaltet	sie haben gefaltet
Sie haben gefaltet	

and the past perfect tense, *I had folded,* etc.:

ich hatte gefaltet	wir hatten gefaltet
du hattest gefaltet	ihr hattet gefaltet
er hatte gefaltet	sie hatten gefaltet
Sie hatten gefaltet	

Not every German verb, however, has **haben** as its perfect-tense auxiliary and in this respect German parallels a usage of older English or of elevated English style. For example, one sometimes sees such sentences as "Christ is risen" instead of "Christ has risen" or "I am come to pronounce judgment" instead of "I have come." In German the verb **sein** *be* is regularly used in the formation of the perfect tenses according to a very definite rule: if a verb is intransitive, that is, if it cannot take an *accusative* object, and if it *also* signifies a change of position or condition, it requires the use of **sein** as its perfect-tense auxiliary, e.g. **Es ist unter den Tisch gerollt** *It has rolled under the table;* **Es war unter den Tisch gerollt** *It had rolled under the table.* If a verb does not fulfill *both* of these conditions it uses **haben** as its auxiliary. The present perfect and the past perfect of **rollen** are:

ich bin gerollt	wir sind gerollt
du bist gerollt	ihr seid gerollt
er ist gerollt	sie sind gerollt
	Sie sind gerollt

ich war gerollt	wir waren gerollt
du warst gerollt	ihr wart gerollt
er war gerollt	sie waren gerollt
	Sie waren gerollt

F. The future perfect tense in German also resembles the future perfect tense in English. Thus, *I will have folded,* etc.:

ich werde gefaltet haben	wir werden gefaltet haben
du wirst gefaltet haben	ihr werdet gefaltet haben
er wird gefaltet haben	sie werden gefaltet haben
	Sie werden gefaltet haben

Notice, however, the use of the perfect-tense auxiliary **sein** by intransitive verbs that show change of position or condition:

ich werde gerollt sein	*I will have rolled*
du wirst gerollt sein	*you will have rolled*
	etc.

III. Strong Verbs

A. The strong verb system follows patterns similar to such English verbs as: *fall, fell, fallen; get, got, gotten; slay, slew, slain.* That is, the pastness is indicated by a change of stem vowel in the simple past tense and in the perfect participle, e.g. **fallen, fiel, gefallen; heben, hob, gehoben.**

B. Strong verbs as well as weak verbs have personal endings and, in fact, the endings for the present tense are exactly the same:*

* Notice however that the 3rd person singular ending -*t* coalesces with the -*t* of the stem in such verbs as:

ich halte	ich rate	ich trete
du hältst	du rätst	du trittst
er hält	er rät	er tritt

ich hebe   wir heben
du hebst   ihr hebt
er hebt   sie heben
        Sie heben

The present tense of strong verbs differs from the present tense of weak verbs, however, in one important respect, namely, that in certain strong verbs there occurs a change in the stem vowel of the second and third persons *singular:*

ich falle   wir fallen
du fällst   ihr fallt
er fällt   sie fallen
        Sie fallen

Here are examples of the changes which can occur: a>ä, ich falle, du fällst, er fällt; ich fahre, du fährst, er fährt; e>i, ich vergesse, du vergißt, er vergißt; ich nehme, du nimmst, er nimmt; e>ie, ich sehe, du siehst, er sieht; o>ö, ich stoße, du stößt, er stößt; au>äu, ich laufe, du läufst, er läuft.

The best way to master this detail is to memorize the third person singular as the fourth principal part of every strong verb, thus:

nehmen   nahm   genommen   er nimmt
heben   hob   gehoben   er hebt

A list of strong verbs will be found in the Appendix.

C.   The simple-past-tense endings of strong verbs differ from those of weak verbs in two persons—the first and third persons singular have no endings:

ich hob   wir hoben
du hobst   ihr hobt
er hob   sie hoben
        Sie hoben

This lack of ending is almost as much a sign of pastness as the change of vowel and much easier to spot. Keep your eyes open for it!

D. What has been said about the formation of the present
perfect, past perfect, future, and future perfect tenses of
weak verbs holds true also for strong verbs.

PRESENT PERFECT:

ich habe	gehoben		ich bin	gefallen
du hast	gehoben		du bist	gefallen
er hat	gehoben		er ist	gefallen
wir haben	gehoben		wir sind	gefallen
ihr habt	gehoben		ihr seid	gefallen
sie haben	gehoben		sie sind	gefallen
Sie haben	gehoben		Sie sind	gefallen

PAST PERFECT:

ich hatte	gehoben		ich war	gefallen
du hattest	gehoben		du warst	gefallen

etc.

FUTURE:

ich werde	heben		ich werde fallen	
du wirst	heben		du wirst fallen	

etc.

FUTURE PERFECT:

ich werde	gehoben haben	ich werde gefallen sein
du wirst	gehoben haben	du wirst gefallen sein

etc.

IV. Mixed Verbs

There is a rather small group of verbs called "mixed" because
their simple past tense and past participle exhibit *both* a change
of vowel and *also* the tense-sign *t*. Thus:

kennen	kannte	gekannt
wenden	wandte	gewandt

As far as endings are concerned, they are just like weak verbs; as
far as auxiliaries are concerned, they exhibit no irregularities.

V. Irregular Verbs

The three most important irregular verbs with their principal
parts are **sein, haben,** and **werden:**

sein	war	(ist) gewesen	er ist
haben	hatte	gehabt	er hat
werden	wurde	(ist) geworden	er wird

You are already familiar with the present and simple past forms of **sein** and **haben** and with the present tense of **werden** from their use as tense auxiliaries. Their compound tenses follow the regular patterns. It is important to distinguish between the use of **werden** as an independent verb and **werden** as the auxiliary of the future:

Es wird kälter. *It is growing* (or *becoming* or *getting*) *colder.* (**wird** is the independent verb)
Es wird kälter werden. *It will grow colder.* (**wird** is the auxiliary of the future and **werden,** the independent verb)

More will be said about **werden** when we discuss the passive voice. See the Seventh Unit, Grammatical Comment I.

Four other important irregular verbs are:

gehen	*walk, go*	ging	(ist) gegangen	er geht
stehen	*stand*	stand	gestanden	er steht
tun	*do*	tat	getan	er tut
wissen	*know*	wußte	gewußt	er weiß

The present tense of **wissen** requires special notice:

ich weiß	wir wissen
du weißt	ihr wißt
er weiß	sie wissen
	Sie wissen

VI. Participles and Infinitives

Each verb has two infinitives and two participles: present and past. The present infinitive of a verb is its first principal part:

fallen *fall*   **falten** *fold*   **kennen** *know*

Every present infinitive ends in *n* or *en*.
The present participle of every verb ends in *nd* or *end*, which is added to the stem of the present infinitive:

fall -end *falling*   **falt -end** *folding*
kenn -end *knowing*   **veränder -nd** *changing*

The past participle of a verb is its third principal part. The past participle of weak and mixed verbs ends in *t:*

gefaltet *folded*   **verändert** *changed*
gekannt *known*

The past participle of a strong verb ends in *n:*

gefallen *fallen*   **gehoben** *raised*

The past participle of most verbs begins with the prefix *ge.* However, those verbs which do *not* bear the stress on the first syllable do not have the participle prefix *ge,* as you can see from the following principal parts:

verän′dern	veränderte	verändert	er verändert
restaurie′ren	restaurierte	restauriert	er restauriert
bekom′men	bekam	bekommen	er bekommt
genie′ßen	genoß	genossen	er genießt

The perfect infinitive of a verb is made up of its past participle and the present infinitive of its tense auxiliary:

gefaltet haben *have folded*   **gerollt sein** *have rolled*

These, of course, are the forms which occur in the future perfect tense:

ich werde gefaltet haben   *I will have folded*
es wird gerollt sein   *it will have rolled*

VII. Imperatives

There are three imperative forms: the familiar singular, the familiar plural, and the conventional, which is both singular and plural. The imperatives of weak and mixed verbs follow the patterns:

SINGULAR	PLURAL	CONVENTIONAL
mache!	macht!	machen Sie!
falte!	faltet!	falten Sie!

Many strong verbs follow this pattern also:

hebe!	hebt!	heben Sie!
falle!	fallt!	fallen Sie!

However, those strong verbs whose stem vowel changes from *e* to *i*
or *ie* in the second and third persons singular of the present tense
exhibit the same change in the singular familiar imperative:

nimm!	**nehmt!**	**nehmen Sie!**
sieh!	**seht!**	**sehen Sie!**

Moreover, the imperative ending *e* of the singular familiar is frequently omitted, especially in strong verbs, and always in those
strong verbs which exhibit the vowel change *e>i* or *e>ie:*

komm!	**nimm!**	**sieh!**

EXERCISES

[The exercises are based on the German Texts, which supply you with the necessary vocabulary and factual information to do what is required. In these and all the following exercises you will be expected to translate *every* sentence with scrupulous accuracy.]

I. *These exercises are printed at page 179, and can be detached and submitted for correction and grading if your instructor so wishes.*

II. *Arrange the following sentences according to the sequence in the text of the events which they describe.*

1. Der Mann im grauen Rock erbat sich die Erlaubnis, Schlemihls Schatten von dem Grase zu lösen und in die Tasche zu stecken.

2. Der Mann redete Schlemihl im Tone eines Bettlers an.

3. Er hatte mit unaussprechlicher Bewunderung den Schatten betrachtet, den Schlemihl in der Sonne gleichsam von sich warf.

4. Er überließ ihm die Wahl unter allen Kleinodien, die er in der Tasche bei sich führte.

5. Er ging auf ihn zu, löste den Schatten leise von dem Grase, hob ihn auf, und steckte ihn ein.

III. *Determine which German sentence best translates the English in each group. Translate each German sentence carefully.*

1. He said nothing and seemed to be very embarrassed, then quickly held out his hand to me.

a. Er sagt nichts und scheint sehr verlegen zu sein, dann hält er mir schnell die Hand hin.

b. Er hat nichts gesagt und scheint sehr verlegen zu sein, denn er hält mir schnell die Hand hin.

   c. Er schweigt und sieht sehr verlegen aus, dann schlägt er schnell ein.

   d. Er schwieg und schien sehr verlegen zu sein, dann hielt er mir schnell die Hand hin.

  2.   However rudely I had spoken to the man, he bowed lower than anybody had ever bowed to me before, for he was probably out of his mind. (See Note 8 to the German Text.)

   a. Habe ich den Mann auch grob angeredet, er verneigt sich so tief, als noch niemand vor mir getan hat, denn er wird wohl verrückt sein.

   b. Wie grob ich den Mann auch angeredet hatte, verneigte er sich so tief, als noch niemand vor mir getan hatte, denn er wird wohl verrückt gewesen sein.

   c. Wenn ich den Mann auch grob anrede, er wird sich so tief vor mir verneigen als noch niemand getan hat, denn er ist ohne Zweifel verrückt.

   d. Ich hatte aber den Mann grob angeredet, da hatte er sich so tief verneigt, als noch niemand vor mir getan hatte, denn er war ohne Zweifel verrückt.

   IV. *In this exercise are a number of words and phrases, each followed by several statements. Determine which statement is in some way associated with the word or phrase. Be sure to translate all the sentences.*

  1. angewurzelt

a. Sein Schatten war immer hinter ihm her.

b. Er erbat sich die Erlaubnis, den Schatten aufheben zu dürfen.

c. Er war wie ein Vogel, den eine Schlange gebannt hat.

d. Greifen Sie nur hinein! Der Beutel ist voller Goldstücke.

  2. passende Demut

a. Er hat das Wünschhütlein restauriert.

b. „Ich habe ein große Bitte an Sie," sagte er im Tone eines Bettelnden.

c. Lieber Herr Schlemihl, der Beweis gilt nicht.

d. Er zog zehn flimmernde Goldstücke aus dem Beutel.

3. abgeneigt

a. Er sieht ihn voller Verachtung an.
b. „Unterbrich mich nicht! Ich gebe dir gern diesen Beutel für deinen Schatten."
c. Er muß verrückt gewesen sein.
d. Er tritt näher und kniet vor mir nieder.

SECOND UNIT

AN ANECDOTE

BY JOHANN PETER HEBEL

(1760-1826)

Hebel was born in his mother's native village of Hausen, which lies northeast of Basel in the valley of the Wiese, a small tributary of the Rhine. No single fact about Hebel, perhaps, is more important than this, because it was the village and peasant life and, above all, the local dialect, which fed the sources of his poetry. And, it must be added, it was Hebel's poetry which demonstrated for the first time in Germany that the native speech of the country man can be an arrestingly beautiful vehicle of artistic expression.

The outline of his life's history is soon told. The date of his birth was 1760, the year after the birth of the Scots poet Robert Burns, who did for the Scottish speech what Hebel did for his native Alemannic. Burns excelled his German contemporary in scope, for Hebel produced only one small volume of poetry, but Hebel is fully the great Scotsman's equal in humor, vividness of narrative, poignancy of insight, and suggestiveness of phrase. There the resemblance ends, however, for Hebel, although early left an orphan, was enabled by stipends and the contributions of various interested persons to attend the *Gymnasium Illustre* in Karlsruhe and later the University of Erlangen, thus laying the foundations for a career as teacher and churchman which eventually culminated in his appointment to the highest post in the Protestant state church of the Grand Duchy of Baden.

The selection from Hebel's work here presented comes from a little book called *Schatzkästlein des rheinischen Hausfreundes.* The material in this collection came from a kind of farmers' almanac of which Hebel became the editor in 1807. Such almanacs were one of the main sources of information and entertainment of which country people availed themselves and therefore had to be full of riddles, charades, tricky arithmetic problems, and short instructive essays and anecdotes. When Hebel became responsible for the contents of the almanac he found it necessary to write a great many things to fill its pages. The result was a permanent enrichment of German literature with a store of masterful short narratives and anecdotes. One of the most famous of these is the one you are about to read.

UNVERHOFFTES WIEDERSEHEN

VON JOHANN PETER HEBEL

In Falun in Schweden küßte vor guten fünfzig Jahren und mehr
ein junger Bergmann seine junge hübsche Braut und sagte zu
ihr: „Auf Sanct Luciä wird unsere Liebe von des Priesters Hand
gesegnet. Dann sind wir Mann und Weib und bauen uns ein
5 eigenes Nestlein." — „Und Friede und Liebe soll darin wohnen!"
sagte die schöne Braut mit holdem Lächeln, „denn du bist mein
einziges und alles, und ohne dich möchte ich lieber im Grab sein
als an einem anderen Ort." Als sie aber vor St. Luciä der Pfarrer
zum zweitenmal in der Kirche aufgerufen hatte: „So nun jemand
10 Hindernis wüßte[1] anzuzeigen, warum diese Personen nicht möchten ehelich zusammen kommen," da meldete sich der Tod. Denn
als der Jüngling den andern Morgen in seiner schwarzen Bergmannskleidung an ihrem Haus vorbei ging — der Bergmann hat
sein Totenkleid immer an — da klopfte er zwar noch einmal an
15 ihrem Fenster und sagte ihr guten Morgen, aber keinen guten
Abend mehr. Er kam nimmer aus dem Bergwerk zurück, und sie
säumte vergeblich selbigen Morgen ein schwarzes Halstuch mit
rotem Rand für ihn zum Hochzeittag, sondern als er nimmer kam,
legte sie es weg und weinte um ihn und vergaß ihn nie. — Unter-
20 dessen wurde die Stadt Lissabon in Portugal durch ein Erdbeben
zerstört, der siebenjährige Krieg ging vorüber, Polen wurde
geteilt, die Kaiserin Maria Theresia starb, Amerika wurde frei,
und die vereinigte französische und spanische Macht konnte
Gibraltar nicht erobern. Die französische Revolution und der
25 lange Krieg fing an, Napoleon eroberte Preußen, die Engländer
bombardierten Kopenhagen, und die Ackerleute säten und schnitten, der Müller mahlte, die Schmiede hämmerten, und die Bergleute gruben nach den Metalladern in ihrer unterirdischen Werk-

26

UNVERHOFFTES WIEDERSEHEN

BY JOHANN PETER HEBEL

A good fifty years ago and more in Falun in Sweden a young miner kissed his pretty young bride-to-be and said to her, "On St. Lucia's day*a* our love will receive the blessing of the church.*b* Then we will be man and wife and will build ourselves a little nest of our own." — "And peace and love shall dwell therein!" said his beau- 5 tiful betrothed with a lovely smile, "for you alone are everything to me,*c* and I would rather be in the grave than in any other place without you." But when the preacher had called out their names in church for the second time before St. Lucia's day: "If now anyone should be able to give a reason why these people might 10 not be joined in matrimony," then Death spoke up. For when on the following morning the young man went by her house in his black miner's costume—the miner always wears his burial clothes— he did indeed knock once more at her window and bade her good morning, but never again a good evening. He never came back 15 from the mine and all for nothing did she on that same morning hem a red border on a black scarf [to give] him on the wedding day, but when he never returned, she put it away and wept for him and never forgot him.—Meanwhile the city of Lisbon in Por- tugal was destroyed by an earthquake,*d* the Seven Years' War 20 came to an end,*e* Poland was divided,*f* the Empress Maria Theresa died,*g* America became independent,*h* and the combined forces of France and Spain were unable to conquer Gibraltar.*i* The French Revolution and the long war commenced,*j* Napoleon de- feated Prussia,*k* the English bombarded Copenhagen,*l* and the 25 farmers sowed and harvested, the miller ground [his grist], the smiths pounded [their iron], and the miners dug for veins of metal in their underground workshop. But in the year 1809, a little

statt. Als aber die Bergleute in Falun im Jahre 1809 etwas vor oder
30 nach Johannis zwischen zwei Schachten eine Öffnung durchgraben wollten,[2] gute dreihundert Ellen tief unter dem Boden,
gruben sie aus dem Schutt und Vitriolwasser den Leichnam eines
Jünglings heraus, der ganz mit Eisenvitriol durchdrungen, sonst
aber unverwest und unverändert war; also daß man seine Ge-
35 sichtszüge und sein Alter noch völlig erkennen konnte, als wenn
er erst[3] vor einer Stunde gestorben oder ein wenig eingeschlafen
wäre an der Arbeit.

Als man ihn aber zu Tag ausgefördert hatte, waren Vater und
Mutter, Gefreunde und Bekannte schon lange tot; kein Mensch
40 wollte[4] den schlafenden Jüngling kennen oder etwas von seinem
Unglück wissen, bis die ehemalige Verlobte des Bergmanns kam,
der eines Tages auf die Schicht gegangen war und nimmer zurückkehrte. Grau und zusammengeschrumpft kam sie an einer Krücke
an den Platz und erkannte ihren Bräutigam; und mehr mit freu-
45 digem Entzücken als mit Schmerz sank sie auf die geliebte Leiche
nieder, und erst als sie sich von einer langen, heftigen Bewegung
des Gemüts erholt hatte, „es ist mein Verlobter,“ sagte sie endlich,
„um den ich fünfzig Jahre lang getrauert hatte, und den mich
Gott noch einmal sehen läßt vor meinem Ende. Acht Tage[5] vor
50 der Hochzeit ist er auf die Grube gegangen und nimmer zurückgekommen.“ Da wurden die Gemüter aller Umstehenden von
Wehmut und Tränen ergriffen, als sie sahen die ehemalige Braut
jetzt in der Gestalt des hingewelkten kraftlosen Alters und den
Bräutigam noch in seiner jugendlichen Schöne, und wie in ihrer
55 Brust nach fünfzig Jahren die Flamme der jugendlichen Liebe
noch einmal erwachte, und wie sie ihn endlich von den Bergleuten
in ihr Stüblein tragen ließ,[6] als die einzige, die ihm angehöre und
ein Recht an ihn habe, bis sein Grab gerüstet war auf dem Kirchhof. Den andern Tag, als das Grab gerüstet war auf dem Kirchhof
60 und ihn die Bergleute holten, schloß sie ein Kästlein auf, legte
ihm das schwarzseidene Halstuch mit roten Streifen um und
begleitete ihn alsdann in ihrem Sonntagsgewand, als wenn es ihr
Hochzeittag und nicht der Tag seiner Beerdigung wäre.

NOTES TO THE GERMAN TEXT

1. **So jemand Hindernis wüßte anzuzeigen** *If anybody were
able to indicate an obstacle.* **So** is archaic and elevated for

before or a little after St. John's day,[m] when the miners were about
to dig an opening through between two shafts, a good three hun- 30
dred ells down below the surface, they dug out of the rubble and
the vitriolated water the body of a young man which was completely impregnated with iron vitriol, but in other respects was
unaltered and preserved, so that his features and his age could still
be fully recognized, as though he had died only an hour before or 35
had gone to sleep a while at his work.

But when he had been brought out into the [light of] day, his
father and mother, friends[n] and acquaintances had long been
dead. Not a [single] person said he knew the sleeping youth or
anything about his mishap until there came the former fiancée of 40
the miner who had gone to work[o] one day and never returned.
Gray and shriveled, [leaning] on a crutch, she came to the place
and recognized her [former] husband-to-be; and she sank down
upon her dead love more in a transport of joy than in grief and
only after she had recovered from a long and violent tempest of 45
feelings did she finally say, "It is my betrothed, for whom I had
mourned fifty years, and whom God [now] lets me see once more
before my end. A week before the wedding he went to the mine
and never returned." Then the feelings of all the people standing
around were seized by sadness and tears when they saw the one- 50
time bride-to-be now in the shape of withered and decrepit age
and her betrothed still in the beauty of his youth, and how, after
fifty years, the flame of youthful love revived once more in her
heart, and how she finally had him taken by the miners to her
little room, as [being] the only one who belonged to him and had 55
a claim to him, until his grave should be readied in the churchyard. The following day, when the grave was ready in the churchyard and the miners came for him, she opened a little box, put the
black silk scarf with the red edge about [his neck] and then went
with him in her Sunday dress, as though it were her wedding day 60
and not the day of his burial.

NOTES TO THE ENGLISH TEXT

a. The thirteenth of December.

b. **wird von des Priesters Hand gesegnet** *is* (i.e. *will be*)
blessed by the hand of the pastor.

wenn. The important part of this expression is the use of *wissen*, *know* in the sense of *be able*, thus: **Der Tod wußte ein Hindernis anzuzeigen** *Death was able to indicate an obstacle.*

2. **Die Bergleute wollten eine Öffnung zwischen zwei Schachten durchgraben** *The miners were about to dig an opening through between two shafts.* This use of **wollen,** *want to* is especially frequent in the past tense.

3. **erst** *for the first time, only, not until;* **jetzt erst recht,** *now for the first time* or *now more than ever.*

4. **kein Mensch wollte den Jüngling kennen:** quite often the verb **wollen** is used where we would use such an expression as *profess* or *say (that).* For example: **Und dieser Mann will Musiker sein** *And this man says he is a musician.*

5. **Acht Tage** *a week.*

6. **sie ließ ihn in ihr Stüblein tragen** *she had him taken to her little room.* This is one of the important special uses of **lassen.** Notice that the meaning is not that she let or allowed him to be carried to her room but that she had him carried there. Thus, **Napoleon ließ Moskau bombardieren** *Napoleon had Moscow bombarded.* Observe also that the active infinitive of the German is very often translated by a passive form in English.

c. **du bist mein einziges und alles** *you are my only and every thing.*

d. 1775

e. 1763

f. 1772

g. 1780

h. 1783

i. 1782

j. 1789

k. 1806

l. 1807

m. The twenty-fourth of June.

n. **Gefreunde:** an archaic collective word, meaning *friends of both sexes;* used here rather than **Freunde und Freundinnen.** Cf. **Geschwister,** meaning *brothers and sisters,* or, in the English of anthropologists, *siblings.*

o. **auf die Schicht gegangen war** *had gone on shift.*

GRAMMATICAL COMMENT—VERBS:
USES OF THE BASIC FORMS

I. The Six Tenses of the Indicative

   A.   As you have seen, English and German are strikingly similar in the basic forms of the indicative verb systems, but in
one respect they are very different: English has a much more
elaborate system than has German. That is, English has developed
so-called progressive and emphatic forms. An English verb may
therefore be said to have in the indicative mood three present-
tense forms, three simple-past-tense forms, and two forms each in
the present perfect, the past perfect, the future, and the future
perfect tenses. The present tense of the verb *knock,* for example,
in the third person singular is *he knocks, he is knocking, he does
knock;* in the past it is *he knocked, he was knocking, he did knock;*
in the present perfect, *he has knocked, he has been knocking;* in
the past perfect, *he had knocked, he had been knocking;* in the
future, *he will knock, he will be knocking;* in the future perfect,
he will have knocked, he will have been knocking. This is not the
situation in German, where a single simple form such as **er klopft**
is used to mean either *he knocks,* or *he is knocking,* or *he does
knock,* as the sense requires. Similarly, there are in standard German no special question forms such as *Does he knock?* or *Is he
knocking?* but the question is asked by putting the subject after
the verb: **Klopft er?**

   B.   Certain smaller differences in the use of the various tenses
         are also worth noting. Let us take up the tenses systemati-
cally one after the other.

   1. *THE PRESENT TENSE.*   The present tense in German has
one use for which English employs the present perfect: to describe
an action which has begun in the past but is still going on in the
present. Sentences of this type frequently employ the adverb
schon *already,* which need not be translated, but which does help
you to identify such a sentence: **Sie trauert schon seit fünfzig**

Jahren um ihren Verlobten *She has been mourning her fiancé for fifty years.*

In other respects the present tense in German has the same uses as the present tense in English, including the possibility of expressing past action and future action, but both these uses occur very much more frequently in German than in English: **Amerika wird im Jahre 1783 frei** *America becomes* (i.e. *became*) *free in the year 1783.* **Morgen geht er noch einmal an ihrem Haus vorbei** *Tomorrow he goes* (i.e. *will go*) *past her house once again.*

2. *THE SIMPLE PAST AND THE PRESENT PERFECT TENSES.* English and German are much alike in the use of these two tenses. The simple past is the regular tense for narrative in the past time: **In Falun in Schweden küßte vor guten fünfzig Jahren und mehr ein junger Bergmann seine junge hübsche Braut** *A good fifty years ago and more in Falun in Sweden a young miner kissed his pretty young bride-to-be.* And the simple past tense is used to express customary or repeated past action: **Die Ackerleute säten und schnitten** *The farmers sowed and harvested.*

In two important respects, however, German and English differ in the use of these two tenses. (1) German uses the simple past to describe an action or condition that had continued from a more remote to a less remote time in the past, whereas English requires the use of the past perfect tense: **Als man ihn aber zu Tag ausgefördert hatte, waren Vater und Mutter, Gefreunde und Bekannte schon lange tot** *But when he had been brought out into the light of day, his father and mother, friends and acquaintances had long been dead.* (2) German very frequently and especially in conversation uses the present perfect tense in statements about the past regardless of whether or not a specific time is mentioned, whereas English, when specific time is mentioned, requires the use of the simple past tense: **Acht Tage vor der Hochzeit ist er auf die Grube gegangen** *A week before the wedding he went to the mine.*

3. *THE PAST PERFECT TENSE.* The past perfect tense in German is used like the past perfect tense in English: **Als man ihn aber zu Tag ausgefördert hatte** *But when they had brought him out into the light of day.*

4. *THE FUTURE AND THE FUTURE PERFECT TENSES.* German and English are much alike in the use of these two tenses:

Wir werden uns ein eigenes Nestlein bauen *We will build ourselves a nest of our own.* **Bis zu der Zeit wird er aus dem Bergwerk
zurückgekommen sein** *By that time he will have come back from
the mine.* But German uses these two tenses in a way which is not
usual in English, to express probability. The future tense tells
what is probably the case in the present, and the future perfect,
what was probably the case in the past: **Der junge Mann wird
wohl ihr Verlobter sein** *The young man is probably her fiancé.*
Der Bergmann wird wohl vor fünfzig Jahren gestorben sein *The
miner probably died fifty years ago.* The use of the adverb **wohl** is
usual in such statements of probability: watch out for it.

II. Other Verb Forms

A. The imperative forms of German verbs are used, as are the
imperatives of English verbs, to express a command or request, although German distinguishes between the singular and
the plural of the familiar form: **Hole die Bergleute!** *Fetch the
miners!* **Holt die Bergleute!** *Fetch the miners!* The conventional
imperative is both singular and plural: **Holen Sie die Bergleute!**
Fetch the miners!

B. The infinitives have a few special uses which require some
brief mention. (1) The present infinitive without the connective **zu** is frequently used as a noun and is, of course, capitalized: **Das Erwachen der jugendlichen Liebe** *The awakening of
youthful love.* (2) The present infinitive without the connective
zu is sometimes used to make a demand or request, that is, as a
less personal imperative: **Nicht weinen, bitte!** *No weeping, please!*
(3) The prepositions **um** *in order,* **ohne** *without,* and **anstatt** or
statt *instead* take an infinitive with **zu**: **Der junge Bergmann ging
an dem Hause vorbei, um seiner Braut guten Morgen zu sagen**
*The young miner went past the house in order to say good morn-
ing to his fiancée.*

C. The participles do not differ greatly from English participles in their use. (1) The past participle enters into the
formation of the perfect tenses: **Sie hatte lange um ihn getrauert.**
She had mourned him for a long time. The present participle, however, cannot be used in this way to form tenses. (2) Both parti-

ciples are used as adjectives: **der schlafende Jüngling** *the sleeping youth,* **die zusammengeschrumpfte Frau** *the shriveled woman.* Sometimes, of course, such an adjective is used as a noun: **der Verstorbene** *the deceased,* **die Gemüter aller Umstehenden** *the feelings of all the people standing around.*

The past participle does, however, have one or two uses which are not paralleled in English. (1) It is used as a brusque and impersonal imperative, usually military: **Das Kästlein aufgeschlossen!** *Open the box!* (2) The past participle of some verbs such as **gehen, laufen, fliegen** and the like will be used with forms of **kommen** where we would expect a present participle in English: **ein Vogel kam geflogen** *a bird came flying.*

D. Participles frequently enter into a construction which, to be sure, exists in a simple form in English, but which in German often attains great and sometimes extraordinary and even baffling complexity. This is the long attribute or, as it is sometimes called, the participial construction. Such a simple example as **die Flamme der plötzlich erwachenden jugendlichen Liebe** is very quickly comprehended and is correctly and easily rendered by a word-for-word translation: *the flame of suddenly awakening youthful love.* But this particular construction can and does assume much more complicated form, such as, **Sie gruben den ganz mit Eisenvitriol durchdrungenen, sonst aber unverwesten und unveränderten Leichnam eines Jünglings hervor.** An acceptable translation might be, *They exhumed the body of a young man, which was completely impregnated with iron vitriol, but was in other respects completely preserved and unaltered.* This is a construction which may be employed with telling artistic effect by a fine writer but which some German scientists and scholars seem to cherish and cultivate with an almost inhuman glee and may constitute the one really great difficulty in reading scholarly German prose. It will be discussed and analyzed at greater length in the next chapter and you will, we trust, learn to unravel it with considerable ease.

EXERCISES

I.   These exercises are at page 181.

*II.   Arrange these eight sentences in chronological sequence. (Be sure
to translate every sentence.)*

1.   Tränen und Wehmut ergriffen die Gemüter der Umstehenden, als die auf die Leiche ihres Geliebten niedergesunkene Frau
endlich sagte: „Er ist mein Verlobter."

2.   Die alte Frau hat den Leichnam des jungen Bergmanns auf
den Kirchhof begleitet.

3.   Die Tränen galten der hingewelkten alten Frau, die erst
jetzt verstand, warum ihr Verlobter nie wieder aus der Grube
zurückgekehrt war.

4.   Die vereinigte spanische und französische Macht wußte
Gibraltar nicht zu erobern.

5.   „Das wird wohl die alte Frau sein," sagte einer der Umstehenden, „die schon seit fünfzig Jahren um ihren Verlobten
trauert."

6.   Acht Tage lang weinte die Frau um ihren Verlobten; dann
legte sie das schwarze Halstuch mit dem roten Rand in ein Kästlein und machte das Kästlein nie wieder auf.

7.   Der junge Bergmann und seine Braut wollten sich ein
eigenes Nestlein bauen lassen.

8.   Jeden Morgen als der Bergmann auf die Schicht ging,
klopfte er an dem Fenster seiner Braut und sagte ihr guten
Morgen.

*III.   Determine which German sentence best translates the English
in each group. (It is possible that more than one sentence is
admissible.)*

1.   On the day of the funeral, the old lady opened the little box
once more and took out the black silk scarf, for she wanted to put
it around her fiancé's neck.

a. Am Tage der Beerdigung wird die alte Frau das Kästlein wohl wieder aufgeschlossen und das schwarzseidene Halstuch wieder herausgenommen haben, welches sie ihrem Bräutigam umlegen wollte.

b. Am Tage der Beerdigung hat die alte Frau das Kästlein wieder aufgeschlossen und das schwarzseidene Halstuch herausgenommen, denn sie wollte es ihrem Bräutigam umlegen.

c. Am Tage der Beerdigung schloss die alte Frau das Kästlein wieder auf und wollte eben das schwarzseidene Halstuch herausnehmen, um es ihrem Bräutigam umzulegen, als sie einen Schwindel bekam.

d. Am Tage der Beerdigung hatte die alte Frau das Kästlein wieder aufgeschlossen und das schwarzseidene Halstuch herausgenommen, denn sie wollte es ihrem Bräutigam umlegen.

2. When the old woman saw the dead miner, her senses reeled, for the young man whom no one professed to know was her fiancé.

a. Da die alte Frau den toten Bergmann sieht, geht es ihr im Kopfe herum, denn der junge Mann, den niemand kennen will, ist ihr Verlobter.

b. Da die alte Frau den verstorbenen Bergmann sah, kam es ihr in den Sinn, daß der junge Mann, den niemand kennen wollte, ihr Verlobter war.

c. Da die alte Frau den toten Bergmann sah, ging es ihr im Kopfe herum, denn der junge Mann, den niemand kennen wollte, war ihr Verlobter.

d. Als die alte Frau den Leichnam des Bergmanns gesehen hatte, kam es ihr in den Sinn, daß der junge Mann, der niemand kennen wollte, ihr Verlobter war.

IV. Determine which statement is in some way associated with the preceding word or phrase. (Be sure to translate each sentence.)

1. das Lächeln

a. Im Jahre siebzehnhundertachtzig ist die Kaiserin Maria Theresia gestorben.

b. Der Bergmann hat gleichsam sein Totenkleid immer an.

c. Es war kein Zweifel: es war derselbe junge Bergmann, der vor fünfzig Jahren auf die Schicht gegangen und nie zurückgekehrt war.

d. Der junge Mann küßte seine Braut und sagte: „In acht Tagen
sind wir Mann und Weib und dann lassen wir uns ein schönes
Haus bauen."

  2. das Wiedersehen

a. „Der Beweis gilt nicht," sagte der Pfarrer verachtungsvoll,
„denn der Mann, der das gesagt hat, ist verrückt."

b. „Ich habe eine Bitte an Sie," sagte die alte Frau; „lassen Sie
ihn in mein Stüblein tragen, denn ich bin die einzige, die
ihm angehört."

c. Der Müller mahlte, die Schmiede hämmerten und die Stadt
Lissabon wurde durch ein Erdbeben zerstört.

d. „Das Kästlein holen!" sagte sie heftig, als sie von einer langen
Bewegung des Gemüts erwachte.

V. Correct the misinformation (in German, of course).

  1. Als sie den Pfarrer zum zweitenmal aufgerufen hatte, da
meldete sich der Tod.

  2. Amerika war schon frei geworden, als der junge Bergmann
auf die Schicht ging.

  3. Wie hingewelkt und kraftlos die alte Frau auch war, sie
kam* in ihrer jugendlichen Schöne an den Platz und erkannte
ihren Bräutigam.

  4. Der Leichnam des Jünglings, den man herausgegraben
hatte, war so mit Eisenvitriol durchdrungen, daß man seine Ge-
sichtszüge und sein Alter gar nicht erkennen konnte.

  5. Die alte Frau hatte fünfzehn Jahre lang um ihren Verlobten
getrauert, der eines Tages auf die Schicht gegangen war und
nimmer zurückkehrte.

* See Unit IV, Note 8 to the German Text, page 60.

THIRD UNIT

A SELECTION FROM

Die deutsche Arbeit

BY WILHELM HEINRICH RIEHL

(1823-1897)

The career of Wilhelm Heinrich Riehl was an almost uninterrupted progress from rather modest beginnings to a position of eminence, respect, and influence. Not a towering genius, but versatile, gifted, and industrious, Riehl caught the favorable attention of King Maximilian II of Bavaria, who made full use of his many talents as a professor, editor, and museum director. Riehl's professional attainments were in the fields of sociology and cultural history, but he was also a novelist of some note.

The present selection is taken from his book *Die deutsche Arbeit,* inspired by and dedicated to King Maximilian. The basic idea of this book is that the mentality of a people is revealed in its ideal of work and in the way it performs its work. Riehl is therefore very much concerned with such topics as honor in work, the treatment of work in popular songs and proverbs, the attitude of the common people toward work. One section of the book is called *"Poesie der Arbeit"* and in this section occurs the chapter *"Mühsal und Genuß des Schaffens,"* from which the following excerpts have been taken.

AUS DIE DEUTSCHE ARBEIT

VON WILHELM HEINRICH RIEHL

In den höheren geistigeren Formen der Arbeit fällt Mühsal und
Genuß in Eins zusammen. Die Arbeit selber wird Genuß, während
beim rein mechanischen Tagewerk, welches ein Tier oder eine
Maschine beinahe ebensogut vollführen könnte als der Mensch,
5 erst nach der Arbeit und in ihren Resultaten der rechte Genuß
kommt. Es geht[1] darum den meisten Handarbeitern wie vielen
Studenten, denen die lange Vakanz als das Schönste an den Universitätsstudien erscheint. Dem schöpferischen Geistesarbeiter ist
kein Feierabend vergönnt, und er träumt wohl gar im Schlafe
10 seine Arbeit weiter; allein für diese Entbehrung ward[2] ihm dennoch reicher Ersatz, denn die Wonne des Feierabends steckt ihm
in der Arbeit. Darum fällt auch dem schöpferischen Manne in
Alter oder Krankheit nichts schwerer als mit der Arbeit aufzuhören. Kluge Leute haben gut predigen,[3] daß der Künstler mit
15 seiner reifsten Blütezeit abschließen solle. Mit dem Schaffen
abschließen heißt für ihn mit dem reinsten Lebensgenusse abschließen, und das mag doch keiner, bevor er wirklich tot ist. Die
seligsten Augenblicke bei der Geistesarbeit sind das Empfangen
und das Vollenden, Anfang und Ende, der erste Wurf und die
20 letzte Hand. In beiden wird die Arbeit zum freien Genuß,
dazwischen liegt der Schweiß und die Mühe der Arbeit. Begabte,
aber strenger Selbstzucht und gesammelter Tatkraft bare Naturen[4]
bleiben daher häufig bei dem bloßen Empfangen, bei den ersten
zündenden Ideen der Geistesarbeit stehen; sie beginnen und ent-
25 werfen ewig um nichts zu Ende zu führen.
  Nicht im Entwurf bleiben die meisten Arbeiten stecken sondern
im ersten Teile der Ausführung; selten dagegen und in der Regel
nur durch ein äußeres Hindernis bleibt ein über die Mitte vor-

40

In the higher, more intellectual forms of work, toil and gratification coincide.[a] Work itself becomes pleasure, whereas in the case
of purely mechanical day-labor, which an animal or a machine
could execute almost as well as a human being, the proper gratification comes only after work and in its results. For this reason 5
most manual laborers feel as many students feel, to whom the long
vacation appears to be the finest thing about studying at a university. The creative intellectual worker is not accorded the right
to relax,[b] and he probably continues to dream of his work even in
his sleep. For this sacrifice, however, he has nonetheless received 10
ample compensation,[c] for the joy of respite from work is embodied
for him in the work itself. For this reason also there is nothing
harder for a creative man in old age or illness than to cease his
work. It is futile for [so-called] sensible people to preach that the
artist should cease [creation] at the time of his most mature flower- 15
ing. For him cessation of his creativity is the same as cessation of
the purest pleasure of living, and, after all, nobody wishes to do
that before he is actually dead. The most ecstatic moments in
intellectual work are conception and completion, beginning and
end, the first projection and the finishing touch. In both, work 20
turns into untrammeled pleasure; in between lie the sweat and
toil of work. Individuals who are talented but devoid of strict self-
discipline and concentrated energy therefore frequently stop at
the mere conception, the first exciting ideas of intellectual work;
they eternally begin and make plans but complete nothing.[d]   25
  Most works do not bog down in the planning [stage] but in the
first part of [their] execution; on the other hand, a work which has
progressed beyond the mid-point rarely remains a fragment and,

geschrittenes Werk[4] Fragment. In der Mitte kommt man über
30 den Berg, und nicht die steilste Stelle, sondern das erste Ansteigen
ist bergauf das sauerste. Den Scheitelpunkt der Gebirgspässe
nennt man in vielen Gegenden „beim fröhlichen Mann;" denn
mag der Wanderer von hüben oder drüben kommen,[5] bei dieser
Stelle ist er allemal fröhlich; und das Hinuntersteigen deucht ihm
35 nur noch ein Spiel. Bevor man aber in einer Arbeit beim "fröhlichen Mann" angelangt ist, kostet es ganz besonderer Willenskraft und Ausdauer. Im Augenblicke des ersten Wurfes sitzen wir
wie ein Feldherr hoch zu Roß, ordnen und mustern unsere Reihen
in keckem Flug und sehen überall schon gewonnenes Spiel. Beim
40 Ausführen aber müssen wir all die Schritte erst erkämpfen, die
wir im Geiste schon weit hinter uns hatten. Es[6] beginnt eine Schule
der Selbsterkenntnis, wir finden tausend ungeahnte Lücken unsers
Wissens, der Stoff trocknet uns ein, oder er wird uns auch
umgekehrt so warm und lebendig, daß er mit unserer Phantasie
45 durchgeht und wir nicht mehr zum geduldigen Sitzen uns nieder-
schlagen können. Allmählich gewinnt man aber auch diese Nöte
und Mühen lieb, und der Zwang der begonnenen Arbeit hilft
durch dick und dünn. Es ist etwas Köstliches um diesen Zwang.
Kein großes Werk wird ohne äußeren Zwang vollendet. Wer un-
50 begrenzte Zeit hat, der tut gewöhnlich gar nichts; nur wenn wir
keine Zeit haben, finden wir Zeit. Man verspricht sich oft Wunder
wie viel[7] von einer Ferienarbeit, und sind die Ferien herum, so
haben wir nichts getan; kommt aber der köstliche Zwang, brennt
es auf dem Nagel,[8] dann verdoppelt sich die Schnellkraft des
55 gesammelten Geistes, und eine gestohlene Stunde reicht weiter
als zwölf geschenkte.

NOTES TO THE GERMAN TEXT

1. **Es geht den meisten Handarbeitern wie vielen Studenten**
   *For most manual laborers it goes as [it does] for many stu-
   dents.* That is: *Most laborers feel as many students feel.*

2. **ward:** an archaic form of **wurde** (usually only in the singular)
   which still may be used to impart a tone of gravity or
   impressiveness.

3. **Kluge Leute haben gut predigen** *Clever people have [it]
   good to preach.* But the meaning is ironical: *There is no good
   in clever people preaching.*

if it does, usually because of some external obstacle. At the mid-point one gets over the hill and it is not the steepest spot but the first upward climb that is the most toilsome part of the ascent.*e* In many regions the divide of the mountain passes is called "at [the sign of] the happy man," for whether the traveler may come from this direction or that, at this point he is always happy, and the descent seems to him to be merely [child's] play. But before one has gotten to the "happy man" in a task, very special will power and perseverance are required.*f* At the moment of the first projection we sit like a general, high on our steed, drawing up and mustering our ranks in a bold sweep, and everywhere we see a game [that is] won. But in the execution we must really struggle to achieve all the steps which in our minds we have already taken. Training in the knowledge of one's self begins, we find a thousand unsuspected gaps in our information, our subject shrivels up, or, on the contrary, it becomes so warm and vital that it runs away with our imagination and we can no longer settle down to sitting quietly. Gradually, however, one gets to love these difficulties and exertions, and the compulsion of work that is begun helps through thick and thin. There is something about this compulsion [that is] invaluable. No great work is completed without external compulsion. A person who has unlimited time usually does nothing at all; only when we have no time, do we find time. Often one promises oneself ever so much from a vacation task and when the vacation is over, we have done nothing. But if that invaluable compulsion comes, if there is a sense of great urgency, then the elasticity of one's concentrated mental power is redoubled and an hour which has been stolen, [so to speak, from other things] often goes further than twelve hours that are given for nothing.

NOTES TO THE ENGLISH TEXT

a. **fallen in Eins zusammen**   *fall together into one.*

b. **Dem Geistesarbeiter ist kein Feierabend vergönnt**   *No respite from work is accorded the intellectual worker.*

c. **ihm ward reicher Ersatz**   *to him there became abundant compensation.*

d. **um nichts zu Ende zu führen**   *in order to bring nothing to an end.*

4. **Begabte, aber strenger Selbstzucht und gesammelter Tatkraft bare Naturen:** for analysis and translation see the Grammatical Comment of this Unit: IV. The Long Attribute Construction. Same reference for **ein über die Mitte vorgeschrittenes Werk.**

5. **denn mag der Wanderer von hüben oder drüben kommen:** for analysis and translation see the Grammatical Comment of this Unit: II C.

6. **Es beginnt eine Schule der Selbsterkenntnis:** The pronoun **es** is an expletive, a "filler," or a way of getting a sentence started similar to the English expletive *there: There begins a training in the knowledge of one's self.* The real subject is **Schule,** and **es** need not be translated in this case. Watch out for instances where **es** introduces a plural subject: **Es haben kluge Leute gut predigen.**

7. **Wunder wie viel**   *a miracle how much.* English will usually prefer some expression such as *ever so much.*

8. **brennt es auf dem Nagel**   *if it burns on the nail.* Usually the plural **Nägel** is used, e.g. **es brennt mir auf den Nägeln** *it burns on my nails,* meaning *I have a sense of great urgency.*

e. **das erste Ansteigen ist bergauf das sauerste**   *the first ascent
    is uphill the most painful [part].*
f. **es kostet ganz besonderer Willenskraft und Ausdauer**   *it is at
    the cost of very special will power and perseverance.* This use
    of the genitive case is not common. See the Ninth Unit, Gram-
    matical Comment III B 2.

GRAMMATICAL COMMENT—WORD ORDER

I. The Position of the Inflected Verb in the Independent Clause

A.   The arrangement of words in a sentence has just as much to do with expressing meaning as have number, case, gender, tense, mood, and all the other categories of grammar that you have studied at one time or another. In the English language, the word order of declarative sentences tends so strongly to be subject-verb-object that the native speaker of English automatically expects the first noun or pronoun in a sentence to be the subject. German usage is so different in this respect that you must make a special effort to overcome this expectation if you are going to understand German with facility and accuracy.

B.   When dealing with the main or independent clause of a German sentence you may, however, be sure that one element in that clause will have a fixed position: the inflected verb—that is, the verb which shows tense, person, number and so on—comes in the second position. This rule is shown in the three following sentences, which, so far as meaning is concerned, differ in emphasis but not in substance:

Reicher Ersatz wird dem Geistesarbeiter für seine Entbehrung.
Dem Geistesarbeiter wird für seine Entbehrung reicher Ersatz.
Für seine Entbehrung wird dem Geistesarbeiter reicher Ersatz.

The first sentence is said to show normal order, and the other two, inverted order; but it must be emphasized that "normal order" is a misnomer and that the subject-verb-nonsubject arrangement is neither more normal nor much more frequently used than the nonsubject-verb-subject arrangement. All three sentences above may be translated *Ample compensation comes to the mental worker for his self-denial.* The rule for the use of inverted order may be stated as follows: When a sentence starts with a word or phrase other than the subject, the subject follows the verb, usually, but not always, coming immediately after it.

C. Direct questions employ inverted order: **Soll der Künstler mit seiner reifsten Blütezeit abschließen?** *Shall the artist cease at the time of his most mature flowering?* Imperatives in the conventional second person plural and also the first person plural likewise employ inverted order: **Führen Sie die Arbeit zu Ende!** *Complete the work!* and **Führen wir die Arbeit zu Ende!** *Let us complete the work!*

II. The Inflected Verb in Complex Sentences

A. The inflected verb of the dependent clause is postponed, frequently, but not necessarily, to the end of the clause:

Das ist rein mechanisches Tagewerk, welches ein Tier oder eine Maschine beinahe ebensogut als der Mensch vollführen könnte.

Das ist rein mechanisches Tagewerk, welches ein Tier oder eine Maschine beinahe ebensogut vollführen könnte als der Mensch.

Both mean *That is merely mechanical day labor which an animal or a machine could perform almost as well as a human being.*

B. When the subordinate clause comes first in a complex sentence, the following main clause usually has inverted order: **Bevor man aber beim „fröhlichen Mann" angelangt ist, kostet es ganz besonderer Willenskraft und Ausdauer.** *Before one has arrived at the sign of the happy man, it will cost very special willpower and perseverance.* See, however, the Fourth Unit, Note 8 to the German Text.

C. A very important use of inverted word order in complex sentences is to state a condition. You are familiar with this construction in English in such sentences as, "Had I known this, I would have acted differently" or "Were he to reform, he would still have a good chance." In German this construction occurs very frequently (there are several examples in the text of this lesson) and it is a persistent source of error. Watch out for it and remember: if the subject follows the verb for no apparent reason, it is almost certain that you are dealing with some form of conditional sentence. Examples:

Kommt aber der köstliche Zwang, dann verdoppelt sich die Schnellkraft des gesammelten Geistes. *But if that invaluable compulsion comes, then the elasticity of one's concentrated mental powers is redoubled.*

Denn mag der Wanderer von hüben oder drüben kommen, bei dieser Stelle ist er allemal fröhlich. *For whether the traveler may come from this direction or that, at this point he is always happy.*

(Observe from the second example that the conjunction **denn** is always considered to be a coördinating conjunction and does not affect the word order.)

Similar to this construction is the use of the verb-subject order after the conjunction **als**, to mean *as if* or *as though*: **als hätte er unbegrenzte Zeit** *as though he had unlimited time.* The important practical rule is: **Als** followed immediately by a verb means *as though.*

III. The Relative Order of Other Elements within the Clause

A. Certain elements are postponed, usually to the end of the clause. These are: the separable prefix, the infinitive, the perfect participle. Examples:

Hören Sie mit der Arbeit auf! *Stop working!*

Eine Maschine könnte diese Arbeit ebensogut vollführen. *A machine could perform this work just as well.*

Er hat das Spiel schon gewonnen. *He has already won the game.*

B. The relative order of adverbial expressions of time and place in German is exactly the reverse of English order: time before place in German, but place before time in English. Thus, **Wir werden heute Nachmittag beim „fröhlichen Mann" anlangen.** *We will arrive at the sign of the happy man this afternoon.*

C. An indirect object usually precedes a direct, i.e., accusative, object: **Ich habe dem Arbeiter Ersatz für diese Entbehrung versprochen.** *I have promised the worker compensation for this self-denial.* But when the direct object is a pronoun it will precede any dative: **Ich habe es ihm versprochen.** *I have promised it to him.*

D. One might go to considerable length formulating rules for the position of various elements in a sentence, but such formulations would probably only be confusing because they would pile exception upon exception. It may be well, however, if you remember these general statements about the structure of sentences in English and German: In an English sentence, unless it is worded for special effect, the important or strong elements come first and the weaker elements straggle along behind, like this: subject, verb, object, modifying and qualifying words. In a German sentence the strong elements come at the beginning and at the end, and the weaker elements come in between. For example, until one gets to the final word in such a sentence as **Kein Feierabend ist dem schöpferischen Geistesarbeiter vergönnt** *No respite is granted the creative mental worker,* it is not possible to tell what the meaning of the sentence is, for the last word might just as well be **versagt** *denied* and the sense of the sentence would then be completely reversed. Remember, then: *Always read a sentence through to the end before making up your mind what it means.*

IV. The Long Attribute Construction

A. In the preceding chapter some mention was made of the long attribute or participial construction and two rather simple examples were given. The first of these not only exhibits the basic structure, but is also capable of being manipulated to serve as a good model for you to operate: **die Flamme der plötzlich erwachenden Liebe** *the flame of suddenly awakening love.*

What lets you know that you are confronted with such a construction is that you have an "impossible" combination of words: **der plötzlich** *of the suddenly.* Let us call this impossible combination the "clash," and break up the long attribute as follows:

der + plötzlich   erwachenden   Liebe
  1   4   3   2

In a complex long attribute the elements may usually best be translated in the order suggested by the numbers above. At any rate, the clash (+) makes you aware that you have to continue

in your sentence until you come to a word (2) which will go with
the introductory word (1).

Now let us expand this example a bit and devise a structure
like this:

der + plötzlich nach fünfzig Jahren im Herzen der alten Frau

   1   4

erwachenden Liebe

      3   2

The problem is basically the same: find the clash, then the introductory word (1), and then the noun (2) which goes with the
introductory word, in this case **Liebe**. A good way to find the noun
is to find the "key word (words)," which is always an adjective
and, very frequently, a participle. Number the key word 3 and
the rest of the construction 4 and then translate in 1, 2, 3, 4 order:

of the love awakening

  1   2   3

suddenly after fifty years in the heart of the old lady.

                 4

You will be able to find the key word more readily when you
realize that it must have the appropriate adjective ending. This
means: (a) if the introductory word is **ein** or an *un*inflected **ein**-
word, the key word will end in **-er** or **-es**; (b) if the introductory
word is a definite article, **dieser**-word, or inflected **ein**-word (e.g.
der, die, das, diesem, eine, eines, einem, etc.) the ending of the
key word will be **-e** or **-en**; (c) if, however, the introductory word
(1) is an adjective, the key word will have the same ending as
the adjective. An example of this last condition occurs in our text:

Begabte, + aber strenger Selbstzucht und gesammelter Tatkraft

    1   4

bare Naturen. *Talented natures [which are] bare, however, of*

  3   2

severe self-discipline and concentrated energy. Observe that, as in the last example, it may frequently be well not to translate the key word as a participle or as an adjective, but to expand it into a whole clause: **ein über die Mitte vorgeschrittenes Werk** *a work [which has] advanced beyond the mid-point.*

In this and the following chapters, there will be a good many examples of the long attribute construction; whenever you seem to have a meaningless jumble of words before you, suspect a long attribute.

EXERCISES

I. These exercises are at page 183.

II. Determine which German sentence best translates the English in each group.

1. If no respite from work is accorded the creative man, he has nonetheless received ample reward for this sacrifice.

a. Dem schöpferischen Menschen ist kein Feierabend vergönnt, aber er hat doch für diese Entbehrung reichen Ersatz.
b. Wenn dem schöpferischen Menschen für diese Entbehrung kein Feierabend vergönnt ist, so hat er doch reichen Ersatz.
c. Ist dem schöpferischen Menschen kein Feierabend vergönnt, so ward ihm doch für diese Entbehrung reicher Ersatz.
d. Wenn dem schöpferischen Menschen kein Ersatz für seine Arbeit vergönnt ist, so ist das keine Entbehrung.

2. In the moment of the first projection the general reviews his lines in a bold sweep, as though everywhere he saw a game already won.

a. In keckem Flug mustert der General im Augenblick des ersten Wurfs seine Reihen, als er überall schon gewonnenes Spiel sieht.
b. Als der Feldherr überall schon im ersten Wurf gewonnenes Spiel sah, musterte er in keckem Flug seine Reihen.
c. Musterte der Feldherr im Augenblick des ersten Wurfes seine Reihen, sah er in keckem Flug schon gewonnenes Spiel.
d. Im Augenblick des ersten Wurfes mustert der General seine Reihen in keckem Flug, als sähe er überall schon gewonnenes Spiel.

III. Determine which statement is in some way connected with the preceding word or phrase. (Translate each sentence.)

1. der Lebensgenuß

a. Schlagen wir uns zum geduldigen Sitzen nieder!

b. Brennt es auf dem Nagel, reicht eine gestohlene Stunde Wunder wie weit.

c. Es fällt dem schöpferischen Manne nichts schwerer als mit der Arbeit aufzuhören.

d. Die seligsten Augenblicke bei der Geistesarbeit sind das Empfangen und das Vollenden.

2. die Selbsterkenntnis

a. Uns geht es wie dem hoch zu Roß sitzenden und seine Reihen in keckem Fluge musternden Feldherrn.

b. Ihm geht es im Kopfe herum, wie einem Künstler, dem die Phantasie eben durchgegangen ist.

c. Tausend ungeahnte Lücken ihres Wissens finden alle Menschen, die ein begonnenes Werk zu Ende führen.

d. Beim „fröhlichen Mann" wird der Wanderer erst recht fröhlich.

IV. Decide which statement in each group is not true.

GROUP 1

a. Der rechte Künstler kann mit der Arbeit nicht aufhören, wenn er auch krank und alt ist.

b. Keine Maschine könnte rein mechanisches Tagewerk ebensogut vollführen wie der Mensch.

c. Hat man unbegrenzte Zeit, so weiß man oft nicht begonnene Arbeit ohne äußeren Zwang zu vollenden.

d. Es hilft der Zwang der begonnenen Arbeit durch dick und dünn.

GROUP 2

a. Vielen Studenten wird wohl die lange Vakanz als das Schönste an den Universitätsstudien erscheinen.

b. Die meisten Arbeiten bleiben nicht oft im ersten Entwurf stehn.

c. Unbegabten Naturen wird die Arbeit zum freien Genuß.

d. Dem Wanderer deucht das Hinuntersteigen nur noch ein Spiel.

GROUP 3

a. Haben wir auch keine Zeit, so finden wir doch Zeit, wenn es uns auf den Nägeln brennt.

b. Vollendet wird kein großes Werk ohne äußeren Zwang.

c. Mag der Stoff uns auch warm und lebendig werden, er geht nie mit unserer Phantasie durch.

d. Die meisten Handarbeiter schlagen sich gern zum geduldigen Sitzen nieder.

V. Rearrange the following words and phrases to make sentences, as in the following example, and translate your sentence.

bei der Geistesarbeit, das Empfinden, die seligsten Augenblicke, das Vollenden, und, sind—Die seligsten Augenblicke bei der Geistesarbeit sind das Empfinden und das Vollenden.

1. Anfang und Ende, der Schweiß, liegt, die Mühe, und, der Arbeit, zwischen.

2. lieb, der Student, allmählich, gewinnt, diese Nöten, auch, und, Mühen.

3. verspricht, weit mehr, sich, von einer gestohlenen Stunde, man, von zwölf geschenkten, als.

4. wohl, im Schlaf, Ihre Arbeit, träumen Sie, weiter?

5. langte ... an, endlich, der von drüben kommende Wanderer, des Gebirgspasses, auf dem Scheitelpunkt.

FOURTH UNIT

A LETTER

BY WOLFGANG AMADEUS MOZART

(1756-1791)

When Wolfgang Amadeus Mozart died before attaining his thirty-sixth birthday he left the world a legacy of music so rich, so varied, so abundant as to challenge belief. His prodigious genius had become apparent at the age of four. By the time he was six there was no longer any doubt of his unique talent. And before he reached the age of twelve he had composed, among many other things, two operas which still give pleasure in performance and one of which (*La Finta Semplice*) is a full-scale work of five hundred fifty-eight pages.

To recount the familiar multitudinous stories of his well-nigh supernatural achievements would be a futile task. Let it be enough to say that what makes the story of his life so infinitely moving is that, although the accomplishments of his manhood far surpassed even the promise of his first years, his life is a chronicle of disappointments, humiliations, drudgery, and defeats caused by the fear, envy, and indifference of those in power, but that through it all from his mind and spirit there emanated a radiance, sweetness of temper, and profound understanding of life that make his music one of the greatest treasures of mankind.

WOLFGANG AMADEUS MOZART

AN DEN BARON * * *

Prag (Herbst) 1790

Ihren Brief hab' ich vor Freude vielmal geküßt. Nur hätten Sie mich nicht so sehr loben sollen; hören kann ich so etwas allenfalls, aber nicht gut lesen. Ihr habt mich zu lieb, ihr guten Menschen; ich bin das nicht wert, und meine Sachen auch nicht. Und was 5 soll ich denn sagen von Ihrem Präsent, mein allerbester Herr Baron! Das kam wie ein Stern in dunkler Nacht, oder wie eine Blume im Winter. Gott weiß, wie ich mich manchmal placken und schinden muß, um das arme Leben zu gewinnen, und Stännerl will doch auch was[1] haben. Wer Ihnen gesagt hat, daß ich faul 10 würde, dem (ich bitte Sie herzlich und ein Baron kann das schon tun) dem versetzen Sie aus Liebe ein paar tüchtige Watschen. Ich wollte ja immer fort arbeiten, dürfte ich nur immer solche Musik machen wie ich will und kann, und wo ich mir selbst was daraus mache.[2] So habe ich vor drei Wochen eine Symphonie 15 gemacht, und mit der morgenden Post schreibe ich schon wieder an Hofmeister und biete ihm drei Klavier-Quatuor an, wenn er Geld hat. O Gott, wär' ich ein großer Herr, so spräch' ich: „Mozart, schreibe du mir, aber was du willst und so gut du kannst; eher kriegst du keinen Kreuzer von mir, bis du was fertig hast, 20 hernach aber kaufe ich dir jedes Manuskript ab." O Gott, wie mich das alles zwischendurch traurig macht und dann wieder wild und grimmig, wo dann freilich manches geschieht, was nicht geschehen sollte. Sehen Sie, lieber guter Freund, so ist es, und nicht wie Ihnen dumme oder böse Lumpen mögen gesagt haben.

25 Und nun komme ich auf den allerschwersten Punkt in Ihrem Brief, und den ich lieber gar fallen ließe, weil mir die Feder für so was nicht zu Willen ist.[3] Aber ich will[4] es doch versuchen, und sollten Sie nur etwas zu lachen drinnen finden. Wie nämlich meine

56

WOLFGANG AMADEUS MOZART

TO BARON***

Prague (Autumn) 1790

I have kissed your letter for joy [many] many times. Only you
should not have praised me so much; at all events, I can listen to
such things, but [I can] not easily read them. You kind people are
too fond of me; I do not deserve*ᵃ* that and my things don't either.
And *what* shall I say about your present, my most excellent Baron! ₅
That came like a star in [a] dark night or a flower in winter.
Heaven knows how I must often pinch and scrape in order to earn
a meager living and, after all, Stännerl*ᵇ* wants to have something
too. Whoever has told you that I was getting lazy, as for him (I
beg you sincerely, and a baron can do that all right) give him a ₁₀
couple of solid whacks out of affection [for me]. I would like to
work on and on and on, of course, if only I might make such music
as I want to and am able to, and that means something to me.
Thus, three weeks ago I made a symphony and in the morning
mail I will be writing to Hofmeister*ᶜ* again and offering him three ₁₅
piano quartets, if he has money. Good Lord, if I were a great
gentleman this is what I would say: "Mozart, you write*ᵈ* for me,
but whatever you want to and as well as you can; you won't get a
red cent from me until you have something finished, but afterwards I'll buy all your manuscripts." Heavens, how sad all this ₂₀
makes me from time to time, or again [it makes] me angry and
furious; and then,*ᵉ* of course, a good many things happen that
ought not to. You see, my dear good friend, *that* is how it is and
not the way stupid or malicious scoundrels may have reported [it]
to you. ₂₅
And now I come to the most difficult point in your letter and
the one I would much rather drop, because my pen simply refuses
to obey me in this kind of thing. But I will try*ᶠ* it anyway, even if

Art ist beim Schreiben und Ausarbeiten von großen und derben
30 Sachen? Nämlich, ich kann darüber wahrlich nicht mehr sagen als
das, denn ich weiß selbst nicht mehr und kann auf weiter nichts
kommen. Wenn ich recht für mich bin und guter Dinge,[5] etwa
auf Reisen im Wagen oder nach guter Mahlzeit beim Spazieren,
und in der Nacht, wenn ich nicht schlafen kann, da kommen mir
35 die Gedanken stromweis und am besten. Woher und wie, das
weiß ich nicht, kann auch nichts dazu.[6] Die mir nun gefallen, die
behalte ich im Kopf und sumse sie wohl auch vor mich hin,[7] wie
mir andere wenigstens gesagt haben. Halt' ich nun fest, so kommt
mir bald eins nach dem andern bei, wozu so ein Brocken zu
40 brauchen wär', um eine Pastete daraus zu machen, nach Contrapunkt, nach Klang der verschiedenen Instrumente etc. Das erhitzt
mir nun die Seele, wenn ich nämlich nicht gestört werde; da wird
es immer größer, und ich breite es immer weiter und heller aus,
und das Ding wird im Kopf wahrlich fast fertig, wenn es auch
45 lang ist, so daß ich's hernach mit einem Blick, gleichsam wie ein
schönes Bild im Geiste übersehe, und es auch gar nicht nacheinander wie es hernach kommen muß, in der Einbildung höre sondern wie gleich alles zusammen. Das ist nun ein Schmaus! Alles
das Finden und Machen geht in mir wie in einem schönen starken
50 Traum vor. Aber das Überhören, so alles zusammen, ist doch das
beste. Was nun so geworden ist, das vergesse ich nicht so leicht
wieder, und das ist vielleicht die beste Gabe, die mir unser Herrgott geschenkt hat. Wenn ich hernach einmal zum Schreiben
komme, so nehme ich aus dem Sack meines Gehirns was vorher
55 hinein gesammelt ist. Darum kommt es hernach auch ziemlich
schnell aufs Papier, denn es ist eigentlich schon fertig und wird
auch selten viel anders als es vorher im Kopf gewesen ist. Darum
kann ich mich auch beim Schreiben stören lassen; und mag um
mich herum mancherlei vorgehen, ich schreibe doch,[8] kann auch
60 dabei plaudern, nämlich von Hühnern und Gänsen, oder von
Gretel und Bärbel und dergleichen. Wie nun aber über dem
Arbeiten meine Sachen überhaupt eben die Gestalt oder Manier
annehmen, daß sie Mozartisch sind, und nicht in der Manier eines
andern, das wird halt eben so zugehen wie daß meine Nase eben
65 so groß und herausgebogen, daß sie Mozartisch und nicht wie bei
andern Leuten geworden ist. Denn ich lege es nicht auf die
Besonderheit an,[9] wüßte die meine auch nicht einmal näher zu
beschreiben; es ist ja aber wohl bloß natürlich, daß die Leute, die

you should only find something to laugh at in it. That is, what is my procedure in writing and working out big, powerful things? 30 Well, of course, I really can't say any more about it than this, for I don't know any more myself and I can't hit upon anything further. When I am really by myself and in a good mood, for instance on [my] travels in a coach or taking a walk after a good meal, and at night when I can't sleep, then the best ideas come to me in 35 torrents.[g] From where and how, I don't know, and I can't do anything about it either. The ones I like I keep in my head and probably hum them to myself, too, as other people have told me at any rate. Now if I persist, then [pretty] soon, one thing after the other occurs to me for which such a fragment could be used[h] to 40 make a pasty of, according to counterpoint, the timbre of the various instruments, etc. Now that excites my imagination, that is, if I am not disturbed, so it gets bigger and bigger and I spread it out farther and clearer and the thing really gets almost finished in my head, even if it is long, so that afterwards I see it all at one 45 glance in my mind, like a beautiful picture, so to speak, and in my imagination I don't hear it in succession as it has to come later but sort of simultaneously all together. Now that is a [real] feast! All the invention and shaping goes on within me, as though in a beautiful compelling dream. But that hearing it all through, everything 50 at once, that's really the best [part]. Now what has come about in this way I don't forget so readily and that is perhaps the best gift that our Lord has given me. When I get around to writing afterwards I pull out of my brain-sack whatever has previously been collected in it. For that reason, it gets down on paper rather 55 quickly afterwards, for, actually, it is already finished and it rarely turns out very different from what it already was in my head. For that reason I can let [people] disturb me while [I am] writing; and [even] if many [odd] things may be going on about me, I write just the same. I can even talk at the same time, that is, about 60 hens and geese and Gretel and Bärbel and the like. But now [as to] how my things take on the shape or manner in working [them out] so that they are Mozartean and not in somebody else's manner, that probably just happens the way that my nose is just so big and hooked, that it turned out Mozartean and not like other 65 people's. For I don't make individuality my aim, and wouldn't even know [how] to describe my own more closely. But it is probably merely natural that people who really have an appearance

wirklich ein Aussehen haben, auch verschieden von einander
70 aussehen, wie von außen so von innen. Wenigstens weiß ich, daß
ich mir das eine so wenig als das andere gegeben habe.

   Damit lassen Sie mich aus für immer und ewig, bester Freund,
und glauben Sie ja[10] nicht, daß ich aus anderen Ursachen ab-
breche, als weil ich nichts weiter weiß.

Mozart

NOTES TO THE GERMAN TEXT

1. **was:** a very common abbreviation of **etwas** *something.*
2. **wo ich mir was daraus mache:** an extraordinarily idiomatic expression. **Was,** of course, is the abbreviation for **etwas** something. **Wo** is a generalized relative pronoun, especially favored in southern German, that can stand for any case, number, or gender: **Der Mann, wo** *The man who or whom, etc.* **Ich mache mir etwas aus dieser Musik,** literally, *I make something out of this music for myself;* in English idiom, *I care about this music.* The whole clause, therefore, means something like: *that I care something about,* or, *that means something to me.*
3. **die Feder ist mir nicht zu Willen** *the pen is not at my will,* that is, *it does not obey me.*
4. **Aber ich will es doch versuchen** *But I will try it just the same.* Occasionally, as here, the modal auxiliary **wollen** *want to,* is used as the future tense auxiliary.
5. **guter Dinge:** a phrase in the genitive plural (genitive of description) meaning literally, *of good things.* English idiom requires a phrase such as *in good spirits.*
6. **ich kann nichts dazu** *I can [do]nothing to it,* i.e., *I cannot change it one way or the other.*
7. **vor mich hin** *to myself.* **Für** may also be used: **er sprach für sich hin** *he talked to himself.*
8. **ich schreibe doch:** notice that after the clause of concession, the conclusion exhibits normal word order, i.e. subject-verb, rather than the inverted order you might expect. This order occurs fairly frequently, especially after concessive clauses that have inverted order, i.e. verb-subject, rather than a conjunction with transposed order.
9. **ich lege es darauf an** *I aim at it.*
10. **ja** has strong stress for particular emphasis.

look different from each other, both inside and outside. At least I know that I haven't given myself the one any more than the other. ₇₀

Let me off with that for ever and always, my very good friend, and do not believe by any means that I am breaking off for any other reason except that that is all I know.

Mozart

NOTES TO THE ENGLISH TEXT

a. **ich bin das nicht wert**   *I am not worthy of it.*

b. **Stännerl:**   Constanze, Mozart's wife.

c. **Hofmeister:**   a prominent publisher of the time.

d. **schreibe du:**   an imperative; unusual in that the subject, **du,** is expressed.

e. **wo:**   the generalized relative form that can stand for almost anything in southern German. Here it refers to Mozart's becoming angry and furious, a circumstance in which many things can happen that shouldn't.

f. **ich will es versuchen:**   an instance, not unusual, of the modal auxiliary **wollen** *want to* serving as the auxiliary of the future tense. This is not the rule, however.

g. **stromweis und am besten**   *in streams and in the best way.*

h. **wozu so ein Brocken zu brauchen wär'**   *whereto such a fragment were to be used,* i.e. *would be usable.*

GRAMMATICAL COMMENT—THE MODAL AUXILIARIES

I. Modal Auxiliaries in English and German

A. An auxiliary verb is one which helps, so to speak, to modify the basic meaning of another verb in some way. Thus **sein**, **haben**, and **werden** help to define the *time* of action just as do the verbs *have* and *will* in English. These are called tense auxiliaries. There are also certain other auxiliary verbs known as modal auxiliaries, because they are used to express distinctions in the *mode* of action. The brief English sentence, "He must work," is a good example for you to analyze to understand how modal auxiliaries are employed: *he must* is the third person singular present tense of the modal auxiliary *must;* and *work* is the present infinitive of the verb *work*. Thus the main verb always appears in the infinitive form (the complementary infinitive) and the modal auxiliary is to be taken with the subject.

B. Now in English the modal auxiliaries are defective, that is, they have only fragmentary tense structures. Thus, the verb *must* exists only in the present tense and in that one form *must:* the past, the future, the three perfect tenses, the infinitives, and the participles all are missing. There is, therefore, no possibility of saying in English "he had musted," or "he will must," or "he is musting." This is not the case in German, for in this language the modal auxiliaries have complete tense systems in both the indicative and subjunctive moods. This difference in the languages means that we have to resort to various circumlocutions in translating the German modals in their various forms. Here they are with their most common English meanings:

dürfen	*be allowed to*	**können**	*be able to*
mögen	*like to*	**sollen**	*be supposed to*
müssen	*have to*	**wollen**	*want to*

II. The Forms of the Modals

A. The principal parts of the modals are:

können	konnte	gekonnt	er kann
dürfen	durfte	gedurft	er darf
mögen	mochte	gemocht	er mag
müssen	mußte	gemußt	er muß
sollen	sollte	gesollt	er soll
wollen	wollte	gewollt	er will

B. As you can tell from the principal parts, the modal auxiliaries are irregular in the present tense:

ich	darf	kann	mag	muß	soll	will
du	darfst	kannst	magst	mußt	sollst	willst
er	darf	kann	mag	muß	soll	will
wir	dürfen	können	mögen	müssen	sollen	wollen
ihr	dürft	könnt	mögt	müßt	sollt	wollt
sie	dürfen	können	mögen	müssen	sollen	wollen
Sie	dürfen	können	mögen	müssen	sollen	wollen

C. When a modal auxiliary is used without a complementary infinitive, that is, as an independent verb, its forms are exactly what you would expect: **er will es** *he wishes it;* **er wollte es** *he wished it;* **er hat es gewollt** *he wished it;* **er hatte es gewollt** *he had wished it;* **er wird es wollen** *he will wish it;* **er wird es gewollt haben** *he will have wished it.* But when a modal auxiliary does take a complementary infinitive, a peculiar form occurs in the present perfect, past perfect and future perfect tenses. That is, the perfect participle of the modal occurs in a form which is identical with the present infinitive. Compare the six tenses of **er will es** *he wishes it* with the six tenses of **er will es tun** *he wishes to do it:*

Er will es	Er will es tun
Er wollte es	Er wollte es tun
Er hat es gewollt	Er hat es tun wollen
Er hatte es gewollt	Er hatte es tun wollen
Er wird es wollen	Er wird es tun wollen
Er wird es gewollt haben	Er wird es haben tun wollen

The combination **tun wollen** in the three perfect tenses is known as a double infinitive and comes at the very end of the clause. Any other element, such as infinitive or past participle, which is postponed will precede the double infinitive.

The verbs **heißen** *order,* **helfen** *help,* **hören** *hear,* **lassen** *let,* **lehren** *teach,* **lernen** *learn,* **machen** *make,* **sehen** see (and sometimes **fühlen** *feel* and **nennen** *name*) may also take the double infinitive construction: **Ich habe es kommen sehen** *I have seen it coming.*

III. Use and Meanings of the Modal Auxiliaries

A. In addition to the basic meanings given early in this chapter, the modals have a great many special idiomatic meanings which can best be learned from careful observation of their use in various contexts. Some of the most common idiomatic meanings are illustrated in the following sentences:

  1. **Das dürfen Sie nicht glauben.** *You must not believe that.*
  2. **Das dürfte der Fall sein.** *That might be the case.*
  3. **Wenn auch mancherlei um Mozart herum vorging, er durfte nur die Musik aus dem Sack seines Gehirns wieder herausnehmen.** *Even though many kinds of things went on round about Mozart, he needed only to take the music back out of his brainsack.* (For word order see this Unit, Note 8 to German Text.)
  4. **Er kann Deutsch.** *He knows German.*
  5. **Das mag wahr sein.** *That may be true.*
  6. **Möchten Sie eine Zigarette?** *Would you like a cigarette?*
  7. **Was soll ich denn davon sagen?** *What am I to say about it?*
  8. **Diese Symphonie soll Mozartisch sein.** *This symphony is said to be Mozartean.*
  9. **Was soll das?** *What is the meaning of that?*
  10. **Er wollte eben gehen.** *He was just about to go.*
  11. **Das will was sagen.** *That means something.*
  12. **Wir wollen jetzt aufhören.** *Let us stop now.* **Wollen wir heute abend ins Kino gehen.** *Let's go to the movies this evening.*
  13. **Der Baron wollte auch Musikkenner sein.** *The baron pretended to be a music expert, too.*

B. It will be noticed that in the preceding list of idiomatic meanings there are two subjunctive forms, in sentence 2 and sentence 6. A general discussion of the subjunctive mood will be given in the next two chapters, but it may be well to anticipate a bit here and point out the difference between the simple past indicative forms of the modals and the subjunctive forms, that is, the present subjunctive II forms, which resemble them.

PAST INDICATIVE		PRESENT SUBJUNCTIVE II	
durfte	*was allowed to*	dürfte	*would be allowed to*
konnte	*was able to*	könnte	*would be able to*
mochte	*liked to*	möchte	*would like to*
mußte	*had to*	müßte	*would have to*
sollte	*was to*	sollte	*ought to*
wollte	*wished to*	wollte	*would wish to*

Notice that in the first four verbs the subjunctive forms are distinguished from the indicative forms by the modified, that is, the umlauted vowel. Whether the forms **sollte** and **wollte** are indicative or subjunctive is made clear only by the context. However, a fairly reliable rule of thumb is that the form **sollte** is usually subjunctive and means *should* or *ought to,* unless it occurs in the context of some adverb or other expression of time which puts it in the past, to mean *was supposed to:* **das sollten Sie nicht tun** *you shouldn't do that,* but **er sollte ursprünglich Musiker werden** *he was originally supposed to become a musician.* **Wollte,** on the other hand, is usually the past indicative form unless the context makes it clear that it is subjunctive, as in this part of a sentence from Mozart's letter: **Ich wollte ja immer fort arbeiten, dürfte ich nur immer solche Musik machen wie ich will und kann** *I would want to work constantly if only I were allowed to make such music as I wish and can.*

   C.   Notice the difference between such pairs of sentences as the following:

1.   a.   **Er hat es tun können.** *He has been able to do it.*
      b.   **Er kann es getan haben.** *He can have done it.*
2.   a.   **Er hat es sagen müssen.** *He has had to say it.*
      b.   **Er muß es gesagt haben.** *He must have said it.*

The first sentence in each group consists of the present perfect tense of the modal auxiliary, hat . . . können, hat . . . müssen, with the complementary present infinitive, **tun, sagen.** The second sentence in each group consists of the present tense of the modal, **kann, muß,** with the complementary perfect infinitive, **getan haben, gesagt haben.** All these sentences are perfectly parallel to the corresponding English sentence.

Sentences of the first type frequently occur also in the subjunctive mood (past subjunctive II). Here are some simple examples with suggested translations.

1. **Das hätte er schon tun dürfen.** *He would have been allowed to do that.*
2. **Ich hätte das tun können.** *I would have been able to do that.* or, *I could have done that.*
3. **Das hätte ich sehen mögen.** *I would have liked to see that.*
4. **Er hätte das tun müssen.** *He would have had to do that.*
5. **Das hätte er nicht tun sollen.** *He should not have done that.*
6. **Ich hätte das tun wollen.** *I would have wished to do that.*

EXERCISES

I.   These exercises are at page 185.

II. Determine which English sentence is the best translation of the German in each group.

   1.   Und was soll ich denn sagen von Ihrem Präsent?

a.   And what am I to say about your present?
b.   Then what will I say about your present?
c.   What should I say about your present?
d.   What shall I say next about your present?

   2.   Er mußte sich manchmal schinden und placken, um das arme Leben zu gewinnen.

a.   He frequently had to pinch and scrape in order to gain a meager living.
b.   He must frequently pinch and scrape in order to gain a meager living.
c.   Occasionally he will be compelled to pinch and scrape in order to win a poor livelihood.
d.   He would frequently have to pinch and scrape in order to win a poor livelihood.

   3.   Dürfte er nur immer solche Musik machen, so wollte er immer fort arbeiten.

a.   He was always allowed to make such music; he always wanted to work on and on.
b.   He may always make such music, if he will only keep on working.
c.   He would always keep on working if only he were allowed always to make such music.
d.   He was always able to make such music, so he always wanted to keep on working.

4. Aber ich will es doch versuchen, und sollten Sie nur etwas zu lachen drinnen finden.

a. But I will try it just the same, and you should simply find something to laugh at in it.
b. But I want to try it all the same, and you shall find merely something to laugh at in it.
c. But let me try it just the same, and you really ought to find something to laugh at in it.
d. But I will try it all the same, and even if you should only find something to laugh at in it.

5. Und mag um mich herum mancherlei vorgehen, ich mache mir nichts daraus.

a. And I like many things going on around me, even if I don't make anything out of it.
b. And I like to go ahead with many kinds of things I make nothing of.
c. And even if many things go on all around me, it means nothing to me.
d. Many kinds like to go ahead of me, but I don't care.

6. Und wenn ich es auch darauf anlegen wollte, ich wüßte meinen Sachen die Gestalt nicht zu geben, daß sie Mozartisch sind.

a. And whenever I wished to aim at that, I never knew what shape to give my things so that they would be Mozartean.
b. And even if I wanted to make that my aim, I would not be able to give my things such a form as to be Mozartean.
c. Whenever I wanted to make that my aim, I forgot to shape my things so as to be Mozartean.
d. And if I wanted to stop at that, I did not know the shape to give my things that were Mozartean.

7. Das hatte ihm die Seele erhitzt und er wollte dem Lump ein paar tüchtige Watschen geben, aber dann mußte er über die ganze Sache lachen.

a. That has infuriated his soul and he wants to give the rascal a couple of sound smacks, but then he must laugh at the whole business.

b. That stirred up his soul and he would wish to give the rascal a few sound blows, but he had to laugh at the whole thing.
c. Even though he was very angry, and intended to give the rascal a few energetic whacks, he had to laugh at the whole thing.
d. That had infuriated him and he was just about to give the rascal a few energetic whacks, but then he had to laugh at the whole thing.

   8. Sie sollte mich nicht so sehr loben.
a. They are not supposed to praise me so much.
b. She ought not to praise me so much.
c. You shouldn't praise me so much.
d. You mustn't praise me so much.

III.   Decide which statement in each group is not true.

GROUP 1
a. War Mozart guter Dinge, kamen ihm die Gedanken stromweis und er konnte nichts dazu.
b. Wenn Mozart guter Dinge war, konnten ihm die Gedanken stromweis kommen und er machte sich nichts daraus.
c. Manchmal konnte Mozart nachts nicht schlafen; da ging er spazieren und ihm kam dann eins nach dem andern bei, bis das Ding ihm im Kopf fast fertig ward.
d. Es müssen diesem einzigartigen Musiker die Gedanken stromweis gekommen sein.

GROUP 2
a. Was von Mozarts Manier in der Musik gilt, gilt auch von seiner Nase: er kann sich das eine so wenig als das andere gegeben haben.
b. Hatte Mozart nun gleichsam alles zusammen überhört, konnte er die Arbeit Wunder wie schnell auf Papier werfen.
c. Es durfte ihn aber niemand stören, obgleich er sehr gerne plaudern mochte.
d. Bei Mozart ging all das Finden und Machen wie in einem schönen starken Traum vor, aber das Überhören wird für ihn doch wohl das beste gewesen sein.

GROUP 3

a. Mozart hatte gut arbeiten:* böse Leute wollten nichts davon wissen, daß er sich manchmal placken und schinden mußte, um das arme Leben zu gewinnen.

b. Mozart hatte eine große Bitte an den Baron: daß er den bösen Leuten ein paar tüchtige Watschen versetzte.

c. Er schrieb dem Baron, daß er vor acht Tagen eine Symphonie gemacht hätte.

d. Mozart brannte es auf den Nägeln, solche Musik zu machen, wie er wollte und konnte.

GROUP 4

a. Wurde Mozart auch beim Ausarbeiten seiner Sachen gestört, er durfte doch nur die Musik, die ihm beigekommen war, aus dem Sack seines Gehirns wieder herausnehmen.

b. Mozart ging es wie es den meisten Musikern beim Ausarbeiten ihrer Sachen geht.

c. Die Feder war ihm meistens zu willen, auch wenn mancherlei um ihn herum vorging.

d. Er wußte seine Besonderheit nicht näher zu beschreiben.

* See Third Unit, Note 3 to the German Text, page 42.

FIFTH UNIT

SELECTIONS FROM THE WRITINGS OF
GEORG CHRISTOPH LICHTENBERG
(1742-1799)

Among the many versatile men of genius of the eighteenth century, Lichtenberg occupies a place of honor. Mathematician, astronomer, chemist, and physicist, he added luster to the brilliant reputation of the University of Göttingen, which had been founded in 1737 by King George II of England. Lichtenberg studied in England for rather long periods of time and communicated his enthusiasm for England to educated circles in Germany; he was commissioned by King George III to make the geodetic calculations for an accurate atlas of the king's German domains; and he was an unofficial faculty adviser to many young English students at the university (including the king's own sons). In his professional sphere, he was one of the first to resort to experiment to test mathematical theory and to set up elaborate and striking chemical and physical demonstrations in the lecture room.

He wrote with great elegance and wit on scientific and other subjects ranging from religious matters to the pseudo-science of physiognomy and to a critical appreciation of the engravings of the English artist Hogarth. Of equal elegance in style and wit are his private journals, in which he jotted down scattered observations, queries, philosophical insights, comments of all kinds. But whereas the published essays and papers were cool, ironical, even rationalistically skeptical, his private notebooks show him in an introspective struggle with the great questions of life: What is God? What is man? What can we know? You will find some of his tentative answers to these questions on the following pages.

APHORISMEN

VON GEORG CHRISTOPH LICHTENBERG

1. Ein Buch ist ein Spiegel: wenn ein Affe hineinguckt, so kann freilich kein Apostel heraussehen. Wir haben keine Worte, mit dem Dummen von Weisheit zu sprechen. Der ist schon weise, der den Weisen versteht.

5 2. Mir ist es immer vorgekommen, als wenn man den Wert der Neuern gegen die Alten auf einer sehr falschen Wage wäge und den letztern Vorzüge einräumte, die sie nicht verdienen. Die Alten schrieben zu einer Zeit, da die große Kunst schlecht zu schreiben noch nicht erfunden war und bloß schreiben hieß gut 10 schreiben. Sie schrieben wahr, wie die Kinder wahr reden. Jetzt ist natürlich schreiben, möcht' ich sagen, fast unnatürlich. Homer hat gewiß nicht gewußt, daß er gut schrieb, so wenig wie Shakespeare. Unsre heutigen guten Schriftsteller müssen alle die fatale Kunst lernen: zu wissen, daß sie gut schreiben.

15 3. Wenn man eine Arbeit vorhat, so ist es gut bei der Ausführung sich nicht gleich das Ganze vorzustellen, denn dieses hat viel Niederschlagendes; sondern man arbeite an dem, was man gerade vor sich hat; und wenn man damit fertig ist, gehe man an das nächste.

20 4. Man schneide die Glieder nicht ab, die man noch heilen kann, wenn sie auch gleich etwas verstümmelt bleiben; der Mensch könnte über der Operation sterben. Und man reiße nicht gleich ein Gebäude ein, das etwas unbequem ist, und stecke sich dadurch in größere Unbequemlichkeiten. Man mache *kleine* 25 Verbesserungen.

APHORISMS

BY GEORG CHRISTOPH LICHTENBERG

1. A book is a mirror: if a monkey looks in, then, to be sure, an apostle cannot look out. We have no words [with which] to talk of wisdom with a stupid man. The [man] who understands the sage is already sagacious.

2. It has always seemed to me as though we balanced the value of the Moderns against the Ancients on very inaccurate scales[a] and conceded to the latter excellences which they do not deserve. The Ancients wrote at a time when the great art of writing badly had not yet been invented, and merely to write was the same as writing well. They wrote truthfully [just] as children speak truthfully. Nowadays, I am tempted to say, writing naturally is almost unnatural. Homer surely did not know that he wrote well, any more than did Shakespeare. Our good writers of today are all under the necessity of acquiring that unfortunate accomplishment: to know when they write well.

3. When one is engaged in a [piece of] work, it is not good, when carrying it out,[b] to picture the whole thing to oneself right away, for this is very depressing; but instead one should work at that which one has right before him, and when one is finished with that, go on to the next thing.

4. One should not cut off limbs which can still be healed, even though they may remain somewhat crippled; the [whole] person could die of the operation. And one should not immediately tear down a building that is a bit uncomfortable and thus lodge oneself in greater discomforts. Make *small* improvements.

5. Wenn Leute ihre Träume aufrichtig erzählen wollten, da ließe sich der Charakter eher daraus erraten[1] als aus dem Gesicht.

6. Mein Körper ist derjenige Teil der Welt, den meine Gedanken verändern können. Sogar eingebildete Krankheiten können wirkliche werden. In der übrigen Welt können meine Hypothesen die Ordnung der Dinge nicht stören.

7. Wie glücklich würde mancher leben, wenn er sich um anderer Leute Sachen so wenig bekümmerte als um seine eigenen.

8. Wenn man auf einer entfernten Insel einmal ein Volk anträfe, bei dem alle Häuser mit scharfgeladenem Gewehr behängt wären und man beständig des Nachts Wache hielte, was würde ein Reisender anders denken können, als daß die ganze Insel von Räubern bewohnt wäre? Ist es aber mit den europäischen Reichen anders? Man sieht hieraus von wie wenigem Einfluß die Religion überhaupt[2] auf Menschen ist, die sonst kein Gesetz über sich erkennen, oder wenigstens, wie weit wir noch von einer wahren Religion entfernt sind.

9. Einer der größten und zugleich gemeinsten Fehler der Menschen ist, daß sie glauben, andere Menschen kennten ihre Schwächen nicht, weil sie nicht davon plaudern hören[3] oder nichts davon gedruckt lesen. Ich glaube aber, daß die meisten Menschen besser von andern gekannt werden, als sie sich selbst kennen.

10. Zweifle an allem wenigstens einmal, und wäre es auch der Satz: zwei und zwei ist vier.

11. Etwas das sich mit der Schnelligkeit des Blitzes oder des Lichts von dem einen Ende eines Sandkörnchens bis zum andern bewegt, wird uns zu ruhen scheinen.

12. Es wäre ein denkendes Wesen möglich, dem das Zukünftige leichter zu sehen wäre als das Vergangene. Bei den Trieben der Insekten ist schon manches, das uns glauben machen muß, daß sie mehr durch das Künftige als das Vergangene geleitet werden. Hätten die Tiere ebenso viel Erinnerung des Vergangenen als Vorgefühl vom Künftigen, so wäre uns manches Insekt überlegen. So aber scheint die Stärke des Vorgefühls immer im umgekehrten Verhältnis mit der Erinnerung an das Vergangene zu stehen.

5. If people were willing to tell their dreams honestly, their characters could be divined from this sooner than from their faces.

6. My body is that part of the world which my thoughts can change. Even imaginary illnesses can become real ones. In the rest of the world my hypotheses cannot disturb the order of things. 30

7. How happily would many a person live if he concerned himself as little about other people's affairs as about his own.

8. If sometime on a distant island one should come upon a people where the houses were all hung full of loaded guns and where they constantly posted sentinels at night, what else would 35 a traveler be able to think than that the whole island were inhabited by robbers? But is it any different with the European nations? One sees from this how little influence religion has, on the whole, upon people who acknowledge no other law above them, or at least [one sees] how far we are still removed from a 40 true religion.

9. One of the greatest and at the same time most common failings of human beings is that they believe other people do not know their weaknesses, because they do not hear [anyone] talk about them or read anything about them in print. I believe, how- 45 ever, that most people are known better by others than they know themselves.

10. Question everything at least once, even if it were the statement, "two plus two is four."

11. Something that moves with the speed of lightning or of 50 light from one end of a grain of sand to the other will seem to us to be at rest.

12. It would be possible [to conceive of] a thinking creature[c] for whom the future would be easier to see than the past. There is a good deal about the drives of the insects that must make us 55 believe that they are guided by the future more than the past. If these animals had as much recollection of the past as premonition of the future, many an insect would be superior to us. As it is, however, the force of premonition always seems to be in inverse proportion to recollection of the past. 60

13.   Wir mögen uns eine Art, uns die Dinge außer uns vorzustellen,[4] denken, welche wir wollen, so wird und muß sie immer
etwas von dem Subjekt an sich tragen. Es ist, dünkt mich, eine
65 sehr unphilosophische Idee, unsere Seele bloß als ein leidendes
Ding anzusehen; nein, sie leihet auch den Gegenständen. Auf
diese Weise möchte es kein Wesen in der Welt geben,[5] das die
Welt so erkennte, wie sie ist. Ich kann mir gar wohl vorstellen,
daß es Wesen geben könnte, für die die Ordnung des Weltge-
70 bäudes eine Musik ist, wonach sie tanzen können, während der
Himmel aufspielt.

14.   Wenn uns ein Engel einmal aus seiner Philosophie erzählte, ich glaube, es müßten wohl manche Sätze so klingen, als
wie zweimal zwei ist dreizehn.

75 15.   Ich bin überzeugt, daß, wenn Gott einmal einen solchen
Menschen schaffen würde, wie ihn[6] sich die Magistri und Professoren vorstellen, er müßte den ersten Tag ins Tollhaus gebracht
werden.

NOTES TO THE GERMAN TEXT

1.   **da ließe sich der Charakter erraten**   *the character would let
itself be* (i.e., *could be*) *guessed.* This is another important
idiomatic use of **lassen** (see Second Unit, Note 6 to the German Text, page 30). It is illustrated in such expressions as:
das läßt sich leicht machen   *that can be easily done;* **er ließ
sich nicht bewegen**   *he could not be moved;* **wir lassen uns
gerne von ihm leiten**   *we are glad to be guided by him.*

2.   **überhaupt:**   a very troublesome word with the dictionary
definitions *in general, generally, at all, on the whole.* But often
these definitions will not suit and it may be necessary to
express the idea by some circumlocution. The following sentence illustrates its meaning rather handily: **Du hättest das
überhaupt nicht tun sollen und besonders nicht jetzt**   *You
should not have done that in any case, and especially not now.*

3.   **weil sie nicht davon plaudern hören**   *because they do not
hear chat about them.* This may be considered an ellipsis for
some such full form as **weil sie die andern nicht davon plaudern hören**   *because they do not hear the others chat about
them.* Or it may be felt that the infinitive **plaudern** is actually

13. We may conceive any way we like of having an idea of the things outside ourselves, it will and must always have something of the subject[d] about it. It is, it seems to me, a very unphilosophical idea to regard our soul merely as a passive thing; no, it also *makes contributions* to objects. In this way there might 65 not be any creature in the world that apprehended the world as it is. I can very well conceive that there could be creatures for whom the order of the world structure is music to which they can dance while the heavens strike up a tune.

14. If an angel were to tell us sometime something out of his 70 philosophy, I believe many propositions would sound like two times two is thirteen.

15. I am convinced that if God were ever to create a human being such as the scholars and professors imagine [man to be], on the [very] first day he would have to be taken to the madhouse. 75

NOTES TO THE ENGLISH TEXT

a. **als wenn man den Wert der Neuern gegen die Alten auf einer sehr falschen Wage wäge** *as though one weighed the value of the Moderns against the Ancients on a very inaccurate balance.* The Ancients are, of course, the old Greeks and Romans. The form **wäge** is the present subjunctive I of **wägen, wog, gewogen, wägt.** The verb may also have weak forms: **wägen, wägte, gewägt.** It may also have the forms **wiegen, wog, gewogen, wiegt,** and **wiegen, wiegte, gewiegt, wiegt.** For such irregularities you will need to consult the list of strong and irregular verbs in this book or in any good dictionary.

b. **bei der Ausführung** *in the execution.*

c. **Es wäre ein denkendes Wesen möglich** *A thinking creature would be possible* that is, it might be possible for such a creature to exist. For **Es,** see Third Unit, Note 6 to the German Text.

d. **das Subjekt** *the subject:* a philosophical term which designates that which perceives, feels, and thinks, the individual mind, and also, in some philosophical systems, the Universal Mind. Here it means the individual mind.

the direct object of **hören** as in the sentence **Ich höre plaudern** *I hear chatting.* Notice that English requires either a noun or pronoun object with the infinitive: *I have heard* HIM *talk about it;* or a verbal substantive, sometimes called a gerund, *I hear* CHATTING.

4. **sich vorstellen** in everyday speech means *imagine:* **Das kann ich mir kaum vorstellen** *I can scarcely imagine that.* But in the language of philosophers it means *form an idea*—just how this is done is, of course, a subject of philosophical debate— and not *perceive* or *sense* or *feel.* The noun based on this verb, **die Vorstellung,** occurs in the title of the chief work of the great philosopher Arthur Schopenhauer, **Die Welt als Wille und Vorstellung** *The World as Will and Idea.*

5. **es möchte kein Wesen in der Welt geben** *it might give no creature in the world.* This is a form of that familiar idiom **es gibt,** which is sometimes hard to recognize when it does not appear in the present indicative. Remember that it can occur in any tense of the indicative or subjunctive and in combination, as here, with the modal auxiliaries.

6. **wie ihn sich die Professoren vorstellen** *as the professors imagine him.* From the point of view of English the pronoun (**ihn**) is unnecessary and the translation is, *such as the professors imagine.*

GRAMMATICAL COMMENT—THE
SUBJUNCTIVE IN DIRECT DISCOURSE

I. Introduction

It has become traditional for students of foreign languages to shiver with apprehension when "the subjunctive mood" is mentioned in their presence. Actually, the subjunctive mood is not as black as it is made out to be, because, in German at any rate, the subjunctive forms are very regular and have English parallels. Thus when Macbeth says, "If it were done when 'tis done, then it were well it were done quickly," he might as well be speaking German except for the vocabulary, and if you fully understand that bit of Shakespearean subjunctive, you have a hold of the basic principles involved.

Before we proceed, however, you should be informed that the terminology employed in any given description of the grammatical structure of a language is not something that is universally accepted. This is especially true about the subjunctive: some grammarians like one set of terms and definitions and some grammarians prefer another. You may or may not be familiar with the terms we are going to use. In any case, please remember that there is nothing sacred or immutable about these terms or any others. You will probably do best if you just accept the ones we use here and work with them. They really *are* as good as any, and, of course, your author has found them the most convenient in the classes he has taught.

Everybody is agreed, however, that when an utterance is expressed in the subjunctive mood it is made subject to some contingency, concession, or doubt, or it conveys a wish, purpose, or imperative. Because the subjunctive mood does not state or assert something flatly, no given subjunctive form, *when isolated,* has a standard translation or meaning. Nobody can tell you the meaning of **wäre**, for example, until that word is used in a context. It can, however, be described grammatically, classified, and set into relation with the entire subjunctive and indicative system of the verb **sein,** of which it is a part. We are now about to set forth a general description of the subjunctive system of German verbs.

II. Forms of the Subjunctive

A. THE TIME DISTINCTIONS

You know, of course, that a German verb in the indicative mood has six tenses. When speaking of the subjunctive system of a German verb, however, it is well to speak of *time distinctions* rather than tenses. These time distinctions are: present, past, future, and future perfect. Each time distinction, moreover, has two forms. If you will stop to think of it, of course, you will soon realize that this is the case in English also: "So be it" and "If it were only so" both employ present subjunctive forms of the verb *be* and the forms are different because the functions of the verb are different in the two sentences. In German these two sentences are expressed: **So sei es!** and **Wenn es nur so wäre!**—a perfect parallel. Notice especially that all these sentences, English as well as German, refer to the *present* time: "So be it (now)" and "If it were only so (now)." You can therefore readily see that the present subjunctive in both German and English has two distinct forms: *were* and *be,* **wäre** and **sei** are all present in meaning. Hence the general statement: A complete German verb has four time distinctions in the subjunctive mood and each time distinction has two forms. The different forms we will merely number I and II. Thus we have in the abstract the following subjunctive system for every complete German verb:

Present I	Future I
Present II	Future II
Past I	Future perfect I
Past II	Future perfect II

Please understand at the outset that the two different forms (I and II) have different functions and are not interchangeable, although they refer to the same time.

B. THE ENDINGS

With one exception, *all* verbs have the same endings in *all* time distinctions and *both* forms. These endings are:

-e	-en
-est	-et
-e	-en

The single exception is the present I of **sein:**

ich sei	wir seien
du seiest	ihr seiet
er sei	sie seien

Sie seien

C. FORMATION OF THE TIME DISTINCTIONS

1. *THE PRESENT SUBJUNCTIVE I* is based upon the present stem of the verb, to which are added the subjunctive endings. Notice that the one really distinctively subjunctive form is the third person singular with the ending **-e** rather than the **-t** of the indicative:

ich hab -e	wir hab -en	ich mach -e	wir mach -en
du hab -est	ihr hab -et	du mach -est	ihr mach -et
er hab -e	sie hab -en	er mach -e	sie mach -en
Sie hab -en		Sie mach -en	

ich geb -e	wir geb -en	ich könn -e	wir könn -en
du geb -est	ihr geb -et	du könn -est	ihr könn -et
er geb -e	sie geb -en	er könn -e	sie könn -en
Sie geb -en		Sie könn -en	

2. *THE PRESENT SUBJUNCTIVE II* is based upon the stem of the simple past indicative, to which are added the regular subjunctive endings. In the case of weak verbs the present subjunctive II is identical with the simple past indicative:

ich macht -e	wir macht -en
du macht -est	ihr macht -et
er macht -e	sie macht -en

Sie macht -en

In the case of the strong verbs not only are the endings added to the simple past stem but also the vowel of the stem is umlauted if possible (i.e., if *a, o,* or *u*):

ich schrieb -e	wir schrieb -en	ich gäb -e	wir gäb -en
du schrieb -est	ihr schrieb -et	du gäb -est	ihr gäb -et
er schrieb -e	sie schrieb -en	er gäb -e	sie gäb -en
Sie schrieb -en		Sie gäb -en	

Notice, however, that a good many strong verbs may have in the present subjunctive II a modified or umlauted vowel different from the vowel of the past stem: **ich half**, but **ich hülfe; ich gewann**, but **ich gewönne; ich warf**, but **ich würfe**. The modal auxiliaries are regular in the formation of the present subjunctive II except that **sollen** and **wollen** have no umlauted vowel: **ich dürfte, könnte, möchte, müßte, sollte, wollte**. In the case of the other mixed verbs the present subjunctive II forms have the vowel of the present stem: indicative **ich kannte**, but subjunctive **ich kennte; ich sandte**, but **ich sendete**. Such irregularities can be found in the list of strong and irregular verbs in this book or in any good German-English dictionary.

3. *THE PAST SUBJUNCTIVE I* is made up of the past participle of the verb in question plus the present subjunctive I of the proper auxiliary:

ich	habe	gemacht	wir	haben	gemacht
du	habest	gemacht	ihr	habet	gemacht
er	habe	gemacht	sie	haben	gemacht

Sie haben gemacht

ich	sei	gekommen	wir	seien	gekommen
du	seiest	gekommen	ihr	seiet	gekommen
er	sei	gekommen	sie	seien	gekommen

Sie seien gekommen

4. *THE PAST SUBJUNCTIVE II* is made up of the past participle of the verb in question plus the present subjunctive II of the proper auxiliary:

ich	hätte	geschrieben	wir	hätten	geschrieben
du	hättest	geschrieben	ihr	hättet	geschrieben
er	hätte	geschrieben	sie	hätten	geschrieben

Sie hätten geschrieben

ich	wäre	gefolgt	wir	wären	gefolgt
du	wärest	gefolgt	ihr	wäret	gefolgt
er	wäre	gefolgt	sie	wären	gefolgt

Sie wären gefolgt

Notice that the past subjunctive is always a compound form: **er habe gemacht, er wäre gefolgt.**

5. *THE FUTURE SUBJUNCTIVE I* is made up of the present infinitive of the verb in question plus the present subjunctive I of the tense auxiliary **werden:**

ich werde	schreiben	wir werden schreiben	
du werdest	schreiben	ihr werdet schreiben	
er werde	schreiben	sie werden schreiben	

Sie werden schreiben

6. *THE FUTURE SUBJUNCTIVE II* is made up of the present infinitive of the verb in question plus the present subjunctive II of the tense auxiliary **werden: ich würde schreiben,** etc.

7. *THE FUTURE PERFECT SUBJUNCTIVE* follows the pattern:

I		II	
ich werde	geschrieben haben	ich würde	geschrieben haben
du werdest	geschrieben haben	du würdest	geschrieben haben
	etc.		etc.
ich werde	gekommen sein	ich würde	gekommen sein
du werdest	gekommen sein	du würdest	gekommen sein
	etc.		etc.

III. Uses of the Subjunctive in Direct Discourse

In *direct* discourse, form I is used rather infrequently, since its functions are restricted very largely to formal expressions and pious phrases. The subjunctive II forms, on the other hand, are used very often indeed, as you have discovered in reading the basic text of this lesson. Let us therefore consider the subjunctive II forms first.

A. THE SUBJUNCTIVE II FORMS IN DIRECT DISCOURSE

1. *EXPRESSING UNREAL CONDITION.* "Unreal condition" is the name we give to that statement of Macbeth which we have already quoted. It is called unreal because the verb forms themselves, that is, the subjunctive forms, clearly indicate that the circumstances under which something would be true do not really exist. To be explicit, by using the *were* in "If it were done when 'tis done," Macbeth tells us that he knows it will not be done, that

is, over and done with, when the murder is accomplished. That choice of mood is completely in accord with modern English usage, except that we no longer say "then it were well it were done quickly" but instead, "then it would be well, if it were done quickly." Notice particularly the possibility of interchanging *it were* and *it would be*, for, as you will see, the precisely analogous possibility exists in German also.

Now the reason for starting off with a study of the unreal condition in German is not only that expressing unreal condition is the most important and common function of the subjunctive form II, but also that many other important functions of this form are based upon it. Let us take a sentence from our text, the twelfth aphorism, and modify it slightly to suit our purposes: **Hätten die Tiere ebensoviel Erinnerung des Vergangenen als Vorgefühl des Künftigen, so wäre uns manches Insekt überlegen.** This can be translated word for word into Macbeth's English: *Had the animals just as much recollection of the past as premonition of the future, then many an insect were superior to us.* In modern English, of course, we would say "then many an insect would be superior to us." This particular German sentence uses the present subjunctive II of **sein** (i.e. **wäre**) in the conclusion, and uses inverted or verb-subject order to express the condition, but it could also be written in a form which is precisely parallel to modern English: **Wenn die Tiere ebensoviel Erinnerung des Vergangenen als Vorgefühl des Künftigen hätten, so würde uns manches Insekt überlegen sein.** *If the animals had just as much recollection of the past as premonition of the future, then many an insect would be superior to us.* That is, the present subjunctive II (**wäre**) of the original conclusion has been replaced by the future subjunctive II (**würde . . . sein**) and the meaning remains the same. If you fix the structure of these sentences and the Macbeth sentence firmly in your mind and use them as a starting point and a model, the following brief systematic formulation of the various uses of subjunctive II in direct discourse should be relatively easy to understand.

PRESENT II

Present subjunctive II in unreal conditions is used to express present or future time.

Present time: **Wenn die Tiere ebensoviel Erinnerung des Ver-**

gangenen als Vorgefühl des Künftigen hätten, so wäre uns manches Insekt überlegen. *If the animals had just as much recollection of the past as premonition of the future, many an insect would be superior to us.*

Future time: **Wenn man auf einer entfernten Insel so ein Volk anträfe, was könnte ein Reisender anders denken, als daß die ganze Insel von Räubern bewohnt wäre?** *If one encountered such a people on a distant island, what else could a traveler think than that the whole island were inhabited by robbers?*

FUTURE II

Future subjunctive II is almost interchangeable with present subjunctive II, especially so in concluding clauses: **manches Insekt würde uns überlegen sein** *many an insect would be superior to us;* **was würde ein Reisender anders denken können?** *what else would a traveler be able to think?*

PAST II

Past subjunctive II in unreal conditions is used to express past time: **Wenn Gott einen solchen Menschen geschaffen hätte, so hätte man ihn den ersten Tag ins Tollhaus gebracht.** *If God had created such a person, one would have taken him to the madhouse the very first day.*

FUTURE PERFECT II

Future perfect subjunctive II is almost interchangeable with past subjunctive II, especially so in concluding clauses: **man würde ihn ins Tollhaus gebracht haben** *one would have taken him to the madhouse.*

2. *USES BASED ON UNREAL CONDITION.* Other uses of the subjunctive II forms based on the unreal conditions are the following.

A conditional clause may be used independently to express a wish: **Wäre das Zukünftige nur eben so leicht zu sehen, wie das Vergangene!** *If only the future were just as easy to see as the past!* **Wenn ich den Weisen nur verstanden hätte!** *If only I had understood the wise man!*

An independent clause with a subjunctive II form expresses what would or might be or what might have been: **Es wäre ein** solches denkendes Wesen möglich *Such a thinking creature would be possible.* Unter diesen Umständen würde mancher glücklich leben. *Under these conditions many a person would live happily.* Ein solches denkendes Wesen wäre möglich gewesen. *Such a thinking creature would have been possible.* Unter diesen Umständen würde mancher glücklich gelebt haben. *Under these conditions many a person would have lived happily.*

A subordinate clause introduced by als ob or als wenn, meaning *as if* or *as though,* may employ the subjunctive II: Mir ist es immer vorgekommen, als wenn man den Alten Vorzüge einräumte, die sie nicht verdienen. *It has always seemed to me as though one conceded merits to the Ancients which they do not deserve.* The wenn or ob of als wenn and als ob may be omitted. In that case the subjunctive verb follows immediately upon als: als räumte man den Alten Vorzüge ein, die sie nicht verdienen.

Auch and gleich are frequently used in conditional clauses employing subjunctive II forms to express a concession: Zweifle an allem wenigstens einmal, und wäre es auch der Satz: zwei und zwei ist vier. *Question everything at least once, even if it were the statement: two and two is four.* The clause may also be written wenn es auch der Satz wäre.

B. THE SUBJUNCTIVE I FORMS IN DIRECT DISCOURSE

The subjunctive I forms are, generally speaking, more formal and ceremonial than the II forms. Hence their use is largely restricted to certain stereotypes. In English they exist only in (1) a few set expressions such as "So be it," "Perish the thought," "Long live the king," "Thanks be to God," and (2) in pious formulas in prayer, for example, "Thy kingdom come," "God bless you," "The Lord lift up his countenance upon you and give you peace." Examples of such formulas in German are: Gott sei Dank! *Thanks be to God;* Es lebe der König! *[Long] live the king;* Möge es dir gut ergehen! *May it go well with you;* Gott segne dich! *God bless you.*

Whereas in English the subjunctive I forms are scarcely more than mere vestigial fragments, in German they are much more generally used. In the third person singular the subjunctive I expresses a formal imperative which we must usually translate by a phrase employing the auxiliary verb *let.* Thus, the subjunctive formula "Perish the thought" can be rephrased as "Let the thought perish." This use of the subjunctive I in German is especially frequent in stating assumptions that should be made or in giving directions in a general way: **AB sei die Seite eines Dreiecks ABC** *let AB be the side of a triangle ABC;* **der Dumme spreche nicht von Weisheit** *let the fool not speak of wisdom.* In the text of this chapter there are several sentences of this kind with the impersonal subject **man.** Such sentences can be translated by a phrase employing the auxiliary *should:* **man mache kleine Verbesserungen** *one should make small improvements;* **man arbeite an dem, was man gerade vor sich hat** *one should work at the thing that one just has before him.* The subjunctive I is also used in the first person plural as a rather formal imperative: **Stellen wir uns die Dinge so vor!** *Let us imagine the things thus.* **Machen wir kleine Verbesserungen!** *Let us make small improvements.* In everyday conversation or less formal language, except for such a phrase as **Gehen wir!** *Let's go,* the tendency is for the first person plural imperative to be expressed by **wollen: wir wollen jetzt aufhören** *let us stop now;* **wollen wir jetzt nach Hause gehen** *let's go home now.*

Certain functions of the subjunctive II are shared with the subjunctive I. The **als wenn** or **als ob** clauses may employ forms of subjunctive I or II: **Es kam ihm vor, als ob die ganze Insel mit Räubern bewohnt wäre** or **sei.** *It seemed to him as if the whole island were inhabited by robbers.* And concessive clauses with **auch** or **gleich** may employ subjunctive I forms: **wie dem auch sei** *however that may be;* **wenn die Religion gleich von wenig Einfluß auf die Menschen sei** *even though religion be (is) of little influence on people.*

EXERCISES

I.   These exercises are at page 189.

II.   Determine which German sentence best translates the English.

1.   If he were already wise himself, he would have understood the wise man.

a.   Wenn er selber schon weise gewesen wäre, so würde er den Weisen verstanden haben.

b.   Wäre er selber schon weise gewesen, so hätte er den Weisen verstanden.

c.   Er würde den Weisen verstehen, wenn er selber schon weise wäre.

d.   Er hätte den Weisen verstanden, wäre er selber schon weise.

2.   How would a traveler feel, if sometime on a distant island he came upon insects which had an interest in music?

a.   Was hätte ein Reisender gedacht, wenn er einmal auf einer entfernten Insel Insekten angetroffen hätte, die sich für die Musik interessierten?

b.   Wie würde es einem Reisenden gehen, wenn er auf einer entfernten Insel einmal Insekten anträfe, die sich etwas aus der Musik machten?

c.   Wie ist es dem Reisenden gegangen, der auf einer entfernten Insel einmal Insekten angetroffen hat, die sich etwas aus der Musik machten?

d.   Wie wäre es einem Reisenden vorgekommen, wenn er einmal auf einer entfernten Insel Insekten angetroffen hätte, die sich für die Musik interessierten?

3.   Let man imagine the things outside him any way he wishes, he will never know the world as it really is.

a.   Läßt man den Menschen sich die Dinge außer sich so vorstellen wie er will, wird er die Welt so erkennen wie sie wirklich ist.

b. Ließe man den Menschen sich die Dinge außer sich so vorstellen, wie er wollte, würde er die Welt nie so erkennen, wie
sie wirklich ist.

c. Stellte sich der Mensch die Dinge außer sich so vor, wie er
wollte, er würde die Welt nie so erkennen, wie sie wirklich ist.

d. Der Mensch stelle sich die Dinge außer sich so vor, wie er will,
er wird die Welt nie so erkennen, wie sie wirklich ist.

*III. Determine which sentence in each group is in some way con-
nected with the preceding word or phrase.*

1. der menschliche Körper

a. Man bekümmere sich nicht mehr um anderer Leute Sachen
als um seine eigenen.

b. Für ihn wäre die Ordnung des Weltgebäudes eine Musik,
wonach er tanzen könnte.

c. Aus der Schnelligkeit der Bewegung ließe sich erraten, warum
die alte Antwort auf die Frage nicht mehr gilt.

d. Er ist der Teil der Welt, der durch bloße Gedanken verändert
wird.

2. die menschliche Seele

a. Die Dinge außer uns können wir nie so erkennen wie sie sind.

b. Man stelle sich vor, was es bedeuten würde, wenn die Insekten
ebensoviel Erinnerung des Vergangenen als Vorgefühl vom
Künftigen hätten.

c. Die große Kunst schlecht zu schreiben mußte in neuerer Zeit
erfunden werden.

d. Man reiße nicht gleich ein Gebäude ein, das etwas unbequem
ist.

*IV. Select the most appropriate clause to make a complete meaning-
ful sentence.*

1. Ist man mit dem fertig, was man gerade vor sich hat,

a. gehe man an das nächste.

b. würde man kleine Verbesserungen machen.

c. bekümmerte man sich wenig um die große Kunst natürlich
zu schreiben.

d. wenn man es darauf anlegt, sich das Ganze vorzustellen.

2. Gäbe es solche Menschen, wie sie sich die Professoren vorstellen,

a. könnten ihre Hypothesen die Ordnung der Dinge überhaupt nicht stören.

b. müßten sie ins Tollhaus gebracht werden.

c. wären die Professoren guter Dinge und würden ihre Träume aufrichtig erzählen.

d. und hätten sie auch keine Worte, mit dem Dummen von Weisheit zu sprechen.

3. Die meisten modernen Schriftsteller, sagt Lichtenberg, schreiben schlecht, nicht weil ihnen die Feder nicht zu willen ist, sondern

a. weil sie an allem zweifeln und wäre es auch der Satz: zwei mal zwei ist vier.

b. weil man sie auf einer falschen Wage wägt.

c. weil sie immer von ihren Schwächen plaudern.

d. weil sie nicht natürlich schreiben könnten, wenn sie es auch wollten.

4. Wenn uns ein Professor einmal aus seiner Philosophie erzählte,

a. müßte er sogleich ins Tollhaus gebracht werden.

b. müßten wir uns daran erinnern, daß er die Welt, so wie sie ist, nicht erkennen kann.

c. müßte er ein Gesetz über sich erkennen.

d. würden wir verstehen, wie weit wir noch von einer wahren Religion sind.

SIXTH UNIT

A SELECTION FROM

Der große Krieg
in Deutschland

BY RICARDA HUCH

(1864-1947)

As the result of an unhappy love Ricarda Huch decided at the age
of twenty-two to exchange her sheltered and secure life for inde-
pendence and an intellectual career. This decision made it necessary for her to leave Germany and go to Switzerland, where she
very speedily prepared herself to enter the University of Zürich.
In 1891 she attained her doctorate in the study of history and was
embarked upon a long career of abundant literary productivity
which included novels, poetry, and literary criticism as well as
history proper.

In all these fields she made a distinguished contribution to German letters. To her creative endeavors she brought penetration
and philosophical insight which had been sharpened by training
in scholarship; to her critical and historical studies she brought
the enthusiasm, sense of form, and understanding of the human
heart which characterize a true artist. These qualities are apparent
in the following selection from her study of the Thirty Years' War.

AUS **DER GROSSE KRIEG**

IN DEUTSCHLAND

VON **RICARDA HUCH**

Der Wind blieb nicht stetig, sondern sprang wechselnd hin und
her, so daß die Fahrt schwieriger war und länger währte als der
König berechnet hatte; aber gegen den Abend des vierten Juli
begann die Küste sanft glühend, mit einer Laubkrone geschmückt,
5 aus dem Meere zu steigen. „Sie biegt sich mir wie eine sehnende
Braut entgegen,"[1] sagte der König fröhlich, „bevor die Sonne
sinkt, sollen sie meine Arme umfangen." Er sprang als erster aus
dem anlandenden Schiffe, kniete nieder und dankte Gott für die
glücklich vollendete Fahrt. Niemand war rings zu sehen[2] als ein
10 paar zaghaft abseits stehende Fischer mit ihren Frauen und Kin-
dern, die die Neugierde aus ihren Hütten getrieben hatte. Gustav
Adolf trat rasch auf sie zu, sagte, daß er der König von Schweden
sei, gekommen um sie bei ihrem Glauben zu schützen, und fragte,
ob kaiserliche Soldaten auf der Insel wären. Nein, antwortete der
15 eine Mann, sie wären durch Gottes Gnade kürzlich abgezogen.
Ob das nicht Schanzen wären, fragte der König, auf eine Befestigung deutend, die aus dem flachen Boden aufstieg. Die Soldaten
hätten sie verlassen, sagte der Mann, es wären keine mehr oder
nur noch wenige auf Usedom. Die Untersuchung ergab, daß der
20 Mann die Wahrheit gesagt hatte, und die Schweden begaben sich
sofort an die Verschanzungsarbeit.

Nachdem der König auf einem kurzen Streifritt Umschau gehalten hatte, kehrte er an den Strand zurück, da wo die Landung
stattgefunden hatte, und warf sich in das hohe, wildwachsende
25 Sommergras. Zu seiner Linken, nicht weit von ihm, sah er einen
breiten Strom in das Meer fließen: es schien ihm, nachdem er

92

DER GROSSE KRIEG
IN DEUTSCHLAND

BY   RICARDA HUCH

The wind did not remain constant but shifted from one quarter to
the other, so that the voyage was more difficult and lasted longer
than the king[a] had calculated. But towards evening on the fourth
of July the coast, decked out in a diadem of foliage, began to
emerge from the sea in a soft glow. "It is leaning towards me like [5]
a yearning bride," said the king happily, "before the sun sinks my
arms shall embrace her." He was the first to leap from the ship as
it landed, knelt down, and thanked God for the safely completed
voyage. There was no one to be seen round about save for a few
fishermen standing timidly off to one side [together] with their [10]
wives and children, whom curiosity had sent forth from their
huts. Gustav Adolf walked swiftly up to them, said that he was
the King of Sweden, had come to defend them in their faith and
asked whether there were Imperial soldiers[b] on the island. No,
said one man, they had, by the Grace of God, recently withdrawn. [15]
The king, pointing to a fortification which rose from the level
ground, asked whether those were not entrenchments. The man
said that the soldiers had abandoned them and that there weren't
any more or only a few still left on Usedom. Investigation showed
that the man had told the truth and the Swedes at once turned to [20]
the work of digging trenches.

After the king had looked around on a short scouting ride, he
returned to the beach where the landing had taken place, and
threw himself into the high wild summer grass. To his left, not
far away from him, he saw a broad river flowing into the ocean. [25]
It seemed to him, after he had looked into [it] for a long time, as

lange hineingeblickt hatte, als stürze die Flut schneller und schneller, um sich in der Unendlichkeit der harrenden See zu verlieren; wendete er aber den Blick ab und schaute nach einer
30 Weile wieder hin, so schien der Fluß stillzustehen, während nur seine Oberfläche schattenhaft zog und strömte. Zwischen dem Fluß und dem Meere stand ein Hirt mit einem Hunde und einer kleinen Herde magerer Schafe, tief in warme, weiche, graublaue Luft versunken. Der König sah eine Weile zu und winkte dann
35 dem Hirten mit der Hand näher heranzukommen; ob eine Kirche in der Nähe sei, fragte er, da er läuten höre. Die nächste Kirche sei wohl eine Stunde weit oder weiter, sagte der Hirt, man höre sie nicht an dieser Stelle, und es sei auch nicht die Stunde. Nachdem er, die Hand am Ohr haltend, gehorcht hatte, sagte er, er
40 höre nichts; vielleicht habe der König die versunkene Stadt aus dem Meere vernommen. Was das sei, fragte Gustaf Adolf. Vor Hunderten von Jahren, berichtete der Hirt, habe an dieser Stelle eine große, reiche Stadt gestanden, und wegen des Übermutes ihrer Bewohner habe das Meer sie verschlungen. Zuweilen, wenn
45 das Meer sehr glatt sei, könne man die goldenen Turmknöpfe und die Dächer, die mit Gold gedeckt gewesen wären, durch das Wasser schimmern sehen, und das Gerede gehe, wenn einer sterben solle, höre er die Glocken von dort unten her läuten. Das wären Märchen, sagte der König, und wer dergleichen gesehen
50 hätte, möchte wohl tief in den Weinbecher statt ins Wasser geblickt haben. Es sei unwahrscheinlich, daß an dieser Stelle jemals eine große Stadt gestanden hätte, von der keine Spur geblieben sei. Er wisse es nicht, sagte der Hirt, und er wünsche auch gar nicht, daß der König das Läuten gehört habe. „Es könnte dir so
55 gut wie mir gelten," sagte der König scherzend; „deine Haare sind weiß, die meinen noch blond." Der Hirt schüttelte den Kopf und sagte, solche Zeichen pflegten große Herren anzugehen, nicht arme namenlose Leute.

NOTES TO THE GERMAN TEXT

1. **entgegen:** It is not easy to say exactly how this word should be taken in this sentence. Perhaps it should be considered a separable prefix, part of a verb **sich entgegenbiegen.** Another explanation might be that **entgegen** is a postposition, that is, a word that is exactly the same as a preposition save that it

though the stream were rushing faster and faster, to lose itself in
the infinitude of the waiting sea, but if he turned his gaze away
and [then] looked back after a while, then the river seemed to be
standing still, while only its surface moved and flowed shadow- 30
like. Between the river and the ocean stood a herdsman with a
dog and a small herd of thin sheep, submerged in warm, soft,
gray-blue air. The king looked on for a while and then beckoned
to the herdsman to come closer. He asked whether there was a
church near by, since he heard [bells] ringing. The shepherd 35
replied that the nearest church was probably an hour away or
[still] farther, that it was not audible[c] at this place, and that it
was not the right hour, either. After he had listened a while, holding his hand to his ear, he said that he heard nothing; perhaps the
king had heard the sunken city from the sea. Gustav Adolf asked 40
what that was. Hundreds of years ago, the herdsman informed
[him], a great wealthy city had stood on this spot and because of
the arrogance of its inhabitants the sea had engulfed it. At times,
when the ocean was very smooth, one could see the golden steeple
knobs and the roofs, which had been covered with gold, gleaming 45
through the water, and the story went that when someone was to
die he heard the bells toll from down there. The king said that
those were fairy tales and that whoever had seen things of that
kind might well have gazed deep into the wine cup rather than
into the water. It was improbable that a large city, of which no 50
trace remained, had ever stood on this spot. The herdsman said
that he did not know, and neither did he have any wish at all[d]
that the king had heard the tolling. "It could be meant for you as
well as for me," said the king jesting; "your hair is white, mine
still blond." The herdsman shook his head and said that such 55
signs usually concerned[e] great lords, not poor nameless people.

NOTES TO THE ENGLISH TEXT

a. Gustav Adolf, who was King of Sweden from 1611 to 1632.
He intervened in the Thirty Years' War (1618-1648) on the
Protestant side, landing on the island of Usedom in the Baltic,
July 4, 1630, with 13,000 men. From there he proceeded to the
mainland and advanced victorious into South Germany. He
died a hero's death in the Battle of Lützen on the sixteenth
of November, 1632.

follows its object: **mir entgegen** *toward me*. The important postpositions are: (1) With preceding accusative object: **entlang** (**den Fluß entlang** *along the river*). (2) With preceding dative object: **entgegen** (**dem Wind entgegen** *on into the wind*); **gegenüber** (**der Kirche gegenüber** *across from the church*); **nach** (**meiner Meinung nach** *according to my opinion*). (3) With preceding genitive object: **halber** (**des Glaubens halber** *for the sake of the faith*. Notice, however, the spelling and meaning of **meinethalber** *as far as I am concerned, for all I care*, **ihrethalber** *as far as she is concerned, for all she cares*); and **wegen** (**der Neugierde wegen** *on account of curiosity*; notice also **meinetwegen**, etc., *as far as I am concerned, for all I care*). Some of these words are often used as prepositions, too: **wegen des Übermutes** *on account of the arrogance.*

2. **Niemand war rings zu sehen** *Nobody was to be seen round about.* Notice that the German active infinitive is correctly translated by the English passive. The sentence does not mean, "Nobody was around to see."

b. Imperial soldiers, or soldiers of the Holy Roman Empire, would, of course, be Catholic and hostile.

c. **man höre sie nicht**   *that one did not hear it.*

d. **und er wünsche auch gar nicht**   *and he did not at all wish either.*

e. **solche Zeichen pflegten große Herren anzugehen**   *such signs were accustomed to concern great lords.*

GRAMMATICAL COMMENT—
INDIRECT DISCOURSE

I. Use of the Subjunctive Mood in Indirect Discourse

A. DISTINCTION BETWEEN SUBJUNCTIVE AND INDICATIVE

When a person reports a statement made by another, what is reported is called an indirect statement. German and English differ considerably in this regard. The big difference between the languages is the fact that German often employs the subjunctive mood in indirect discourse, whereas English, of course, does not. The really interesting thing is that the choice of mood in German indirect discourse implies the attitude of the speaker to what he is reporting. That is, a person reporting a statement or question or request made by another may use either the indicative or the subjunctive in the reported statement. If he wishes to disclaim responsibility for the truth of the statement or validity of the question, or to dissociate himself in some way from what he is reporting, perhaps merely to imply a certain formal or ceremonial distance, he will use the subjunctive mood. The use of the indicative implies that he sees no reason to dissociate himself from what he is reporting.

This conversation will illustrate what has just been said:

DER HIRT: **Zuweilen, wenn das Meer sehr glatt ist, kann man die goldenen Turmknöpfe und die Dächer, die mit Gold gedeckt waren, durch das Wasser schimmern sehen.** *At times, when the sea is very smooth, one can see the golden steeple knobs and the roofs, which were covered with gold, shimmering through the water.*

DER KÖNIG: **Was sagt er?** *What is he saying?*

EIN DOLMETSCHER (AN INTERPRETER): **Er sagt, zuweilen, wenn das Meer sehr glatt sei, könne man die goldenen Turmknöpfe und die Dächer, die mit Gold gedeckt gewesen wären, durch das Wasser schimmern sehen.** *He says that at times, when the sea is very smooth one can see the golden steeple knobs*

*and the roofs, which were covered with gold, shimmering
through the water.*

In the above sentence the interpreter uses the subjunctive
mood, indicating that he wishes to dissociate himself from the
shepherd's statement. If the interpreter had said: **Er sagt,
zuweilen, wenn das Meer sehr glatt ist, kann man die goldenen
Turmknöpfe und die Dächer, die mit Gold gedeckt waren, durch
das Wasser schimmern sehen,** then he would imply that he saw
no reason to question the statement.

Sometimes a person reporting a statement made by another will
use the subjunctive mood merely for reasons of formal or ceremonial distance. An instance of such usage can be found in such
a sentence as the following, taken from a sermon: **Christus sagte,
er sei gekommen um die Menschen zu erlösen** *Christ said he had
come to save humanity.* The subjunctive does not imply that the
preacher doubts the truth of his message, but it does create a sense
of distance or reverence, which would be shattered by the use of
the indicative.

B. EFFECT OF THE INTRODUCTORY VERB

In German the *tense* of the introductory verb, that is, the verb
of saying, thinking, reporting, etc., has no effect on the *time distinction* of the subjunctive verb. (More will be said about this
matter in a subsequent paragraph.) The tense of the introductory
verb does, however, help to determine which mood will be used in
the reported statement.

If the introductory verb is in the present, the verb of the indirect
statement is likely to be in the indicative mood unless the speaker
wishes specifically to disclaim responsibility as has already been
explained.

If the introductory verb is in the past, the verb in the indirect
statement is more likely to be in the subjunctive, because of the
feeling of distance inherent in statements made in the past. The
subjunctive is used so consistently in the indirect statements of
the text of the present lesson in order to evoke this sense of distance or hearsay in the reader.

If the introductory verb implies certainty, e.g., **wissen** *know,*
es ist sicher *it is certain,* the indicative mood is used in the indirect
statement.

Frequently the verb of saying, thinking, or the like, is omitted or understood and the use of the subjunctive alone indicates that the sentence is an indirect statement. Thus it happens very often that a verb of saying or the like is used just once to introduce a series of sentences employing the subjunctive. There are several examples of this in the text of this lesson.

II. Time and Form Distinctions of the Subjunctive in Indirect Discourse

A. CHOICE OF TIME DISTINCTIONS

You will remember that every complete German verb has four subjunctive time distinctions and each time distinction has two forms. That is, there are two present subjunctive time distinctions, two past, two future, and two future perfect. The question we wish to consider here is, Under what circumstances are a given time distinction and a given form used? In this respect German differs widely from English. Therefore it may be well to recall briefly what the situation is in English, for indirect discourse in English exhibits a peculiarity that is apt to confuse you unless you are on guard against it.

The peculiarity is that English indirect discourse very often causes a certain sequence of tenses to be employed; that is, the tense of the introductory verb affects the tense of the verb of indirect statement. Specifically, if the introductory verb is in the past, then the verb of indirect discourse is in the past also, regardless of the logic of the situation. To make this clear let us consider the following scene: The time is now; it is raining; this conversation takes place among three people within a fraction of a minute.

ANNA *(looking out through the window):* It is raining.
OSCAR *(who didn't hear her):* What did she say?
RICHARD *(to* OSCAR*):* She said it was raining.

You will observe that even though it is still raining when Richard tells Oscar what Anna said, Richard uses a past tense to report Anna's statement. He does so because he introduced his report by the past tense "said."

In German the subjunctive time distinction used in a reported statement is determined by the tense which that statement had or would have had in its direct form. Thus, a statement originally made in the present is reported in the present subjunctive, a statement originally made in the past is reported in the past, and so on, regardless of the tense of the introductory verb. Therefore it will frequently be proper for you to translate a German present subjunctive by an English past tense: **Er sagte, daß es unwahrscheinlich sei** *He said that it was improbable.*

B. CHOICE OF FORMS (SUBJUNCTIVE I OR II)

In indirect statements sometimes the subjunctive I forms are used and sometimes subjunctive II. The subjunctive I forms are used in more formal style and subjunctive II in more colloquial style.

Formal style: **Er sagte, daß es unwahrscheinlich sei.**
Colloquial style: **Er sagte, daß es unwahrscheinlich wäre.**

Both sentences are translated: *He said that it was improbable.*
Sometimes, however, it is necessary to use subjunctive II forms even in formal style. This is the case when a subjunctive I form is indistinguishable from an indicative form. To make this clear let us compare the present indicative forms and the present subjunctive I forms of **haben**:

INDICATIVE		SUBJUNCTIVE I	
ich habe	**wir haben**	**ich habe**	**wir haben**
du hast	**ihr habt**	**du habest**	**ihr habet**
er hat	**sie haben**	**er habe**	**sie haben**
Sie haben		**Sie haben**	

From this we can see that only the underlined forms, the second and third persons singular, are unmistakably subjunctive, and the second plural, although it differs from the indicative, is not really distinctively subjunctive. Since the forms which are not unmistakably subjunctive will necessarily be taken as indicative, they cannot be used at all in indirect statements from which the speaker wishes to withhold his endorsement and he must therefore use subjunctive II forms even in formal style. Illustration:

Der Hirt: **Der Soldat hat die Stadt verlassen.** *The soldier has left the city.*

DER KÖNIG: **Was sagt er?** *What is he saying?*
DER DOLMETSCHER: **Er sagt, der Soldat habe die Stadt verlassen.**
He says that the soldier has left the city.

In this conversation the interpreter very properly, in a formal statement, implies that he takes no responsibility for the truth of what he is reporting. But observe what happens if the shepherd speaks of a number of soldiers.

DER HIRT: **Die Soldaten haben die Stadt verlassen.**
DER KÖNIG: **Was sagt er?**
DER DOLMETSCHER: **Er sagt, die Soldaten hätten die Stadt verlassen.**

Now the interpreter must use the less formal subjunctive **hätten,** for if he said **Er sagt, die Soldaten haben die Stadt verlassen,** the king would be justified in holding him responsible for the truth of the statement, because **Die Soldaten haben . . . verlassen** is necessarily taken as an indicative.

It may, of course, happen that the required person of both form I and form II of a particular verb cannot be distinguished from an indicative. In that case form II is preferred.

C. EXAMPLES OF HOW STATEMENTS WITH VARIOUS INDICATIVE TENSES ARE REPORTED IN INDIRECT DISCOURSE

Present tense in the direct form requiring present subjunctive:

Direct: **Ich bin der König.**
Indirect: **Er sagt** (or **sagte, hat gesagt, hatte gesagt, wird sagen, wird gesagt haben**) **daß er der König sei** (or **wäre**).

Simple past, present perfect, or past perfect in the direct form, all requiring past subjunctive:

Direct: **Die Glocken läuteten früh und spät.**
    Die Glocken haben früh und spät geläutet.
    Die Glocken hatten früh und spät geläutet.
Indirect: **Er sagt** (or **sagte, etc.**)**, daß die Glocken früh und spät geläutet hätten.**

Future in the direct form, requiring future subjunctive:

Direct: **Sie wird in ihrer letzten Stunde die Glocken hören.**

Indirect: **Er** sagt (or sagte, etc.), **daß sie in ihrer letzten Stunde die Glocken hören werde** (or **würde**).

Future perfect in the direct form, requiring future perfect subjunctive:

Direct: **Bis zu der Zeit wird der König schon längst gestorben sein.**

Indirect: **Er sagt** (or **sagte**, etc.), **daß der König bis zu der Zeit schon längst gestorben sein werde** (or **würde**).

III. Imperatives in Indirect Discourse

A command or request is reported by means of the present subjunctive either I or II of **sollen** or **mögen**.

OSCAR (*to* RICHARD): **Erzählen Sie mir mehr davon.** *Tell me more about it.*

RICHARD (*to* ANNA): **Was hat er gesagt?** *What did he say?*

ANNA (*to* RICHARD): **Er hat gesagt, daß Sie ihm mehr davon erzählen sollten.** *He said that you should tell him more about it.*

The use of **möchte** is especially common in transmitting requests such as the following:

ANNA (*to* RICHARD): **Ich habe soeben Oscar Schmidt gesprochen. Sie möchten ihn bitte anrufen.** *I have just talked to Oscar Schmidt. You should please call him.* (i.e., *He wants you to call him.*)

IV. Concluding Consolatory Remark

As you will observe, the grammatical description of a language at certain points inevitably becomes concerned with questions of style, logical implications, emotional inferences, overtones of attitude and value. Such concerns enter particularly into a description of indirect discourse in German: here the problem pivots less on correct and incorrect forms and more on what is meant to be understood between the lines, on intangibles, on atmosphere. Here you become concerned with the most primitive and the most subtle aspect of language, that is, language as artistic expression.

EXERCISES

I. These exercises are at page 193.

II. These exercises are at page 194.

III. Arrange in proper sequence.

1. Dem König sagte der Hirt, er könne das Läuten der Kirchglocken einer vor Hunderten von Jahren im Meer versunkenen Stadt hören.

2. Der Hirt hatte gut erzählen: der König glaubte nicht, daß das Läuten ihm gelte.

3. Als der König die sich ihm wie eine sehnende Braut entgegenbiegende Insel sah, brannte es ihm auf den Nägeln aus dem Schiff zu springen und Umschau zu halten.

4. Dem auf die aus dem flachen Boden aufsteigenden Festungen deutenden König antwortete der Fischer, daß die Soldaten die Insel schon verlassen hätten.

5. Der Hirt wollte wissen ob der König nicht davon habe erzählen hören, daß das Meer die einst so schöne Stadt wegen des Übermutes ihrer Bewohner verschlungen habe.

6. Der König wollte sich aus dem Gerede, daß einer, der sterben solle, die Glocken der versunkenen Stadt höre, nichts machen.

IV. Determine which German sentence best translates the English in each group.

1. If he turned his gaze away and looked back after a while, he could almost believe that only the surface of the river was moving shadowlike towards the ocean.

a. Wendete er den Blick ab und schaute nach einer Weile wieder hin, so konnte er fast glauben, nur die Oberfläche des Stromes ziehe schattenhaft dem Meer entgegen.

b. Wenn er den Blick abgewendet hat und nach einer Weile

wieder hinschaut, so kann er fast glauben, daß nur die Oberfläche des Flusses dem Meere schattenhaft entgegenziehe.

c. Wenn er den Blick abgewendet hatte und nach einer Weile
   wieder hingeschaut hatte, so konnte er fast glauben, daß nur
   die Oberfläche des Stromes dem Meere schattenhaft ent-
   gegenzöge.

d. Hätte er den Blick abgewendet und nach einer Weile wieder
   hingeschaut, so könnte er fast glauben, nur die Oberfläche des
   Stromes zöge schattenhaft dem Meer entgegen.

2. According to the king's calculations the landing would have
had to take place on the evening of the third of July, but night fell
and still no trace of the shore was to be seen.

a. Des Königs Berechnungen nach muß die Landung schon am
   Abend des dritten Juli stattfinden, aber es wird Nacht und
   vom Strande ist noch keine Spur zu sehen.

b. Des Königs Berechnungen nach mußte die Landung schon
   am Abend des dritten Juli stattfinden, aber es wurde Nacht
   und vom Strand war noch keine Spur zu sehen.

c. Des Königs Berechnungen nach hätte die Landung schon am
   Abend des dritten Juli stattfinden müssen, aber es ward Nacht
   und noch war vom Strande überhaupt nichts zu sehen.

d. Des Königs Berechnungen nach würde die Landung schon
   am Abend des dritten Juli stattfinden müssen, aber es wird
   Nacht und noch ist vom Strande überhaupt nichts zu sehen.

*V. Supply with quotation marks the one German sentence in each
group that makes the correct translation of the English. Translate
each sentence.*

1. "Those are fairy tales," said the king, "and anybody who
says he has seen things of that kind has probably looked deep into
the wine cup rather than into the water."

a. Das wären Märchen, sagte der König, und wer dergleichen
   gesehen hätte, möchte wohl tief in den Weinbecher statt ins
   Wasser geblickt haben.

b. Das seien Märchen, sagte der König, und wer dergleichen
   gesehen habe, habe wohl tief in den Weinbecher statt ins
   Wasser geblickt.

c. Das sind Märchen, sagte der König, und wer dergleichen

sehen will, der blicke nur tief in den Weinbecher statt ins Wasser.

d. Das sind Märchen, sagte der König, und wer dergleichen gesehen haben will, wird wohl tief in den Weinbecher statt ins Wasser geblickt haben.

2. The shepherd shook his head and said, "Such signs usually concern great lords and do not apply to poor nameless people."

a. Der Hirt schüttelte den Kopf und sagte, solche Zeichen pflegten große Herren anzugehen und gälten nicht armen namenlosen Leuten.

b. Der Hirt schüttelte den Kopf und sagte, solche Zeichen pflegten große Herren anzugehen und hätten armen namenlosen Leuten nicht gegolten.

c. Der Hirt schüttelte den Kopf und sagte, solche Zeichen pflegen große Herren anzugehen und gelten nicht armen namenlosen Leuten.

d. Der Hirt schüttelte den Kopf und sagte, solche Zeichen pflegten große Herren anzugehen und hatten armen namenlosen Leuten nicht gegolten.

3. "She bent towards him like a yearning bride," said the soldier, "and before the sun sank, his arms had embraced her."

a. Sie hätte sich ihm wie eine sehnende Braut entgegengebogen, sagte der Soldat, und bevor die Sonne gesunken wäre, hätten sie seine Arme umfangen.

b. Sie biege sich ihm wie eine sehnende Braut entgegen, sagte der Soldat, und bevor die Sonne sinken würde, würden sie seine Arme umfangen.

c. Sie biegt sich ihm wie eine sehnende Braut entgegen, sagt der Soldat, und bevor die Sonne sinkt, werden sie seine Arme umfangen.

d. Sie bog sich ihm wie eine sehnende Braut entgegen, sagte der Soldat, und bevor die Sonne sank, hatten sie seine Arme umfangen.

VI. Select the untrue statement in each group.

GROUP 1

a. Gustav Adolf trat rasch auf den Hirten zu und fragte ihn, ob eine Kirche in der Nähe sei, da er läuten höre.

b. Der König sagte, er hätte eine Bitte an den Hirten: er möchte ihm sagen, ob eine Kirche in der Nähe sei.

c. Der Hirt antwortete, die Glocken der nächsten Kirche ließen sich an dieser Stelle nicht hören.

d. „Hat der König die Glocken der versunkenen Stadt vernommen," mag der Hirt gedacht haben, „wird er bald sterben müssen."

GROUP 2

a. Die Fahrt war schwieriger als der König sie sich vorgestellt hatte.

b. Er wäre gern als erster aus dem anlandenden Schiffe gesprungen, hätte er nicht niederknieen müssen und Gott für die glücklich vollendete Fahrt danken.

c. Die zaghaft abseits stehenden Fischer hätten gerne gewußt, wer der große Herr sei, der mit dem Schiffe soeben angekommen.

d. Einer der Fischer sagte, daß es jetzt auf der ganzen Insel keine Soldaten mehr gäbe; sie wären alle kürzlich abgezogen.

GROUP 3

a. Dem in dem hohen, wildwachsenden Sommergras liegenden König schien es, als stürze die Flut schneller und schneller, um sich in der Unendlichkeit der harrenden See zu verlieren.

b. Nachdem die Schweden auf einem kurzen Streifritt Umschau gehalten hatten, kehrten sie an den Strand zurück und begaben sich sofort an die Verschanzungsarbeit.

c. Nachdem der König eine Weile zugesehen hatte, wie der Hirt mit seinen Schafen zwischen dem Fluß und dem Meere stand, winkte er mit der Hand, als wollte er sagen, der Hirt sollte näher herankommen.

d. Nachdem der Hirt auf des Königs Fragen geantwortet hatte, sagte er, es sei nicht sein Wunsch, daß der König das Läuten gehört habe.

A SELECTION FROM

Das Tropenaquarium

BY JAKOB VON UEXKÜLL

(1864-1944)

Jakob von Uexküll was born in 1864 in Esthonia, the scion of one of those distinguished aristocratic families of German origin which for centuries had constituted the governing class of the Baltic countries. As a young man he decided not to follow the life of a landed nobleman but to devote himself to research in zoology and physiology. He received his training at the universities of Dorpat and Heidelberg and the marine experiment station at Naples. Always an independent scholar, he was until 1925 a private scholar also. As a private scholar he wrote many technical articles and also books of greater scope and philosophical import, such as *Umwelt und Innenwelt der Tiere* (1909) and *Theoretische Biologie* (1920). In 1925 the University of Hamburg established for him the *Institut für Umweltsforschung* of which he was the director until 1940.

Here is a rough approximation of how Uexküll arrives at his theory of environment or *Umwelttheorie:*

Every human being, every animal, sits in the center of a number of concentric environmental spheres which that human being or that animal itself creates. For the human being the biggest sphere is the sphere of vision, which is bounded by the horizon. The next sphere is the sphere of hearing, then the sphere of scent, then of touch. Hence in the natural world whatever is beyond the horizon is outside our environment: for us it does not exist. As it approaches us it becomes first a sight-thing and then as it comes closer the number of its qualities increases and it becomes a sound-thing, a scent-thing, a touch-thing, and even a taste-thing. But always its qualities are products of the perceptive powers of the human being or animal which sits in the precise center of all those spheres.

In the selection from his writings which you are about to read you will gain some insight into how Uexküll's *Umwelttheorie* helps to explain the difference in outlook between an Eskimo and an Australian Bushman, between a Japanese and an African Pygmy, between an Arab and a Parisian, between yourself and a German. By inference, the theory helps to show that for the Parisian to understand the Arab he must feel and think his way out of his narrowly personal sphere into the Arab sphere, a difficult thing to do at best, but really impossible unless the Parisian studies the Arabic language, the key to the Arab's heart and mind.

In addition to this, you will be introduced to a theory of life which may seem strange and foreign to you. If it interests you, however, you can read more about it in Uexküll's various books, including his book of memoirs *Niegeschaute Welten* (Frankfurt 1936, 1949) and the English translation of *Theoretische Biologie*, *Theoretical Biology*, published by Kegan Paul, Trench, Trubner and Co. Ltd. London, 1926, in the *International Library of Psychology, Philosophy and Scientific Method*.

AUS DAS TROPENAQUARIUM

VON JAKOB VON UEXKÜLL

Es gibt zwei kleine, wahre, moderne Geschichten, die beide von einem Waschbottich handeln und die einzeln bloß unbedeutende Anekdoten sind, zusammen aber eine tiefe Lehre enthalten.

5 Ein kleines hessisches Bauernmädel fragt seinen Bruder: „Wo hat der Vater den neuen Waschbottich her?"[1] — „Ach," sagt das Brüderlein, „er ist bloß tiefer in den großen Wald hineingegangen, da gibt es einen Baum, an dem die Waschbottiche an den Zweigen hängen, wie in unserem Garten die Äpfel."

10 Und die zweite Geschichte handelt von einem kleinen Berliner Dienstmädchen, das nach Hause kam und der Hausfrau erzählte, wie die Waschbottiche „jemacht werden, habe ich heute jesehen. Aber wie wird denn das Holz jemacht?" — „Das Holz," antwortet die Hausfrau, „das nimmt man von den Bäumen, wie sie draußen 15 im Tiergarten stehen."[2] — „Aber wo macht man denn die Bäume?" erwiderte die Kleine. — „Die werden gar nicht gemacht, die wachsen von selbst." — „Ach was," antwortete die kleine Berlinerin, „irgendwo werden die auch schon jemacht werden."[3]

Leben sie nicht in zwei verschiedenen Welten, so entfernt wie 20 der Mars von der Erde, diese beiden kleinen deutschen Kinder, der hessische Bauernbursch und das Berliner Stadtmädchen? In der einen Welt entsteht alles von selbst, und in der andern wird alles gemacht.

In einer Gemäldeausstellung steht ein junges Paar vor zwei 25 Bildern neuer deutscher Schulen. „Sieh, dieses Bild hier," sagt der Herr, „wie ist das wunderbar gemacht. Jeder Fleck sitzt an seiner Stelle, kalte und warme Töne in wechselvollem kräftigem Gegensatz." Und sie antwortet: „Was geht mich die Technik an? Hier

FROM DAS TROPENAQUARIUM

BY JAKOB VON UEXKÜLL

There are two short, true modern stories, both [of] which are concerned with a washtub and which [taken] separately are merely insignificant anecdotes, but [taken] together contain a profound truth.

A little Hessian peasant girl asked her brother: "Where did 5 Father get the new washtub from?" "Oh," said the little brother, "he just went out deeper into the big woods; there is a tree there, on which washtubs are hanging on the branches, like apples in our garden."

The second story tells about a little Berlin servant girl who came 10 home and told her mistress, "Today I saw how washtubs are made. But how is the wood made?"ᵃ "They take the wood from trees," said the mistress, "like the ones standing out in the Tiergarten."ᵇ "But where do they make the trees?" countered the little girl. "They are not made at all, they grow by themselves." "I don't be- 15 lieve it,"ᶜ answered the little Berlin girl, "they are bound to be made someplace, too."

These two little German children, the Hessian peasant lad and the Berlin city girl, aren't they living in two separate worlds, as distant as Mars from the earth? In the one world everything comes 20 into being spontaneously, and in the other everything is made.

A young couple at an art exhibit is standing before two pictures of modern German schools [of painting]. "Look," says the gentleman, "this picture, how wonderfully that is done. Every spot [of paint] is in its place, cold and warm shades in strong reciprocal 25 contrast." And she answers, "What do I care about the technique? Here in this picture I have a vivid experience [of] how the picture came into being out of the painter's soul."

111

in diesem Bilde erlebe ich, wie das Bild aus der Seele des
30 Künstlers entstanden ist."

Wieder die beiden Welten. Ihre Bewohner sind gezwungen
neben- und durcheinander[4] zu leben. Sie verstehen sich nie. In
der Welt, wo alles entsteht, sind die Leute, die sich mit dem
Machen der Dinge abgeben, lächerlich. Sie sind blind und sehen
35 das Wesentliche nicht, den Zusammenhang des großen wunderbaren Gesamtwerdens.

In der Welt, in der alles gemacht wird, sind die Leute, die auf
das Entstehen warten, unglücklich. Denn von allen Seiten ruft
man ihnen zu: „Seid doch keine Träumer, keine Faselhänse, greift
40 zu und macht etwas Neues!"

Willst du erfahren, in welcher der beiden Welten deine Freunde
leben, so brauchst du sie nur zu fragen: ob sie an den Fortschritt
glauben. Fortschritt gibt es nur dort, wo Dinge besser oder
schlechter gemacht werden. In der Welt, wo alles entsteht, ist
45 alles gleich vollkommen. Dort glaubt man auch nicht an Fortschritt.

Die Dampfmaschinen von heute sind sicher besser als die vor
fünfzig Jahren, aber ein Ei ist weder besser noch schlechter als
eine Henne.

50 Eine Zeitlang hat man es versucht, auch in die Welt des Naturgeschehens den Fortschritt hineinzubringen. Man sagte sich, vor
Jahrmillionen hat es nur einfache kleine Lebewesen auf der Erde
gegeben, und jetzt gibt es große und vielgestaltige Tiere und
Pflanzen. Also ist ein riesiger Fortschritt vorhanden. Die ersten
55 einfachen Strukturen haben nach und nach immer reichere Strukturen gebaut, und nach vielen Mißgriffen ist schließlich die
menschliche Struktur gemacht worden.

Es wurde eine Stufenleiter der Tiere aufgebaut. Von der Amöbe
durch alle Tierarten hindurch bis zum Säugetier. Und dann die
60 Behauptung aufgestellt, der Kampf ums Dasein habe dauernd
für die Erhaltung der besseren Strukturen gesorgt, und dadurch
den Fortschritt verbürgt. Das ist in der Tat die richtige Lehre für
die Leute, die glauben wollen, daß alles „jemacht" wird.

Aber die Leute, die in der Welt leben, in der alles entsteht,
65 sehen die gleichen Dinge ganz anders an. Sie können beim besten
Willen keine besseren oder schlechteren Strukturen finden. Im
Gegenteil ist jedes Tier, mag es einfach oder kompliziert sein,[5]

Again the two worlds. Their inhabitants are compelled to live side by side and intermingled. They never understand each other. [30] In the world where everything comes into being the people who are occupied with the making of things are ridiculous. They are blind and do not see the essential thing, the continuity of the great wonderful total process of becoming.

In the world in which everything is made the people who wait [35] for [things to] come into being are unhappy. For on every side they are admonished.[a] "Don't be dreamers, don't be fools, set to work and make something new!"

If you wish to find out in which of the two worlds your friends are living, you only need to ask them whether they believe in [40] progress. Progress exists only where things are made better or poorer. In the world where everything comes into being, everything is equally perfect. There one does not believe in progress either.

The steam engines of today are surely better than those [of] [45] fifty years ago, but an egg is neither superior nor inferior to a hen.

For a time the attempt was made to bring [the idea of] progress into the world of natural process also. People told themselves, millions of years ago there were only simple small organisms on earth and now there are large and multiform animals and plants. [50] Therefore tremendous progress is evident. Gradually the first simple structures built more and more complicated structures and after many failures the human structure was finally made.

A graduated scale of animals was built up. From the amoeba through all the animal species to the mammal. And then the [55] assertion [was] made that the struggle for existence had constantly cared for the preservation of the better structures and thus guaranteed progress. That is indeed the proper theory for the people who want to believe that everything is "made."

But the people who live in the world in which everything comes [60] into being look at the same things very differently. With the best of intention they can find neither superior nor inferior structures. On the contrary, every animal, whether it is simple or complicated, is just as perfectly adapted to its environment [as every other animal]. The environment of the simple animals is simple and that [65] of the complex animals is complex. Environment and animal reciprocally constitute each other's conditions [of existence]. They

gleich vollkommen in seine Umwelt eingepaßt. Die Umwelt der
einfachen Tiere ist einfach, und diejenige der vielseitigen Tiere
70 vielfältig. Umwelt und Tier bedingen sich gegenseitig. Sie sind
zusammen da, und eines gewinnt nur Sinn durch das andere. Das
Fell des Eisbären hat nur einen Sinn im Schnee Grönlands, und
der Springfuß des Känguruh gehört zu den Steppen Australiens.
In vergangenen Erdepochen, da es andere klimatische und Vege-
75 tationsbedingungen gab, gab es auch andere Tiere; der Ichthyo-
saurus schwand mit den großen Sümpfen der Kreidezeit.

Während alle Bewegungswerkzeuge der Tiere durch die Umgebung geformt zu sein scheinen: die Flosse durch das Wasser, der
Flügel durch die Luft, so formen ihrerseits alle Sinneswerkzeuge
80 die Umgebung. Von all den zahllosen Wirkungen der Außenwelt
wählt jedes Sinnesorgan jedes Tieres die für es passende Reizanzahl aus. Tausende von mechanischen und chemischen Vorrichtungen gibt es, die dafür sorgen, daß nur ganz bestimmte auserlesene Reize der Außenwelt eindringen.[6] Sie allein schaffen die
85 Umwelt des Tieres. Nur was zum Leben wichtig ist, dringt bis
zum Nervensystem und erzeugt dort den Impuls, der die passenden Bewegungswerkzeuge in passender Weise bewegt.

Ebenso unlösbar durch Wechselwirkung verknüpft ist die
Amöbe mit dem Wassertropfen, wie die Forelle mit dem Fluß und
90 der Hai mit dem Meer. Keiner ist besser, keiner ist schlechter.
Alle sind sie mit ihrer Umgebung entstanden und werden mit ihr
verschwinden.

Wie ist das zu verstehen?

Eine allgemeine Lebenssubstanz liegt allem Leben zugrunde.
95 Aus ihr entstehen alle einzelnen Tiere, sie selbst aber wird unverändert von Generation zu Generation weitergegeben. Sie
scheint die Fähigkeit zu besitzen sich den verschiedensten Be-
dingungen anzupassen, denn sie vermochte es in den heißen
Sümpfen der Vorzeit die riesigen phantastischen Reptilien zu
100 schaffen,[7] wie in der Neuzeit den Malariaparasiten des Menschen,
der zwei Wirte braucht, um sein verderbliches Dasein zu führen.
Überall passen Verfolger und Verfolgter zusammen, Wirt und
Parasit, Pflanze und Tier, und beide zum Erdboden.

Wo die Möglichkeit einer neuen Existenz vorhanden ist, ent-
105 steht eine neue Existenz. Sie entsteht aus diesem unheimlichen
unerforschlichen Urgrund, den wir lebendige Substanz nennen.

SEVENTH UNIT: PASSIVE VOICE　　　

exist together and the one takes on meaning only through the other. The polar bear's fur has meaning only in the snow of Greenland and the kangaroo's back legs belong on the Australian steppes. In past ages of the earth, when there were different conditions of climate and vegetation, there were different animals, too. The ichthyosaur*e* disappeared with the great swamps of the Cretaceous period.

While all the instruments of movement of the animals seem to be shaped by the environment, the fin by water, the wing by air, all the instruments of perception, on the other hand, give shape to the environment. From all the innumerable effects of the external world each sense organ of every animal selects the number of stimuli appropriate for it. There are thousands of mechanical and chemical contrivances which take care that only very specific selected stimuli of the outer world penetrate. They alone create the animal's environment. Only that which is important for life penetrates to the nervous system and there produces the impulse which excites the appropriate instruments of movement in [the] appropriate way.

Through action and reaction the amoeba is just as indissolubly united with the drop of water as the trout with the brook and the shark with the ocean. None is superior, none is inferior. They have all come into being with their environment and will disappear with it.

How is that to be understood?

A universal vital substance underlies all life. From it all individual animals come into being, but it itself is transmitted unchanged from generation to generation. It seems to possess the capacity to accommodate itself to the most diverse conditions, for it was able to create the colossal fantastic reptiles in the hot swamps of primeval time, just as in modern times [it has created] the human malaria parasite, which needs two hosts in order to carry on its pernicious existence. Everywhere pursuer and pursued are adapted to one another, host and parasite, plant and animal, and both [are adapted] to the earth.

Where the possibility of a new [form of] existence is at hand, a new [form of] existence comes into being. It comes into being from this mysterious inscrutable primal cause, which we call vital substance. Nothing is made, everything comes into being. Is there

Nichts wird gemacht, alles entsteht. Ist ein Fortschritt vorhanden?
Ebensowenig oder ebensoviel wie vom Ei zur Henne. Das Ei ist
zwar selbst strukturlos, aber es birgt alle Möglichkeiten der Struk-
110 tur der Henne. So ist die Lebenssubstanz strukturlos, aber sie birgt
die Möglichkeit aller Strukturen überhaupt. Und ist die Möglichkeit zu neuer Bildung auch äußerlich gegeben, so wird sie gebildet.
Kann man da von einem andern Fortschritt reden, als von der
fortschreitenden Durchbildung des einzelnen Individuums! Wohl
115 kaum. Alles entsteht zu seiner Zeit und an seinem Orte. So sieht
es aus in der Welt, in der alles entsteht.

In diese Welt ist aber die moderne Naturwissenschaft zurückgekehrt. „Ein Tier ist ein bloßes Geschehnis," sagt ein führender
amerikanischer Forscher. Jedes Tier, jede Pflanze ist nur ein
120 Erlebnis der lebenden Substanz. Und diese Erlebnisse bilden
gemeinsam das große Gesamterlebnis, das wir Natur nennen.
Diese Harmonie der Natur, das Zusammenklingen aller Einzelheiten zu einem großen Ganzen, das sich über Raum und Zeit
erstreckt, ist wieder zum Hauptproblem der Naturwissenschaft
125 geworden.

NOTES TO THE GERMAN TEXT

1. **Wo hat der Vater den neuen Waschbottich her?** *Where has
    Father the new washtub from?* **Woher** is frequently broken
    up this way. Observe especially that the particles of direction
    her and **hin** are essential to the meaning even where they seem
    superfluous from the viewpoint of English: *Where are you
    going?* is in German **Wo gehen Sie hin?** Notice the use of the
    definite article: **der Vater** = *Father.*

2. **von den Bäumen, wie sie draußen im Tiergarten stehen** *from
    the trees as they stand out there in the Tiergarten.* An idio-
    matic formal translation is: *from trees such as are standing,
    etc.* See the Fifth Unit, Note 6 to the German Text.

3. **irgendwo werden die auch schon jemacht werden** *they will
    undoubtedly be made somewhere or other also.* The future
    tense with an adverbial expression of probability (**wohl**) or
    confidence (**schon**) is frequently used to express the likelihood
    of something being true at the present time (see the First
    Unit, Note 7 to German Text; also the Second Unit, Comment
    I, B 4). The form **irgend** is distributive or generalizing:

progress? Just as little or just as much as [there is progress] from the egg to the hen. The egg itself is, to be sure, unstructured, but it harbors all the possibilities of the hen's structure. Thus the vital substance is unstructured, but it harbors the possibility of all struc-110 tures whatever. And if external conditions make a new formation possible, then it is realized.*ꟷ* Can one, then, speak of any other progress than the advancing development of the single individual? Probably not. Everything comes into being in its [own] time and its [own] place. This is how it looks in the world in which every-115 thing comes into being.

Modern natural science has returned to this world. "An animal is merely an event," says a leading American researcher. Every animal, every plant is only an experience of the vital substance. And these experiences together constitute the great total experi-120 ence which we call nature. This harmony of nature, the accord of all separate individuals in a great total which extends over space and time, has again become the main problem of natural science.

NOTES TO THE ENGLISH TEXT

a. **Jemacht, jesehen:** Berlin dialect for **gemacht, gesehen.** The substitution of the sound represented by *j* for the sound represented by *g* is the most obvious characteristic of uncultivated Berlin speech.

b. **der Tiergarten:** a famous park in Berlin.

c. **Ach was!** *Nonsense!* or *Quit your kidding!* or *Impossible!*

d. **Denn von allen Seiten ruft man ihnen zu.** *For from all sides one calls out to them.*

e. The ichthyosaur was a large marine animal which combined characteristics of reptiles and fishes and in some respects resembled whales. It had a large head, a tapering body, four paddles and a long tail. Now extinct.

f. **Und ist die Möglichkeit zu neuer Bildung auch äußerlich gegeben, so wird sie gebildet.** *And if the possibility of a new formation is given externally as well, then it is formed.* That is, the vital substance is just waiting, so to speak, to assume the specific form which the external environment makes appropriate.

irgendwo *somewhere or other;* irgendwie *somehow or other.*
The negative nirgend is exclusive: nirgendwo *nowhere at all.*

4. neben- und durcheinander = nebeneinander und durch-
    einander *side by side and pell mell.* Similarly, Skulptur- und
    Gemäldeausstellung *exhibition of sculpture and painting;*
    Tier- und Pflanzenwelt *world of animals and plants.*

5. mag es einfach oder kompliziert sein *may it be simple or
    complicated.* An important idomatic use of mögen to express
    concession.

6. die dafür sorgen, daß nur ganz bestimmte auserlesene Reize
    der Außenwelt eindringen *which provide for it that only
    very definite selected stimuli of the outer world penetrate.*
    From the point of view of English the dafür *for it* seems un-
    necessary and even a bit confusing. But it has a precise parallel
    in the following translation, which is a perfectly acceptable
    alternative: "which see to it that only very definite, etc." In
    other words, the da *it* anticipates and introduces the clause
    to come. A very frequent construction in German.

7. sie vermochte es in den heißen Sümpfen der Vorzeit die rie-
    sigen phantastischen Reptilien zu schaffen *it was able to
    create the colossal fantastic reptiles in the hot swamps of
    primeval time.* Es, the grammatical object of vermochte, an-
    ticipates the infinitive phrase zu schaffen. Notice that ver-
    mögen *be able,* even though based on a modal auxiliary
    (mögen), is complemented by an infinitive with zu.

GRAMMATICAL COMMENT—
THE PASSIVE VOICE

I. Introductory Remarks

The verb **werden** is extraordinarily important and useful in German: it is used as an independent verb (**es wird kalt** *it is getting cold*), as the auxiliary of the future tense (**er wird einen Waschbottich machen** *he is going to make a washtub*), and as the auxiliary of the passive voice (**wie wird das Holz gemacht?** *how is the wood made?*). Study the following outline of its forms so that you can recognize any one of them instantly.

INDICATIVE MOOD

PRESENT		SIMPLE PAST	
ich werde	wir werden	ich wurde	wir wurden
du wirst	ihr werdet	du wurdest	ihr wurdet
er wird	sie werden	er wurde	sie wurden
Sie werden		Sie wurden	

PRESENT PERFECT

ich bin geworden	wir sind geworden
du bist geworden	ihr seid geworden
er ist geworden	sie sind geworden
Sie sind geworden	

PAST PERFECT

ich war geworden	wir waren geworden
du warst geworden	ihr wart geworden
er war geworden	sie waren geworden
Sie waren geworden	

FUTURE	FUTURE PERFECT
ich werde werden	ich werde geworden sein
du wirst werden	du wirst geworden sein
etc.	etc.

SUBJUNCTIVE MOOD

(The forms in **bold face** type are unmistakably subjunctive; the others, practically speaking, are only theoretical forms.)

PRESENT I		PRESENT II	
ich werde	wir werden	ich **würde**	wir **würden**
du **werdest**	ihr werdet	**du** **würdest**	ihr **würdet**
er **werde**	sie werden	er **würde**	sie **würden**
Sie werden		Sie **würden**	

PAST I

ich sei geworden	**wir seien geworden**
du seiest geworden	**ihr seiet** geworden
er sei geworden	**sie seien geworden**
Sie seien geworden	

PAST II

ich wäre geworden	**wir wären geworden**
du wärest geworden	**ihr wäret** geworden
er **wäre** geworden	**sie wären geworden**
Sie wären geworden	

FUTURE I

ich werde werden	wir werden werden
du **werdest werden**	ihr werdet werden
er **werde** werden	sie werden werden
Sie werden werden	

FUTURE II

ich **würde** werden	wir **würden werden**
du **würdest werden**	ihr **würdet werden**
er **würde** werden	sie **würden werden**
Sie **würden werden**	

FUTURE PERFECT I

ich werde geworden sein	wir werden geworden sein
du **werdest geworden sein**	ihr werdet geworden sein
er **werde** geworden sein	sie werden geworden sein
Sie werden geworden sein	

FUTURE PERFECT II

ich würde geworden sein	wir würden geworden sein
du würdest geworden sein	ihr würdet geworden sein
er würde geworden sein	sie würden geworden sein
	Sie würden geworden sein

INFINITIVES

PRESENT	PAST
werden	geworden sein

II. Formation of the Passive Voice

By passive voice, of course, we mean the system of verb forms, the subjects of which receive the action expressed by the verb. Any transitive verb, that is, any verb which takes an object, has a passive as well as an active system. For example, the sentence, "They took him away in an ambulance," employs the active voice of the verb "take," but "He was taken away in an ambulance" employs the passive voice.

If you will analyze the passive sentence just quoted, you will realize that the passive system of a verb, in German as well as in English, consists of its past participle in association with an auxiliary verb. The past participle *never* varies in form; therefore it is the auxiliary verb which makes the distinctions not only of voice but also of mood, tense or time, person, and number. Since the auxiliary of the passive voice in German is *werden,* knowing the indicative and subjunctive systems of *werden* given above will enable you to recognize any and all passive forms of any given verb of which you know the principal parts. Let us take, for example, the strong verb *fangen, fing, gefangen,* meaning "capture" or "catch," and give a synopsis of it in the third person singular passive indicative and subjunctive, merely supplying *gefangen* in the appropriate places in the paradigms of *werden.*

INDICATIVE MOOD

PRESENT	SIMPLE PAST
er wird gefangen	**er wurde gefangen**
he is caught	*he was caught*

PRESENT PERFECT	PAST PERFECT
er ist gefangen worden	**er war gefangen worden**
he has been caught	*he had been caught*

FUTURE	FUTURE PERFECT
er wird gefangen werden	**er wird gefangen worden sein**
he will be caught	*he will have been caught*

You will notice that in the three perfect tenses the past participle of **werden** appears in the shortened form **worden** rather than the full form **geworden**. Use of this form avoids the immediate repetition of the prefix **ge-**.

SUBJUNCTIVE MOOD

PRESENT I	PRESENT II
er werde gefangen	**er würde gefangen**

PAST I	PAST II
er sei gefangen worden	**er wäre gefangen worden**

FUTURE I	FUTURE II
er werde gefangen werden	**er würde gefangen werden**

FUTURE PERFECT I	FUTURE PERFECT II
er werde gefangen worden sein	**er würde gefangen worden sein**

INFINITIVES

PRESENT	PAST
gefangen werden	**gefangen worden sein**

No translations are given for the subjunctive forms because, as you learned in the chapters on the subjunctive, the meaning of a subjunctive form depends almost entirely on the context.

Passive imperatives, oddly enough, do not usually employ **werden** as the auxiliary. Instead, the imperative forms of **sein** are used as the passive auxiliary: **Sei gegrüßt!** *Be greeted!* **Seid umschlungen, Millionen!** *Be embraced, ye millions!* **Seien Sie davor gewarnt!** *Be warned about this!*

III. Constructions Used with the Passive

In such a sentence as "A graduated scale of animals was set up by certain investigators," the noun *investigators* is made the object of the preposition *by* to denote the personal agent by whom the action was performed. In German the preposition **von** with the dative is used for the same purpose: **Eine Stufenleiter der Tiere wurde von gewissen Forschern aufgebaut.** Impersonal means or instrument, however, is often expressed by **durch** with the accusative: **Der Fortschritt wird durch den Kampf ums Dasein verbürgt.** *Progress is guaranteed by the struggle for existence.*

The passive voice is often used without an expressed subject,* especially in such formula-like expressions as **Für Unterkunft wird gesorgt** and **Um Antwort wird gebeten.** (The second expression is often abbreviated **U.A.w.g.** and is the equivalent of our *R.S.V.P.*) The passive forms **wird gesorgt** and **wird gebeten** mean *is provided* and *is requested* respectively. But they have no subject, or, viewed differently, they have an impersonal subject **es** understood. The best way to translate such expressions is to take the basic idea of the verb, make a noun of it, and use this noun as the subject of some passive form like *is made* or *is done.* Thus the sentences above can be translated "Provision is made for lodgings," and "A request is made for an answer."

The passive is sometimes used with what seems to be a subject in the dative case: **ihm wurde geholfen** *he was helped.* The explanation is that the verb **helfen** in the active voice takes a dative object: **ich habe ihm geholfen** *I have helped him.* From this construction the feeling seems to have developed that the recipient of help, for example, must be mentioned in the dative case. Of course, it is also possible to look at **wurde geholfen** as an impersonal passive with the subject **es** omitted and an object **ihm.** But it is scarcely more logical that a passive verb should have an object than that the subject of a verb should be in the dative case. As you must have noticed before this, language is not only or even chiefly logical in structure, but psychological.

* Cf. subjectless passive clauses in English: "as has been said," "as has been shown."

EXERCISES

I. These exercises are at page 197.

II. Determine which German sentence in each group best translates the English. (Translate each sentence.)

1. "If washtubs are made, then wood must be made somewhere too," thought the little Berlin girl.

a. „Wenn Waschbottiche gemacht worden sind, so muß das Holz auch irgendwo gemacht worden sein," dachte die kleine Berlinerin.

b. „Waschbottiche werden gemacht, also muß das Holz auch irgendwo gemacht worden sein," dachte die kleine Berlinerin.

c. „Wenn Waschbottiche gemacht werden, so wird wohl das Holz auch irgendwo gemacht werden," dachte die kleine Berlinerin.

d. „Werden die Waschbottiche gemacht, so muß das Holz auch irgendwo gemacht werden," dachte die kleine Berlinerin.

2. For a time the attempt was made to introduce progress into the world of natural events also.

a. Eine Zeitlang wurde versucht, auch in die Welt des Naturgeschehens den Fortschritt hineinzubringen.

b. Eine Zeitlang wird der Versuch gemacht werden, auch in die Welt des Naturgeschehens den Fortschritt hineinzubringen.

c. Eine Zeitlang wurde auch der Fortschritt in die Welt des Naturgeschehens hineingebracht.

d. Wäre der Versuch eine Zeitlang gemacht worden, so hätte man den Fortschritt auch in die Welt des Naturgeschehens hineingebracht.

3. It seems as though the instruments of movement of animals had been formed by the environment.

a. Es schien, daß die Bewegungswerkzeuge der Tiere durch die Umgebung geformt werden würden.
b. Es scheint, daß die Bewegungswerkzeuge der Tiere durch die Umgebung geformt werden.
c. Es sieht so aus, als ob die Bewegungswerkzeuge der Tiere durch die Umgebung geformt worden wären.
d. Es sieht so aus, als ob die Bewegungswerkzeuge der Tiere durch die Umgebung geformt werden müssen.

4. The environment of the animal is created by the mechanical and chemical contrivances which provide that only very definite selected stimuli of the outer world penetrate.

a. Die Umwelt des Tieres wird von den mechanischen und chemischen Vorrichtungen geschaffen, die dafür sorgen, daß nur ganz bestimmte auserlesene Reize der Außenwelt eindringen.
b. Die Umwelt des Tieres wurde von den mechanischen und chemischen Vorrichtungen geschaffen, die dafür sorgten, daß nur ganz bestimmte auserlesene Reize der Außenwelt eindrangen.
c. Die Umwelt des Tieres sei von den mechanischen und chemischen Vorrichtungen geschaffen, die dafür sorgen, daß nur ganz bestimmte auserlesene Reize der Außenwelt eindringen.
d. Die Umwelt des Tieres ist von den mechanischen und chemischen Vorrichtungen geschaffen worden, die dafür sorgen, daß nur ganz bestimmte auserlesene Reize der Außenwelt eindringen.

III. *Select the appropriate continuation.*

1. Nur was zum Leben wichtig ist, dringt bis zum Nervensystem

a. und sorgt dafür, daß die passenden chemischen und mechanischen Vorrichtungen gemacht werden.
b. wo eine Stufenleiter der Tiere von der Amöbe durch alle Tierarten hindurch bis zum Säugetier aufgebaut wird.
c. und erzeugt dort den die passenden Bewegungswerkzeuge in passender Weise bewegenden Impuls.
d. weil die Amöbe ebenso unlösbar mit dem Wassertropfen verknüpft ist, wie die Forelle mit dem Fluß.

2. Allem Leben liegt eine allgemeine Lebenssubstanz zugrunde,

a. die selbst unverändert von Generation zu Generation weitergegeben wird.

b. die aus dem unheimlichen unerforschlichen Urgrund entstanden ist.

c. die mit den Möglichkeiten ihrer Existenz verschwunden ist.

d. die nach und nach immer reichere Strukturen gebaut hat und nach vielen Mißgriffen schließlich die menschliche Struktur gemacht hat.

IV. Determine which statement in each group is in some way associated with the preceding word or phrase.

1. die Dampfmaschine

a. Sie birgt die Möglichkeit aller Strukturen überhaupt.

b. Sie ist wieder zum Hauptproblem der Naturwissenschaft geworden.

c. Die Möglichkeit ihrer Existenz wird durch die Umwelt bedingt.

d. Sie gehört in die Welt, wo man an den Fortschritt glaubt.

2. die Sinneswerkzeuge der Tiere

a. Sie vermögen eine Stufenleiter der Tiere aufzubauen und die Behauptung aufzustellen, der Kampf ums Dasein habe dauernd für die Erhaltung der besseren Strukturen gesorgt.

b. Uexküll behauptet, von ihnen werde die Umgebung der Tiere geformt.

c. Die in den heißen Sümpfen der Vorzeit aus der allgemeinen und unverändert von Generation zu Generation weitergegebenen Lebenssubstanz entstandenen riesigen Reptilien sind jetzt verschwunden.

d. Der Springfuß des Känguruh gehört zu den Steppen Australiens.

V. Supply with quotation marks the one German sentence in each group that makes the correct translation of the English.

1. "The wood," answered the mistress, "is taken from trees such as are growing out in the Tiergarten."

a. Das Holz, antwortete die Hausfrau, werde von den Bäumen genommen, wie sie draußen im Tiergarten ständen.

b. Das Holz, antwortete die Hausfrau, sei von den Bäumen genommen worden, wie sie draußen im Tiergarten ständen.

c. Das Holz, antwortete die Hausfrau, wird von den Bäumen genommen, wie sie draußen im Tiergarten stehen.

d. Das Holz, antwortete die Hausfrau, ist von den Bäumen genommen worden, die draußen im Tiergarten standen.

2. "In past periods of the earth's history," said the professor, "there were different conditions of climate and vegetation."

a. In vergangenen Erdepochen, sagte der Professor, habe es andere Klima- und Vegetationsbedingungen gegeben.

b. In vergangenen Erdepochen, sagte der Professor, hätte es andere Klima- und Vegetationsbedingungen gegeben.

c. In vergangenen Erdepochen, sagte der Professor, gab es andere Klima- und Vegetationsbedingungen.

d. In vergangenen Erdepochen, sagte der Professor, wird es andere klimatische und Vegetationsbedingungen gegeben haben.

3. "It is scarcely possible to talk of any other progress," Uexküll maintains, "than the progressive development of the individual."

a. Von einem andern Fortschritt als von der fortschreitenden Durchbildung des Individuums, behauptet Uexküll, wäre kaum die Rede.

b. Von einem andern Fortschritt als von der fortschreitenden Durchbildung des Individuums, behauptet Uexküll, könne man kaum sprechen.

c. Von einem andern Fortschritt als von der fortschreitenden Durchbildung des Individuums, behauptet Uexküll, kann wohl kaum gesprochen werden.

d. Von einem andern Fortschritt als von der fortschreitenden Durchbildung des Individuums, behauptet Uexküll, könne wohl kaum gesprochen werden.

EIGHTH UNIT

A SELECTION FROM

Ansichten der Natur

BY ALEXANDER VON HUMBOLDT

(1769-1859)

When Alexander von Humboldt died in the spring of 1859 shortly before attaining the age of ninety, he was in the midst of completing his monumental work, *Cosmos*, a complete objective and historical description of the physical universe as it was then known. Some notion of the scope and wealth of this book can be gathered from the fact that the index, which was prepared by Humboldt's collaborators, comprises 1,117 pages. *Cosmos*, however, although it was the crowning synthesis of Humboldt's labors, is a relatively small part of his life's work, for he made basic original contributions to the sciences of anthropology, astronomy, botany, geography, geology, geophysics, meteorology, oceanography, physiology, and zoology. At odd moments he performed diplomatic services and contributed to the enlightenment of kings.

The high points of his career were two great journeys of exploration and scientific investigation. The first journey, undertaken at the age of thirty, took him for a period of five years to Central and South America and Mexico, where, among many other things, he discovered the interconnection between the river systems of the Orinoco and the Amazon, first recognized the relationship between vulcanism and earth structures, pointed the way to the anthropological study of the Inca, Aztec, and Maya civilizations, revolutionized European agriculture by recommending the use of guano as fertilizer, and collected about 60,000 plant specimens and described about 3,500 new species. The second journey, undertaken at the age of sixty, took him for one year through Russia and Siberia to the borders of China. On this trip he mapped the geology of Russia and central Asia, greatly extended knowledge of earth magnetism, uncovered vast new natural resources including gold and diamonds, and established a new science, limnology, or the study of the conditions of freshwater life.

He wrote his scientific works in Latin, English, and French, as well as his native German, had perfect command of Spanish, wrote private letters in Hebrew, read Greek and Sanskrit, and gained some knowledge of the native languages of the Americas. The selection which you are about to read is taken from *Ansichten der Natur,* written in German, and is characteristic of the partly poetic, partly philosophic approach to nature which characterizes not only Humboldt but so many of the greatest German scientists.

AUS ANSICHTEN DER NATUR

VON ALEXANDER VON HUMBOLDT

Unterhalb der Mission von Santa Barbara de Arichuna brachten
wir die Nacht wie gewöhnlich unter freiem Himmel, auf einer
Sandfläche am Ufer des Apure zu. Sie war von dem nahen, undurchdringlichen Walde begrenzt. Wir hatten Mühe, dürres Holz
5 zu finden, um die Feuer anzuzünden, mit denen nach der Landessitte jedes Bivouac wegen der Angriffe des Jaguars umgeben
wird. Die Nacht war von milder Feuchte und mondhell. Mehrere
Krokodile näherten sich dem Ufer. Ich glaube bemerkt zu haben,
daß der Anblick des Feuers sie ebenso anlockt wie unsre Krebse
10 und manche andere Wassertiere. Die Ruder unserer Nachen wurden sorgfältig in den Boden gesenkt, um unsere Hangematten
daran zu befestigen. Es herrschte tiefe Ruhe; man hörte nur bisweilen das Schnarchen der Süßwasserdelphine, welche dem Fluß-
netze des Orinoko wie dem Ganges bis Benares hin eigentümlich
15 sind und in langen Zügen aufeinanderfolgten.

Nach elf Uhr entstand ein solcher Lärmen im nahen Walde, daß
man die übrige Nacht hindurch auf jeden Schlaf verzichten mußte.
Wildes Tiergeschrei durchtobte die Forst. Unter den vielen Stimmen, die gleichzeitig ertönten, konnten die Indianer nur die
20 erkennen, welche nach kurzer Pause einzeln gehört wurden. Es
waren das einförmig jammernde Geheul der Aluaten (Brüllaffen),
der winselnde, fein flötende Ton der kleinen Sapajous, das schnar-
rende Murren des gestreiften Nachtaffen, das abgesetzte Geschrei
des großen Tigers, des Kuguars oder ungemähnten amerikanischen
25 Löwen, des Pecari, des Faultiers und einer Schar von Papageien
und anderen fasanenartigen[1] Vögeln. Wenn die Tiger dem Rande
des Waldes nahe kamen, suchte unser Hund, der vorher ununterbrochen bellte, heulend Schutz unter den Hangematten. Bis-

130

FROM **ANSICHTEN DER NATUR**

BY **ALEXANDER VON HUMBOLDT**

Below the mission of Santa Barbara de Arichuna we spent the
night as usual under the open sky on a [bit of] level sand on the
bank of the Apure. It was bordered by the nearby impenetrable
forest. We had trouble finding dry wood to light the fires by
which, according to the custom of the country, every bivouac is 5
encircled on account of the attacks of the jaguar. The night was
mild and humid and bright with moonlight. Several crocodiles
drew near the bank. I believe I observed[a] that the sight of fire
attracts them just as [it does] our own crayfish and many other
water animals. The oars of our boats were set carefully into the 10
ground in order to fasten our hammocks to them. Profound quiet
reigned; only occasionally did we hear the snorting of the freshwater dolphins, which are peculiar to the river network of the
Orinoco just as [they are] to the Ganges up to Benares, [and
which] followed each other in long processions.   15
   After eleven o'clock there arose such a din in the nearby forest
that for the rest of the night we had to give up all [thought of]
sleep. Wild-animal roaring raged through the woods. Among the
many voices which resounded simultaneously the Indians were
able to recognize only those which were heard individually after 20
a short pause. These were the monotonously complaining howl of
the aluates (howler monkeys), the whimpering, delicately fluting
sound of the little sapajous,[b] the rasping growl of the striped nocturnal monkey, the intermittent[c] roar of the great tiger, the cougar
or unmaned American lion, of the peccary, the sloth, and of a host 25
of parrots and of other pheasantlike birds. When the tigers came
close to the edge of the forest, our dog, which previously had been
barking uninterruptedly, howled and sought protection under the

131

weilen kam das Geschrei des Tigers von der Höhe eines Baumes
30 herab. Es war dann stets von den klagenden Pfeifentönen der
Affen begleitet, die der ungewohnten Nachstellung zu entgehen
suchten.

Fragt man die Indianer, warum in gewissen Nächten ein so
anhaltender Lärmen entsteht, so antworten sie lächelnd: „Die
35 Tiere freuen sich der schönen Mondhelle, sie feiern den Vollmond." Mir schien die Szene ein zufällig entstandener, lang fortgesetzter, sich steigernd entwickelnder Tierkampf. Der Jaguar
verfolgt die Nabelschweine und Tapirs, die dicht aneinandergedrängt das baumartige Strauchwerk durchbrechen, welches ihre
40 Flucht behindert. Davon erschreckt, mischen von dem Gipfel der
Bäume herab die Affen ihr Geschrei in das der größeren Tiere.
Sie erwecken die gesellig horstenden Vogelgeschlechter, und so
kommt allmählich die ganze Tierwelt in Aufregung. Eine längere[2]
Erfahrung hat uns gelehrt, daß es keineswegs immer die „gefeierte
45 Mondhelle" ist, welche die Ruhe der Wälder stört. Die Stimmen
waren am lautesten bei heftigem Regengusse oder wenn bei
krachendem Donner der Blitz das Innere des Waldes erleuchtete.
Der gutmütige, viele Monate schon fieberkranke Franziskanermönch, der uns begleitete, pflegte zu sagen, wenn bei einbrechen-
50 der Nacht er ein Gewitter fürchtete: „Möge der Himmel, wie uns
selbst, so auch den wilden Bestien des Waldes eine ruhige Nacht
gewähren!"

Mit den Naturszenen, die ich hier schildere und die sich oft für
uns wiederholten, kontrastiert wundersam die Stille, welche unter
55 den Tropen an einem ungewöhnlich heißen Tage in der Mittagsstunde herrscht. Ich entlehne meinem Tagebuche eine Erinnerung
an die Flußenge des Baraguan. Hier bahnt sich der Orinoko einen
Weg durch den westlichen Teil des Gebirges Parime. Was man
an diesem merkwürdigen Paß eine Flußenge nennt, ist ein Was-
60 serbecken von noch fünftausenddreihundertvierzig Fuß[3] Breite.
Ein Thermometer, im Schatten beobachtet, aber bis auf einige
Zolle der Granitmasse turmartiger Felsen genähert, stieg auf mehr
als 40° Réaumur. Alle ferne Gegenstände hatten wellenförmig
wogende Umrisse, eine Folge der Spiegelung oder optischen Kim-
65 mung. Kein Lüftchen bewegte den staubartigen Sand des Bodens.
Die Sonne stand im Zenith; und die Lichtmasse, die sie auf den
Strom ergoß und die von diesem, wegen einer schwachen Wellen-

hammocks. Occasionally the tiger's roar came down from the top
of a tree. Then it was always accompanied by the complaining 30
fluting sound of the monkeys which were trying to escape from
the unusual pursuit.

If one asks the Indians why on certain nights such a continuous
din arises, they answer with a smile: "The animals are rejoicing in
the beautiful brightness of the moon, they are celebrating the full 35
moon." To me the scene seemed to be an accidentally caused, long
continued struggle of the animals rising in crescendo.*ᵈ* The jaguar
pursues the peccaries and tapirs, which, crowding close together,
break through the treelike underbrush which impedes their flight.
Frightened by this, the monkeys from the tops of the trees mingle 40
their cries with those of the larger animals. They arouse the bird
tribes roosting in companionship and thus gradually the entire
animal world becomes excited. Rather long experience taught us
that it is by no means always the "celebration of the moon's brightness" which disturbs the peace of the forests. The voices were 45
loudest during a violent rain squall or when the lightning lit up
the interior of the forest to the accompaniment of crashing thunder. The good-natured Franciscan monk, ill of a fever for several
months, who accompanied us, was accustomed to say when he
feared a storm at the fall of night,*ᵉ* "May Heaven grant the wild 50
beasts of the forest, just as ourselves, a peaceful night!"

In marvelous contrast with the nature scenes which I am de-
scribing here and which were often repeated for us is the silence
which prevails in the tropics at noon on an unusually hot day. I
will take from my diary a reminiscence of the narrows of the 55
Baraguan. Here the Orinoco opens up a course through the west-
ern part of the Parime mountain range. What is called a narrows
in this remarkable pass is a basin of water five thousand three hundred forty feet broad. A thermometer, observed in the shade, but
placed within a few inches of the granite mass of towering rocks 60
climbed to more than 40° Réaumur.*ᶠ* All distant objects had undulating outlines, a result of the reflection or mirage. Not a breeze
stirred the dustlike sand of the ground. The sun was at the zenith;
and the mass of light which it poured on to the stream and which
was reflected from it, sparkling in the slight motion of the waves, 65
made still more noticeable the misty redness which veiled the distance. All the boulders and bare stone rubble were covered with

bewegung funkelnd, zurückstrahlte, machte bemerkbarer noch
die nebelartige Röte, welche die Ferne umhüllte. Alle Felsblöcke
70 und nackten Steingerölle waren mit einer Unzahl von großen,
dickschuppigen Iguanen, Gecko-Eidechsen und buntgefleckten
Salamandern bedeckt. Unbeweglich, den Kopf erhebend, den
Mund weit geöffnet, scheinen sie mit Wonne die heiße Luft einzuatmen. Die größeren Tiere verbergen sich dann in das Dickicht
75 der Wälder, die Vögel unter das Laub der Bäume oder in die
Klüfte der Felsen; aber lauscht man bei dieser scheinbaren Stille
der Natur auf die schwächsten Töne, die uns zukommen, so vernimmt man ein dumpfes Geräusch, ein Schwirren und Sumsen
der Insekten, dem Boden nahe und in den unteren Schichten
80 des Luftkreises. Alles verkündigt eine Welt tätiger, organischer
Kräfte. In jedem Strauche, in der gespaltenen Rinde des Baumes,
in der von Hymenopteren bewohnten, aufgelockerten Erde regt
sich hörbar das Leben. Es ist wie eine der vielen Stimmen der
Natur, vernehmbar[4] dem frommen, empfänglichen Gemüte des
85 Menschen.

NOTES TO THE GERMAN TEXT

1. **fasanenartig** *pheasantlike*. The suffix -artig comes from **die
   Art,** meaning *kind, species*. Cf. **vogelartig** *birdlike;* **felsenartig**
   rocklike, and similar words.

2. **eine längere Erfahrung** *a longer experience*, that is, *a rather
   long experience*. The comparative degree of an adjective is
   sometimes used to indicate a rather high degree: **eine ältere
   Frau** is *an older woman*, but by no means *an old woman*. See
   the Tenth Unit, Grammatical Comment III, B.

3. **fünftausenddreihundertvierzig Fuß Breite** *a width [of]* 5340
   feet. **Fuß** is the accusative singular of measure. We employ
   the same construction in English when we speak of a "twelve-
   inch (*not* inches) ruler," an "eight-foot (*not* feet) ceiling,"
   a "ten-ounce (*not* ounces) glass" and so on.

4. **vernehmbar** *audible*. The suffix -bar may be added to a verb
   stem to make a "passive adjective." It is like the English (from
   Latin) suffix -able or -ible; **fühlbar** *perceptible;* **unbeant-
   wortbar** *unanswerable;* **bewohnbar** *inhabitable*.

a great number of large heavy-scaled iguanas, geckos, and gaily spotted lizards. Motionless, holding up their heads, their mouths opened wide, they seem to breathe in the hot air with ecstasy. The 70 larger animals then hide in the forest thicket, the birds under the foliage of the trees or in the clefts of the rocks; but if, during this apparent silence of nature, one listens to the faintest sounds that come to us, then he will hear a dull noise, a buzzing and humming of the insects, near to the ground and in the lower layers of the 75 atmosphere. Everything proclaims a world of active organic forces. In every bush, in the cracked bark of the trees, in the loosened earth inhabited by the hymenoptera, life stirs audibly. It is like one of the many voices of nature, perceptible to the reverent, responsive soul of man.   80

NOTES TO THE ENGLISH TEXT

a. **Ich glaube bemerkt zu haben**   *I believe to have observed.* A Latinized form of indirect statement. Normal English requires some such translation as *I believe I observed.*

b. sapajou: a South American monkey.

c. **abgesetzt**   *interrupted, broken off, coming at intervals.*

d. **ein . . . sich steigernd entwickelnder Tierkampf**   *a struggle of animals intensifyingly developing itself.*

e. **bei einbrechender Nacht**   *at night breaking in.*

f. Réaumur: a thermometer or scale of measurement of temperature. It is so graduated that 0° marks the freezing point and 80° the boiling point of water. To convert to Fahrenheit multiply by 9/4 and add 32.

GRAMMATICAL COMMENT—COMPOUND, REFLEXIVE, IMPERSONAL VERBS

I. Compound Verbs

You cannot have failed to notice how frequently in German familiar simple verbs appear in close connection with syllables, words, or even phrases which modify or perhaps completely alter the meaning of the verb. This association is not unusual in English either: think of the verbs or verb phrases *stand* and *understand; turn* and *turn in; draw* and *draw near; stay, overstay,* and *stay over; go, undergo,* and *go under;* and so on. Indeed, German and English are very comparable in this respect, but German resorts to compound formation with a much greater readiness, even exuberance, than does English.

A. INSEPARABLE COMPOUNDS

1. Inseparable compounds are made up of the regular verb forms preceded by certain syllables, called the inseparable prefixes. These prefixes are: **be-, ge-, ent-, er-, ver-, zer-.** (The prefix **ent-** appears as **emp-** in the three verbs **empfangen, empfinden,** and **empfehlen.**) These syllables appear only in compounds, never as independent words, and never bear the main stress in the word of which they are a part. The inseparable compounds exhibit only one peculiarity in conjugation: **ge-** is not prefixed to the past participle. Thus, the principal parts of two inseparable compounds are: **bewegen, bewegte, bewegt; vernehmen, vernahm, vernommen.** (Incidentally, there are other verbs which likewise have no prefixed **ge-** in the past participle, for example, **kontrastieren, kontrastierte, kontrastiert.** The rule governing both these cases is very definite: If the first syllable of a verb does not bear the main stress, **ge-** is not prefixed to the past participle.)

2. Naturally, what students most want to know is how the prefixes affect or change the meaning of a verb. Unfortunately, a complete enumeration of the possibilities would be so complex and extensive as to be confusing. However, the following general statements about prefixes, with examples, may be useful.

be- tends to make a verb transitive: **steigen** *climb;* **besteigen** *mount*

ent- tends to give the meaning *out of* or *away from* as in **entsteigen** *emerge, arise from*

er- tends to suggest accomplishment or fulfillment as in **ersteigen** *scale, climb to the top*

ge- may suggest thoroughness or emphasis: **denken** *think;* **gedenken** *bear in mind, intend, make mention of*

ver- tends to suggest transience, passing away: **gehen** *go, walk;* **vergehen** *perish, pass away*

zer- signifies *to pieces;* **zergehen** *go to pieces*

But there are very many instances of a prefix changing the meaning of a verb in a way that may be rather hard to understand at first. Let us take the common verbs **gehen** *go, walk* and **stehen** *stand* and consider their inseparable compounds.

gehen: begehen *commit;* **entgehen** *escape;* **sich ergehen** *indulge in;* **vergehen** *pass away;* **zergehen** *go to pieces, disintegrate*

stehen: bestehen *consist, exist, endure;* **gestehen** *confess;* **entstehen** *arise, originate;* **erstehen** *buy;* **verstehen** *understand*

As you observe, some of these compounds can readily be guessed but others cannot.

B. SEPARABLE COMPOUNDS

1. A great many prepositions and adverbs, the particles **hin** and **her** and their compounds, e.g., **hinaus, herein,** and various other words and phrases may be used in such close association with a verb as to form a single verbal idea with it, but in certain forms they are separated from the verb. Hence, of course, they may be called separable prefixes or separable modifiers. The principal parts of two such separable compounds are: **zurückstrahlen, strahlte . . . zurück, zurückgestrahlt; zubringen, brachte . . . zu, zugebracht.** In the simple tenses (present and simple past) in an independent clause the separable prefix is postponed, usually to the end of the clause: **Er bringt (brachte) die Nacht auf der Sandfläche zu.** *He spends (spent) the night on the patch of sand.* In every other instance this separable modifier is spoken and written as an actual prefix to the verb form. Thus, the past participle is **zugebracht,** the present participle is **zubringend,** the infinitive is

zubringen, and the infinitive with connective zu is zuzubringen. In this last form, of course, the first zu is the prefix and the second one, the connective. Moreover, the separable modifier is prefixed to the postponed simple tense forms in dependent clauses: **Sagen Sie mir, warum er die Nacht auf der Sandfläche zubringt (zubrachte).** *Tell me why he spends (spent) the night on the patch of sand.* The separable modifier always bears the main stress: **zu'bringen, zurück'strahlen, herab'kommen, zu'bringt, zurück'strahlend, zu'gebracht, herab'zukommen.**

2. As has been indicated above, not only prefixes properly so called, but also various other words and phrases are used in such close association with the verb as to become to all intents and purposes separable modifiers. One of the most common expressions of this kind, which, however, does not appear in this unit, may be written **zu Grunde gehen** in order to break it up into the parts of which it is composed: **zu** *to,* **Grunde** *bottom,* **gehen** *go.* The meaning is *perish, be destroyed.* In more modern spelling the form is written **zugrundegehen** and the phrase **zugrunde** is in effect a separable prefix. In the text of this unit there are several examples of this kind of separable modifier, for instance: **und so kommt allmählich die ganze Tierwelt in Aufregung** *and thus the whole animal world gradually becomes excited,* where **in Aufregung kommen** is obviously parallel to **zu Grunde gehen.**

3.   The meaning of a separable compound can often readily be inferred from the meaning of the components: **herab** *down,* **kommen** *come,* **herabkommen** *come down;* **zurück** *back,* **strahlen** *shine,* **zurückstrahlen** *be reflected.* Sometimes, however, the meaning of the separable compound seems far removed from the combined meaning of the components: **aus** *out,* **legen** *lay,* **auslegen** *interpret.*

C. VARIABLE COMPOUNDS

As has already been pointed out, English verbs are also frequently used very closely with certain adverbs and prepositions to form verb associations comparable to the separable compounds you have just been studying. Think, for example, of *turn, turn out* (The cake turned out well.), *turn in* (It's time to turn in.), and *turn up* (He turned up ten minutes late.). Consider also *go* and *go under* (The guard reached him just as he was going under.).

Consider *stay* and *stay over* (It is too late to go back tonight, so we will have to stay over.). *Go* and *under*, however, and *stay* and *over* can be combined in a different way and with an entirely different meaning to form the compounds *undergo* (He had to undergo an operation.) and *overstay* (*Let's not overstay our welcome.*). As you can see, *undergo* and *overstay* are inseparable compounds.

The same possibility exists in German. Certain prefixes, namely **durch, über, um, unter, wieder,** may form either separable or inseparable compounds with verbs. When the prefix is separable it bears the main stress, **wie'derholen** *fetch back;* but when it is inseparable the verb bears the stress, **wiederho'len** *repeat.* These compounds present no peculiarities in conjugation: the separable form is conjugated like any other separable compound, and the inseparable form like any other inseparable compound:

wiederholen,	**holte . . . wieder,**	**wiedergeholt**
wiederholen,	**wiederholte,**	**wiederholt**

II. Reflexive Verbs

A reflexive object is a pronoun object in either the dative or accusative referring to the same thing as the subject: **er wäscht sich** *he is washing himself;* **ich mache mir große Sorgen** *I cause myself great worry;* **ich habe mir die Haare schneiden lassen** *I have had my hair cut;* **er hat sich das Bein gebrochen** *he has broken his leg.* In German there is only one form which is exclusively reflexive and that is **sich,** which is used for both dative and accusative cases in the third persons singular and plural and in the conventional form of address. Following are the reflexive pronouns:

	SINGULAR			PLURAL—DATIVE
	DATIVE	ACCUSATIVE		AND ACCUSATIVE
(ich)	mir	mich	(wir)	uns
(du)	dir	dich	(ihr)	euch
(er, sie, es)	sich	sich	(sie)	sich
(Sie)	sich	sich	(Sie)	sich

In the English phrase "I enjoyed myself," the word *myself* is a reflexive pronoun which has no logical but only grammatical function. In German, there are very many similar instances where a reflexive pronoun is grammatically necessary but seems logically superfluous. Examples are: **ich fürchte mich** *I am afraid;* **du freust dich** *you are happy;* **er begeistert sich** *he is enthusiastic;* **wir erinnern uns** *we remember;* etc.

There are various somewhat odd impersonal uses of the reflexive voice in German. For example: **es hört sich gut an** *it sounds good;* **das versteht sich von selbst** *that is understood, that is self-evident;* **es tanzt sich hier gut** *this is a good place to dance.* Especially important is the impersonal reflexive use of **lassen** to express what can or cannot be done: **das läßt sich schon machen** *that can be done all right;* **der Jaguar ließ sich nicht fangen** *the jaguar could not be caught.*

III. Impersonal Verbs

Impersonal verbs are verbs that are used without a personal subject such as **es schneit** *it is snowing;* **es regnet** *it is raining.* Impersonal verbs of other kinds are rather common in German: **es gibt Brüllaffen in Südamerika** *there are howler monkeys in South America;* **es handelt sich um sehr viel Geld** *it is a question of very much money;* **es gefällt mir** *it pleases me, I like it;* **es freut mich** *it makes me happy, I am glad.* Sometimes verbs are used impersonally in the passive voice: **auf Schlaf wird verzichtet** *no claim is made to sleep, there can be no thought of sleep;* **um Antwort wird gebeten** *a request is made for an answer.* (See the Seventh Unit, Grammatical Comment III, second paragraph.)

EXERCISES

I. *These exercises are at page 199.*

II. *These exercises are at page 200.*

III. *Determine which sentence in each group is not true.*

GROUP 1

a. Die Indianer sagten, daß die Tiere sich der schönen Mondhelle freuten.

b. Humboldt aber meinte, die Szene sei ein zufällig entstandener, lange fortgesetzter, sich steigernd entwickelnder Tierkampf.

c. Den Jaguar verfolgen die Nabelschweine und Tapirs, die das baumartige Strauchwerk durchbrechen.

d. In gewissen Nächten entsteht ein anhaltender Lärm.

GROUP 2

a. Unter den vielen Stimmen, die gleichzeitig ertönten, ließen sich nur die erkennen, welche nach kurzer Pause einzeln vernehmbar wurden.

b. Nach elf Uhr schlief es sich immer sehr gut auf der Sandfläche.

c. Die in langen Zügen aufeinanderfolgenden Süßwasserdelphine ließen sich vom Ufer aus sehr gut beobachten.

d. Mehrere durch den Anblick des Feuers angelockte Krokodile kamen dem Ufer nahe.

GROUP 3

a. Das in jedem Strauche, in der gespaltenen Rinde des Baumes, in der von Hymenopteren bewohnten, aufgelockerten Erde sich hörbar regende Leben vernimmt der fromme empfängliche Mensch.

b. In der Mittagsstunde an einem ungewöhnlich heißen Tage verbergen sich die Eidechsen in das Dickicht der Wälder.

c. Die auf den Strom ergossene und von diesem zurückgestrahlte Lichtmasse machte die nebelartige Röte noch bemerkbarer.

d. Alle ferne Gegenstände hatten wellenartig wogende Umrisse, eine Folge der optischen Kimmung.

IV. *Rearrange to make correct sentences:*

1. wegen der Angriffe, mit Feuern, jedes Bivouac, die Indianer, umgeben, des Jaguars

2. die gesellig horstenden Vogelgeschlechter, der Affen, werden . . . erweckt, der Bäume, von dem Geschrei, in dem Gipfel

3. Humboldt, eine Erinnerung, unter den Tropen, hat . . . entlehnt, seinem Tagebuch, an die ungewöhnlich heißen Tage

4. hätte . . . gelauscht, auf die schwächsten Töne, man, so, ein dumpfes Geräusch, man, hätte . . . vernommen

5. die Krokodile, des Feuers, die, des Orinoko, dem Flußnetz, werden . . . angelockt, durch den Anblick, sind, eigentümlich

V. *Select the appropriate continuation:*

1. Die Indianer umgeben jedes Bivouac mit Feuern

a. obgleich die Süßwasserdelphine dem Flußnetz des Orinoko eigentümlich sind.

b. weil die Jaguare sich der schönen Mondhelle freuen.

c. während die größeren Tiere sich in das Dickicht der Wälder verbergen.

d. wegen der Angriffe des Jaguars.

2. Fragt man die Indianer, warum in gewissen Nächten ein so anhaltender Lärm entsteht,

a. feiern sie den Vollmond.

b. scheinen sie mit Wonne die heiße Luft einzuatmen.

c. entsteht ein sich steigernd entwickelnder Tierkampf.

d. antworten sie, daß die Tiere sich der schönen Mondhelle freuen.

3. Wo gehen die größeren Tiere hin,

a. welche dem Ganges bis Benares hin eigentümlich sind?

b. wenn die Sonne im Zenith steht?

c. um die gesellig horstenden Vogelgeschlechter zu erwecken?

d. und werden dem frommen, empfänglichen Gemüte des Menschen vernehmbar?

4. Alles verkündigt eine Welt tätiger organischer Kräfte,

a. die der optischen Kimmung wegen wellenförmig wogende Umrisse haben.

b. die sich bei einbrechender Nacht vor dem Gewitter fürchten.

c. obgleich die größeren Tiere und die Vögel sich verborgen haben.

d. wenn der Hund unter den Hangematten heulend Schutz sucht.

NINTH UNIT

A SELECTION FROM

Parerga und Paralipomena

BY ARTHUR SCHOPENHAUER

(1788-1860)

In 1819 a young man of thirty-one published a massive philosophical work which he entitled *Die Welt als Wille und Vorstellung (The World as Will and Idea)*. For forty years almost nobody took the trouble to read this book and its author, Arthur Schopenhauer, was known merely as a well-to-do eccentric, son of the famous authoress, Johanna Schopenhauer.

For Arthur, who was the slave of an inordinate lust for fame, the years of obscurity were bitter. Never during all this time, however, did he waver in his belief that his book would eventually be recognized as a philosophical masterwork. Secure in the conviction that he had spoken the truth once and for all, he wrote little else, but by the middle of the century he was beginning to attract sufficient attention to warrant the publication of a book of essays on miscellaneous subjects, *Parerga und Paralipomena*, which might be very loosely translated as *Chips from a Philosopher's Workbench*. This book soon became popular and contributed a great deal to the awakening of interest in Schopenhauer. In 1859 he had the great pleasure of seeing a new edition of his main work published and of enjoying widespread acclaim.

After Schopenhauer's death his fame and influence continued to grow and it can be said that he is one of the best known and most influential philosophers of the last century and a half as well as one of the best writers of German prose.

AUS SELBSTDENKEN (PARERGA UND PARALIPOMENA)

VON ARTHUR SCHOPENHAUER

Zu einem Selbstdenker verhält sich der gewöhnliche Bücherphilosoph wie zu einem Augenzeugen ein Geschichtsforscher.
Jener redet aus eigener, unmittelbarer Auffassung der Sache.
Daher stimmen alle Selbstdenker im Grunde doch überein, und
5 ihre Verschiedenheit entspringt nur aus der des Standpunktes; wo
aber dieser nichts ändert, sagen sie alle dasselbe; denn sie sagen
bloß aus, was sie objektiv aufgefaßt haben. Oft habe ich Sätze,
die ich ihrer Paradoxie wegen nur zaudernd vor das Publikum
brachte, nachmals zu meinem freudigen Erstaunen in alten Werken
10 großer Männer ausgesprochen gefunden. Der Bücherphilosoph
hingegen berichtet, was dieser gesagt und jener gemeint und was
dann wieder ein anderer eingewandt hat usw. Das vergleicht er,
wägt es ab, kritisiert es und sucht so hinter die Wahrheit der
Sachen zu kommen, wobei er dem kritischen Geschichtsschreiber
15 ganz ähnlich wird. Man könnte sich wundern über die viele Mühe,
die so einer sich gibt, da es scheint, daß, wenn er nur die Sache
selbst ins Auge fassen wollte,[1] er durch ein wenig Selbstdenken
bald zum Ziele gelangen würde. Allein damit hat es einen kleinen
Anstand,[2] indem solches nicht von unserm Willen abhängt: man
20 kann jederzeit sich hinsetzen und lesen, nicht aber — und denken.
Es ist nämlich mit Gedanken wie mit Menschen: man kann nicht
immer nach Belieben sie rufen lassen, sondern muß abwarten, daß
sie kommen. Das Denken über einen Gegenstand muß sich von
selbst einstellen,[3] durch ein glückliches, harmonierendes Zusam-
25 mentreffen des äußern Anlasses mit der innern Stimmung und
Spannung; und gerade das ist es, was jenen Leuten nie kommen

SELBSTDENKEN (PARERGA UND PARALIPOMENA)

BY ARTHUR SCHOPENHAUER

The ordinary book philosopher stands in the same relation to an independent thinker as a researcher in history [stands] to an eye-witness. The latter[a] speaks from his own immediate grasp of the matter. For this reason all independent thinkers are basically in agreement, and their difference arises only from the [difference] 5 of point of view. But where this does not affect anything, they all say the same thing, for they merely assert what they have objectively grasped. Often, to my happy amazement, I have subsequently found propositions expressed in old works of great men which I had only hesitatingly brought before the public because 10 of their paradoxical quality. The book philosopher, on the other hand, reports what this man has said and that man has thought and what objections a third man has made, etc.[b] This he compares, he weighs it, criticizes it, and tries in this way to get at the truth of things, in which [endeavor] he becomes very much like the 15 critical historian. One could be amazed at the great trouble to which such a person goes, since it seems that if he only would fix his eyes upon the thing itself he would soon get to his goal by means of a little independent thinking. But there is a little difficulty about this, inasmuch as this sort of thing[c] does not depend 20 upon our will; one can sit down and read at any time but not [sit down] and think. With ideas it is the same as with people, one cannot always summon[d] them at one's pleasure, but must wait for them to come. Thinking about a subject must take place of its own accord by means of a fortunate, harmonious coincidence of 25 the external occasion with inner mood and interest. And this is

will. Sogar der größte Kopf ist nicht jederzeit zum Selbstdenken
fähig. Daher tut er wohl, die übrige Zeit zum Lesen zu benutzen,
welches ein Surrogat des eigenen Denkens ist und dem Geiste
30 Stoff zuführt, indem dabei ein anderer für uns denkt, wiewohl
stets auf eine Weise, die nicht die unsrige ist. Dieserhalb eben soll
man nicht zu viel lesen, damit nicht der Geist sich an das Surrogat
gewöhne und darüber die Sache selbst verlerne, also damit das
Gehn eines fremden Gedankenganges ihn nicht dem eigenen ent-
35 fremde. Am allerwenigsten soll man des Lesens wegen dem
Anblick der realen Welt sich ganz entziehn, da der Anlaß und die
Stimmung zum eigenen Denken ungleich öfter bei diesem als
beim Lesen sich einfindet. Denn das Anschauliche, das Reale, in
seiner Ursprünglichkeit und Kraft ist der natürliche Gegenstand
40 des denkenden Geistes und vermag am leichtesten ihn tief zu
erregen. Nach diesen Betrachtungen wird es uns nicht wundern,
daß der Selbstdenker und der Bücherphilosoph schon am Vortrage
leicht zu erkennen sind; jener am Gepräge des Ernstes, der Unmittelbarkeit und Ursprünglichkeit, am Autoptischen aller seiner
45 Gedanken und Ausdrücke; dieser hingegen daran, daß alles aus
zweiter Hand ist, überkommene Begriffe, zusammengetrödelter
Kram, matt und stumpf, wie der Abdruck eines Abdrucks; und
sein aus konventionellen, ja, banalen Phrasen und gangbaren
Modeworten bestehender Stil gleicht einem kleinen Staate, dessen
50 Zirkulation aus lauter[4] fremden Münzsorten besteht, weil er nicht
selbst prägt.

NOTES TO THE GERMAN TEXT

1. **die Sache ins Auge fassen**   *set the thing into the eye,* i.e., *fix
the eye upon the thing.*
2. **es hat einen kleinen Anstand**   *it has a little difficulty,* i.e.,
there is a little difficulty.
3. **sich einstellen**   *turn up, put in an appearance.*
4. **lauter**   *nothing but.* This is an indeclinable adjective, that is,
it has no declensional endings when it has this meaning. When
it means *pure* or *undefiled,* however, it takes the regular adjective endings: **eine lautere Quelle** *a pure spring.*

precisely what never will come to those*e* people [we have mentioned]. Even the most intelligent man is not capable of independent thinking at all times. For this reason he does well to use his spare time for reading, which is a substitute for one's own 30 thinking and supplies the mind [with] material, inasmuch as another is then thinking for us, although always in a way which is not our own. For this reason, one must not read too much, so that the mind will not become used to the substitute and because of this unlearn the thing itself, that is to say, so that it will not grow 35 accustomed to beaten paths, and so that following the path of another person's thought*f* will not estrange it from its own. Least of all should one because of reading withdraw completely from the contemplation of the actual world, since the occasion and mood for independent thinking is produced much more often by 40 this than by reading. For what is seen directly, what is actual, is, because of its original force and power, the natural object of the thinking mind and can most readily stimulate it deeply. After these reflections it will not amaze us that the independent thinker and the book philosopher can be recognized even by their manner 45 of oral delivery: the former, by the stamp of seriousness, immediacy, and originality, by the autoptic*g* [quality] of all his thoughts and expressions; the latter, on the other hand, by the fact that everything is second hand: handed-down ideas, rubbish accumulated [from everywhere], feeble and dull, like the copy of a copy, 50 and his style, which consists of conventional, even banal, phrases and currently fashionable words, is like a small country, the currency of which consists of nothing but foreign coins, because it has no mint of its own.

NOTES TO THE ENGLISH TEXT

a. **jener** *the former.* But here it must be translated *the latter* because the order of the nouns **Selbstdenker** and **Bücherphilosoph**, **Augenzeugen** and **Geschichtsforscher** has been reversed for the sake of smoother English.

b. **was dieser gesagt und jener gemeint und was dann wieder ein anderer eingewandt:** supply **hat** as the tense auxiliary for all the past participles. This is a very common type of ellipsis.

c. **solches** *such, the like, such a thing.* Refers here to **Selbstdenken.**

d. man kann sie rufen lassen *one can have them called.*

e. jene Leute: jener is not the simple demonstrative *that*, but usually has some overtones of meaning such as *yon, that famous one, the one that has been mentioned, the former.*

f. das Gehn eines fremden Gedankenganges *the walking of a strange* (i.e. *a stranger's*) *thought path.*

g. autoptisch *autoptic, based on personal observation.*

GRAMMATICAL COMMENT—
NOUNS AND PRONOUNS

I. Gender of Nouns

An American who has never studied a foreign language usually finds it very surprising that German nouns have grammatical gender and that there is no logical way of deciding what the gender of an unfamiliar noun must be. Indeed, he must reconcile himself to the hard fact that the best method of mastering the gender of nouns in German is to memorize the definite article as part of the noun: **der Kopf, die Hand, das Werk, der Wille, die Mühe, das Auge,** etc. Eventually, as he gains a feeling for the language, he will discover that certain forms or endings indicate gender with complete or almost complete regularity. We will give here only the most practically helpful rules.

A.   GENDER DETERMINED BY ENDINGS

Masculine are:

1. Nouns ending in -ich, -ig, -ing, -ling, -rich: **der Bottich** *the tub;* **der König** *the king;* **der Hering** *the herring;* **der Jüngling** *the youth;* **der Gänserich** *the gander*
2. Nouns ending in -er signifying *a doer* or *performer:* **der Spieler** *the player;* **der Lehrer** *the teacher;* **der Arbeiter** *the worker.*

Neuter are:

1. Nouns with the diminutive endings -chen and -lein: **das Mädchen** *the girl;* **das Fräulein** *the young lady*
2. Nouns ending in -tum: **das Altertum** *antiquity;* (Two nouns ending in -tum, however, are masculine: **der Irrtum** *the error;* **der Reichtum** *the wealth.*)
3. Nouns with the prefix **Ge-** and the suffix -e: **das Gebirge** *the mountain range.* Sometimes the final **e** is omitted: **das Gewölk** *the cloud-bank.*

Feminine are:

1. Nouns ending in -ei, -in, -heit, -keit, -ung, -schaft: **die Bücherei** *the library;* **die Königin** *the queen;* **die Verschiedenheit** *the*

difference; die **Unmittelbarkeit** *the immediacy;* die **Freund-schaft** *the friendship;* die **Spannung** *the tension.*

2.   Nouns of foreign origin ending in -age, -ie, -ik, -ion, -tät: die **Courage** *the courage;* die **Paradoxie** *the paradox;* die **Musik** *the music;* die **Zirkulation** *the circulation, currency;* die **Autorität** *the authority.*

B.   INFINITIVES, ADJECTIVES, COMPOUNDS

Infinitives used as nouns are always neuter: **das Gehen** *the walking.*

Adjectives used as nouns have the "natural" gender: **der Gute** *the good man;* die **Gute** *the good woman;* das **Gute** *the good.*

Compound nouns have the gender of the last element: **das Auge** *the eye* + **der Zeuge** *the witness* → **der Augenzeuge** *the eye-witness.*

II. Declension of Nouns

In a language like Latin the various cases of a noun are indicated by forms of the noun itself, but in German the cases are indicated by various forms of the whole noun phrase, which is composed of the noun and its modifier or modifiers. Just how important knowledge of the gender of a noun is to understanding its use can be seen in a comparison of the three noun phrases **der Affe, der Sache, der Gebirge:** the one form of the article, **der,** indicates that the noun **Affe** is nominative and singular, that **Sache** is either genitive or dative and singular, and that **Gebirge** is genitive and plural. This information follows immediately and directly from the fact that **Affe** is masculine, **Sache** is feminine, and **Gebirge** is neuter. That is, it follows immediately and directly if you know the declensions of the noun modifiers.

A.   The two basic types of noun modifiers are: (1) the **der-** and **dieser-**words and (2) the **kein-**words.

The **der-**words are, of course, the various forms of the definite article:

	MASCULINE	FEMININE	NEUTER	PLURAL
N	der	die	das	die
G	des	der	des	der
D	dem	der	dem	den
A	den	die	das	die

The dieser-words are dieser *this*, jener *that*, jeder *each*, welcher *which*, mancher *many a*, solcher *such*. In declension they are very similar to the der-words:

	MASCULINE	FEMININE	NEUTER	PLURAL
N	dieser	diese	dieses	diese
G	dieses	dieser	dieses	dieser
D	diesem	dieser	diesem	diesen
A	diesen	diese	dieses	diese

The kein-words are the indefinite article ein; kein *not a, no;* mein *my;* dein *your* (singular); sein *his, its;* ihr *her, its, their;* unser *our;* euer *your* (plural); Ihr *your* (singular and plural). They have the following declensional pattern:

	MASCULINE	FEMININE	NEUTER	PLURAL
N	mein	meine	mein	meine
G	meines	meiner	meines	meiner
D	meinem	meiner	meinem	meinen
A	meinen	meine	mein	meine

You will observe from these paradigms that there is no gender in the plural and that instead of there being sixteen different forms for the sixteen different gender-case-number functions, there are only five forms for the dieser-words and six for each of the others. In consequence, you must learn to instantly perceive and understand the meaning of every significant element in a noun phrase: dieses Gebirge is not the same as dieses Gebirges.

B. From noun modifiers we turn to the declensional forms of the nouns themselves. Let us consider first the singular and then go to the plural.

1. Feminine nouns are unchanged in the singular: die Sache, der Sache, der Sache, die Sache.

2. Neuter nouns regularly add -s or -es in the genitive singular, and neuter monosyllables and certain polysyllables may or may not add an -e in the dative singular: das Publikum, des Publikums, dem Publikum, das Publikum; das Ziel, des Ziel(e)s, dem Ziel(e), das Ziel. Mention might also be made of certain neuters which add -s in the genitive singular but -(e)n in the plural: das Auge, des Auges, die Augen; das Hemd, des Hemd(e)s, die Hemden. Notice especially das

Herz, des Herzens, dem Herzen, das Herz; die Herzen, der Herzen, den Herzen, die Herzen.

3. Masculine nouns are of two kinds. One group of masculines is exactly like the neuters first described: **der Denker, des Denkers, dem Denker, den Denker; der Geist, des Geist(e)s, dem Geist(e), den Geist.** The other group adds -(e)n or -(e)ns in the genitive singular and also -(e)n in the dative and accusative singular: **der Mensch, des Menschen, dem Menschen, den Menschen; der Gedanke, des Gedankens, dem Gedanken, den Gedanken.** All nouns of this last type add -(e)n for the plural.

C. Nouns are made plural in various ways such as by modification of the stem vowel or the addition of various endings, and may be classified into five groups: (1) no ending; (2) ending -e; (3) ending -er; (4) ending -(e)n; (5) miscellaneous: -en, -ien, or -s. Nearly all German nouns belong to the first four groups. Here are examples of each group:

1. No ending: **der Denker, die Denker; der Vater, die Väter; die Mutter, die Mütter.**

2. Ending -e: **der Pfad, die Pfade; der Kopf, die Köpfe; die Kraft, die Kräfte.**

3. Ending -er: **der Geist, die Geister; der Mann, die Männer; das Buch, die Bücher.**

4. Ending -(e)n: **der Mensch, die Menschen; der Gedanke, die Gedanken; die Zeit, die Zeiten; die Sache, die Sachen; das Auge, die Augen.**

5. Miscellaneous: (a) Ending -en replacing singular ending -um: **das Individuum, die Individuen.** (b) Ending -ien added to the nominative singular: **das Reptil, die Reptilien.** (c) Ending -s: **das Auto, die Autos; der Chef, die Chefs.**

The following paradigms illustrate the plural declension. Observe that, as has been said, there is no gender in the plural, and that all nouns except the -n-plurals and the -s-plurals add an -(e)n in the dative.

N	die Väter	die Kräfte	die Augen	die Autos
G	der Väter	der Kräfte	der Augen	der Autos
D	den Vätern	den Kräften	den Augen	den Autos
A	die Väter	die Kräfte	die Augen	die Autos

Any rules that can be given for determining the plurals of nouns are so complicated as to be confusing and apply only in a limited way, and no rules can be made to enable the student to determine from inspection, for example, that the plural of **der Pfad** is **die Pfade**, of **der Kopf** is **die Köpfe**, and of **der Geist** is **die Geister.** The only safe rule is: Learn the principal parts, namely, the nominative and genitive singular and the nominative plural.

III. Use of the Cases

Since the four cases of German substantives obviously cannot correspond exactly to the three cases of English substantives, some comment on the use of the cases in German is needed.

A. The uses of the nominative case in German are the same as the uses of the nominative case in English and require no discussion.

B. Among the uses of the genitive case are the following:

1. It expresses the relationship of possession and other more or less analogous relationships and corresponds both to the English possessive case in *'s* and also to many uses of the English preposition *of:* **die Werke dieses Philosophen** *this philosopher's works;* **die unmittelbare Auffassung einer Sache** *the immediate grasp of a thing;* **das Gepräge des Ernstes** *the stamp of seriousness.*

2. It is sometimes used as the object of certain verbs: **Das bedarf keiner weiteren Erklärung** *That requires no further explanation.*

3. It is used with certain prepositions such as **außerhalb, innerhalb, oberhalb, unterhalb, diesseits, jenseits, statt, anstatt, trotz, während, wegen,** and **um . . . willen,*** and with the postpositions **halber** and **wegen.**

4. It is used with many adjectives: **Er ist keiner großen Tat fähig** *He is not capable of a great deed.*

5. It has various idiomatic adverbial uses: **leichten Herzens** *lightheartedly;* **eines Abends** *one evening;* **letzten Endes** *in the final analysis.*

---

* It should be pointed out, however, that there is a very strong tendency to use some of these prepositions with the dative case or to avoid their use as prepositions altogether.

C. Among the uses of the dative case are the following:

1. It is the case of the indirect object of a verb: **Das Lesen führt dem Geiste Stoff zu.** *Reading supplies material to the intellect.*

2. It is used as the sole object of many verbs: **Das gleicht einem kleinen Staat.** *That resembles a small state.*

3. It is used with a good many adjectives: **Er ist einem kritischen Geschichtsschreiber ganz ähnlich.** *He is very much like a critical historian.*

4. It is very often used, in a way which frequently seems unnecessary from the viewpoint of English, to specify the person or thing concerned: **Ich möchte mir dieses Buch ansehen.** *I would like to look at this book.*

5. It is always used with the prepositions **aus, außer, bei, mit, nach, nebst, samt, seit, von, zu,** and with the postpositions **entgegen, gegenüber, nach.**

6. It is used with the prepositions **an, auf, hinter, in, neben, über, unter, vor,** and **zwischen** to indicate station or locality: **Das steht in alten Büchern.** *That is to be found in old books.* **Der Kanarienvogel flog in dem Zimmer herum.** *The canary was flying around in the room.*

D. The uses of the accusative case include the following:

1. It is the case of the direct object of a verb: **Er liest ein gutes Buch.** *He is reading a good book.*

2. It is used adverbially to express definite time and duration of time or extent of space: **diesen Monat** *this month;* **drei Tage lang** *for three days;* **einen Fuß hoch** *one foot high.*

3. It is always used as the object of the prepositions **bis, durch, für, gegen, ohne, um, wider,** and of the postposition **entlang.**

4. It is used with the prepositions **an, auf, hinter, in, neben, über, unter, vor,** and **zwischen** to set a goal or limit to the motion expressed or implied by the verb: **Er bringt gern paradoxe Sätze vor das Publikum.** *He likes to bring paradoxical principles before the public.*

5. It is used with the prepositions **an, auf,** and **über** in some other sense than the literal or concrete one: **Man könnte sich über die viele Mühe wundern.** *One could be amazed at the great exertion.*

IV. Pronouns

As you know, a pronoun is a word which may stand for a noun, or function as its equivalent. Now, if a pronoun is to function as the equivalent of a noun it must have certain features in common with it, that is, it must agree in person and number, and pronouns of the third person singular must agree in gender also. Almost always the pronoun has the grammatical gender of the noun it represents: **der Gegenstand, er; die Wahrheit, sie; das Buch, es.** Sometimes, however, a pronoun may have the natural gender of its antecedent: **das Mädchen, sie.** The case of a pronoun, of course, will be determined by its own function in the particular context in which it occurs.

V. The Personal Pronouns

SINGULAR

	FIRST PERSON	SECOND PERSON	*Masc.*	*Fem.*	*Neut.*
			THIRD PERSON		
N	ich	du	er	sie	es
G	meiner	deiner	seiner	ihrer	seiner
D	mir	dir	ihm	ihr	ihm
A	mich	dich	ihn	sie	es

PLURAL

			All Genders
N	wir	ihr	sie
G	unser	euer	ihrer
D	uns	euch	ihnen
A	uns	euch	sie

The conventional pronoun of address **Sie** is both singular and plural and has the declension of the third personal pronoun plural, save that it is capitalized: **Sie, Ihrer, Ihnen, Sie.** The intimate pronoun **du** is used in addressing the Deity, members of the family, intimate friends, children, and animals. A very common and very important use of the neuter pronoun **es** is as an anticipative subject or expletive like the English word *there*. The verb agrees with the actual subject: **Es waren einmal drei schöne Prinzessinnen.** *Once upon a time there were three beautiful princesses.*

The genitive case of the personal pronoun is seldom used, but it does sometimes occur: (1) as the object of a verb, **niemand achtete seiner** *nobody paid attention to him;* or (2) of a preposition, **statt meiner** *in place of me;* or (3) as the so-called partitive genitive, **ihrer dreißig** *thirty of them.*

VI. The Demonstrative Pronouns

The demonstrative pronouns are:

der, die, das	a strongly stressed *he, she, it*
dieser, diese, dieses	*this*
jeder, jede, jedes	*every*
jener, jene, jenes	*yonder, that*
derjenige, diejenige, dasjenige	*that one*
derselbe, dieselbe, dasselbe	*the same*

When **der, die, das** are used as demonstrative pronouns they have long forms in the genitive singular (**dessen, deren, dessen**), in the genitive plural (**deren**), and in the dative plural (**denen**). Each part of the compounds **derjenige** and **derselbe** is declined: the first part has the regular declension of the definite article and the second part ends in **-n** in every form *except* in the nominative singular of all three genders and the accusative singular of the feminine and neuter where the ending is **-e.** The forms **das** and **dies** (or **dieses**) may be used as expletives: **Das sind die natürlichen Gegenstände des denkenden Geistes.** *Those are the natural objects of the thinking intellect.*

VII. The Relative Pronouns

The relative pronouns are: **der, die, das** and **welcher, -e, -es.** The relatives **der, die, das** have the long forms **dessen, deren, dessen** in the genitive singular, **deren** in the genitive plural, and **denen** in the dative plural. **Welcher, -e, -es** used as a relative pronoun has no genitive forms. The only genitive forms of the relative pronoun, accordingly, are **dessen** (masculine and neuter singular) and **deren** (feminine singular and also plural). Except that the forms of **der** tend to be more frequently used than the forms of **welcher** they are not differentiated in function.

VIII. Wer and was

The words **wer** and **was** may be used as relative pronouns or as interrogatives. As relatives they signify *the one who* or *whoever* and *that which* or *whatever*. **Wer** has what may be considered dual gender and **was** is neuter. As interrogatives they mean *who* and *what*. They have no plural, the full declension being:

MASCULINE AND FEMININE		NEUTER
N	wer	was
G	wessen	wessen
D	wem	(wo + preposition: womit, wozu, etc.)
A	wen	was

IX. The Intensives

Selbst and **selber** are never declined and are used to heighten the force of nouns or pronouns: **der Junge hat das selber gemacht** *the boy did that himself;* **selbst Schopenhauer könnte es nicht besser machen** *even Schopenhauer couldn't do it better.* As you can see from the second example, when **selbst** precedes, the best translation is *even.*

EXERCISES

I. *These exercises are at page 203.*

II. *In this exercise each German sentence is followed by two English sentences. Using the original sentence as a model, translate the English sentences into German.*

1. Zu einem Selbstdenker verhält sich der gewöhnliche Bücherphilosoph wie zu einem Augenzeugen ein Geschichtsforscher.

a. Ordinary book philosophers stand in the same relation to independent thinkers as research historians stand to eyewitnesses.

b. Every ordinary book philosopher stood in the same relation to this independent thinker as a research historian stands to an eyewitness.

2. Alle Selbstdenker stimmen doch im Grunde überein und ihre Verschiedenheit entspringt nur aus der des Standpunktes.

a. At bottom every independent thinker agrees with every other independent thinker and their disagreement arises only from that of their point of view.

b. At bottom every independent thinker will agree with this one and their difference can arise only from that of their point of view.

3. Selbst die größten Köpfe wird es wundern, welche Mühe ein solcher Geschichtsschreiber sich gibt, hinter die Wahrheit der Sachen zu kommen.

a. Even the greatest mind will be amazed at what pains such historians have taken to get at the truth of the affair.

b. Such an historian is amazed at what pains the greatest minds take to get at the truth of things.

III. *Rearrange to make sentences:*

1. nach diesen Betrachtungen, uns, wird . . . wundern, daß, es, ist, am Vortrag, zu erkennen, leicht, der Selbstdenker, nicht

2. jenen Leuten, was, kommen will, ist, nie, des äußern Anlasses, der innern Stimmung, mit, das harmonisierende Zusammentreffen

3. das Lesen, des Denkens, welches, ein Surrogat, ist, dem
Geiste, Stoff, führt . . . zu

4. wegen, man, sich, des Lesens, soll, entziehen, der realen
Welt, dem Anblick, nicht

5. an, der Bücherphilosoph, seinen banalen Phrasen, zu erkennen, und, ist, gangbaren Modeworten

IV. Complete by means of the suitable clause or phrase.

1. Der Anlaß zum eigenen Denken findet sich oft ein,
a. wenn was dieser gesagt und jener gemeint verglichen wird.
b. beim Anblick der realen Welt.
c. weil er einem kleinen Staate gleicht, der nicht selbst prägt.
d. obgleich der zusammengetrödelte Kram aus Abdrücken alter
Abdrücke besteht.

2. Mit dem Selbstdenken hat es immer einen kleinen Anstand,
a. weil ein natürlicher Gegenstand den denkenden Geist tief zu
erregen vermag.
b. der aber nur aus banalen Phrasen besteht.
c. dessen Werke von Bücherphilosophen so oft verglichen
werden.
d. weil nicht jeder Kopf dazu fähig ist.

3. Könnten wir nur die Gedanken nach Belieben rufen lassen,
a. würden wir alle große Geister sein.
b. müßte man sich dem Anblick der realen Welt ganz entziehen.
c. wäre der Bücherphilosoph schon am Vortrag leicht zu
erkennen.
d. könnten wir uns wundern über die Mühe die so einer sich gibt.

TENTH UNIT

A SELECTION FROM

"Der blonde Eckbert"

BY LUDWIG TIECK

(1773-1853)

In the early summer of 1793 two university students went on a hiking trip which was destined to have a significant effect upon the history of German literature. For on this trip the two students, Ludwig Tieck and Wilhelm Wackenroder (1773-1798), saw with the fresh gaze of enthusiastic youth the ancient city of Nürnberg and the forests, fields, clear streams, and fantastic rock formations in the mountains of southeast Germany. It was their portrayal of great artists of the past and their glorification of the magic power of nature that was hailed by the young Romantic critics as an exemplification of their theories. Indeed, it can be said that Tieck and Wackenroder discovered the beauty of the late medieval city and the landscape of the German fairy tale.

Whereas Wackenroder died very young, Tieck had a long and influential career and is remembered as one of the finest writers of the German Romantic Movement. Indeed, for a while in his own day he was felt to be the equal, if not actually the superior, of Goethe. Although this is a judgment which has not stood the test of time, there are few readers who can resist the spell which he weaves in such stories as *"Der blonde Eckbert."* In the selection which you are about to read, Eckbert's wife, Bertha, is telling the story of her childhood.

Als der Tag graute, stand ich auf und öffnete, fast ohne daß ich
es wußte, die Tür unsrer Hütte. Ich stand auf dem freien Felde,
bald darauf war ich in einem Walde, bald mußte ich über Hügel
klettern und erriet nun, daß ich mich in dem benachbarten
5 Gebirge befinden müsse. Meine Angst trieb mich vorwärts. Die
Felsen wurden immer furchtbarer,[1] und endlich hörte sogar der
Weg auf. Nun brach die Nacht herein, und ich suchte mir eine
Moosstelle aus, um dort zu ruhen. Ich hörte die seltsamsten Töne,
bald[2] hielt ich es für wilde Tiere,[3] bald für den Wind, der durch
10 die Felsen klage. Ich schlief nur spät gegen Morgen ein. Ich
erwachte, als mir der Tag ins Gesicht schien. Vor mir war ein
steiler Felsen; ich kletterte hinauf in der Hoffnung von dort den
Ausgang aus der Wildnis zu entdecken. Als ich aber oben stand,
war alles, so weit mein Auge reichte, mit einem nebligen Dufte
15 überzogen; und keinen Baum, keine Wiese konnte mein Auge
erspähn. Zugleich fühlte ich einen peinigenden Hunger, ich war
müde und erschöpft. Ich wünschte kaum noch zu leben, als mir
plötzlich war, als hörte ich ein leises Husten. Ich ging näher und
ward eine alte Frau gewahr. Sie war schwarz gekleidet, und eine
20 schwarze Kappe bedeckte ihren Kopf; in der Hand hielt sie einen
Krückenstock. Ich näherte mich ihr und bat um ihre Hilfe. Sie gab
mir Brot und sagte, ich möchte ihr folgen. Wir stiegen einen
Hügel hinan, von oben sah man in ein kleines Tal. Ein munteres
Bellen kam uns entgegen, und bald sprang ein kleiner Hund die
25 Alte an und wedelte. Dann kam er zu mir, besah mich von allen
Seiten und kehrte dann zu der Alten zurück. Als wir vom Hügel
hinuntergingen, hörte ich einen wunderbaren Gesang, der aus der
Hütte zu kommen schien, wie von einem Vogel; es sang also:

164

FROM DER BLONDE ECKBERT

BY LUDWIG TIECK

When day broke I got up and, almost without knowing it, opened
the door of our hut. I stood in an open field, next I was in a forest,
and soon had to clamber over hills, and then I guessed that I must
be in the nearby mountains. My terror drove me on. The cliffs
became more and more terrible and finally even the path stopped. 5
Now night descended and I found a mossy spot to rest. I heard
the strangest sounds: at one time I took them for wild animals,
at another for the wind wailing through the rocks. I did not fall
asleep until the small hours of the morning.^a I woke up when daylight shone into my face. Before me was a steep cliff. I climbed up 10
in the hope of discovering from there the way out of the wilderness. But when I got up there, everything, so far as my eye
reached, was covered by a misty vapor, and I could not catch a
glimpse of a tree or a meadow. At the same time I felt tormenting
hunger; I was tired and exhausted. I had scarcely any wish to go 15
on living when it suddenly seemed to me that I heard a faint
cough. I approached and caught sight of an old woman. She was
dressed in black and a black hood covered her head. She held a
crooked walking stick in her hand. I went up to her and asked for
her help. She gave me bread and said that I should follow her. We 20
climbed a hill, from the top we looked into a little valley. Cheerful
barking came toward us and soon a little dog was jumping up on
the old woman and wagging his tail. Then he came to me, in-
spected me from all sides, and then returned to the old woman.
As we were walking down from the hill I heard a wonderful song 25
that seemed to be coming from a hut; it was like a bird's song. It
went like this:

Waldeinsamkeit,
30 Die mich erfreut,
So morgen wie heut'
In ew'ger Zeit;
O wie mich freut
Waldeinsamkeit.

35 Ohne daß ich auf den Befehl der Alten wartete, trat ich mit[4] in die
Hütte. Die Dämmerung war schon eingebrochen; fremdartige
Gefäße standen auf einem Tische, in einem kleinen glänzenden
Käfig hing ein Vogel, und er war es,[5] der die Worte sang. Die Alte
keuchte und hustete, bald streichelte sie den Hund, bald sprach
40 sie mit dem Vogel. Indem ich sie so betrachtete, überlief mich
mancher Schauer, denn ihr Gesicht war in einer ewigen Bewegung,
indem sie dazu mit dem Kopfe schüttelte, so daß ich gar nicht
wissen konnte, wie ihr eigentliches Aussehen war. Nach dem
Abendessen wies sie mir in einer engen Kammer ein Bett an. In
45 der Nacht hörte ich die Alte husten und mit dem Hunde sprechen
und den Vogel dazwischen, der im Traume immer einzelne Worte
von seinem Liede sang. Am Morgen weckte mich die Alte und
wies mich bald nachher zur Arbeit an. Ich mußte spinnen, und
dabei hatte ich noch für den Hund und den Vogel zu sorgen. Ich
50 lernte mich schnell in die Wirtschaft finden,[6] und alle Gegenstände umher wurden mir bekannt. Ich dachte gar nicht mehr
daran, daß die Alte etwas Seltsames an sich habe, und daß an dem
Vogel etwas Außerordentliches sei. Seine Schönheit fiel mir zwar
immer auf, denn seine Federn glänzten mit allen möglichen Far-
55 ben, das schönste Hellblau und das brennendste Rot wechselten
an seinem Halse und Leibe, und wenn er sang, blähte er sich stolz
auf, so daß sich seine Federn noch prächtiger zeigten.

NOTES TO THE GERMAN TEXT

1. **immer furchtbarer** *always more terrible,* i.e. *more and more
   terrible.*
2. **bald . . . bald** *at one time . . . at another time, now . . . then.*
3. **ich hielt es für wilde Tiere** *I held it for wild animals,* i.e.
   I took it to be wild animals.
4. **trat ich mit in die Hütte** *I stepped into the hut along with
   [her].* This is a common use of **mit,** to signify that the subject

Forest solitude
Which will make me happy
Tomorrow as well as today   30
In everlasting time;
Oh how it gladdens me,
Forest solitude.

Without waiting for the old woman's instructions I stepped into
the hut along [with her]. Dusk had already fallen; peculiar vessels 35
were standing on a table; in a small gleaming cage there hung a
bird and it was he that sang the words. The old woman panted
and coughed; first she stroked the dog and then she talked with
the bird. While I was looking at her thus, many a shudder ran
over me, for her face was constantly moving, while she shook her 40
head at the same time so that I had no way of knowing how she
really looked.ᵇ After supper she showed me a bed in a cramped
room. In the night I heard the old woman coughing and talking
with the dog and at intervals [I heard] the bird, which in its
dreams kept singing disconnected words of its song. In the morn- 45
ing the old woman waked me and soon afterwards instructed me
in my work. I had to spin and besides I had to care for the dog
and the bird. I soon became accustomed to the household and all
the objects around became familiar to me. I no longer thought at
all about the fact that the old woman had something odd about 50
her or that there was something extraordinary about the bird. To
be sure, his beauty always amazed me, for his feathers gleamed
in all possible colors; the loveliest light blue and the most flaming
red interplayed on his throat and body, and when he sang, he
puffed up proudly so that his feathers showed off still more 55
magnificently.

NOTES TO THE ENGLISH TEXT

a.   **Ich schlief nur spät gegen Morgen ein.**   *I went to sleep only
late towards morning.*

b.   **wie ihr eigentliches Aussehen war**   *how her actual appearance was.*

joins in the action, e.g. **Ich kletterte mit hinauf** *I was one of those who climbed up.*

5. **er war es** *he was it.*

6. **Ich lernte mich schnell in die Wirtschaft finden** *I quickly learned to find myself into the household,* i.e. *I quickly grew accustomed to the household.* **Sich in etwas finden** is a rather frequent idiomatic expression, meaning something like *catch on to, adjust oneself to.*

GRAMMATICAL COMMENT—ADJECTIVES

You have probably often wondered how anybody ever gets a feeling of instantaneous certainty about adjective endings. The answer to this as to all similar questions is "Practice," and it does take a good deal of practice to achieve perfection. But you can take comfort in the reflection that you will be able to read German with fair understanding before you attain mastery of the adjective declension. For this reason consideration of the adjective declension has been put off until now. However, from time to time you will come across passages the meaning of which you will not be able to understand unless you know the adjective endings. And, to be sure, you will not be able to speak or write German well until you can handle them easily. It will pay you well to master this aspect of German grammar.

I. The Case Endings

A. Predicate adjectives have no case endings: **das Mädchen war müde und erschöpft** *the girl was tired and exhausted.* Attributive adjectives, however, that is, adjectives before nouns, do have case endings: **das erschöpfte Mädchen** *the exhausted girl.*

B. It may be said that there are three systems of case endings for adjectives, the so-called strong, weak, and mixed. The strong system is:

	MASC.	FEM.	NEUTER	PLURAL
N	-er	-e	-es	-e
G	-en	-er	-en	-er
D	-em	-er	-em	-en
A	-en	-e	-es	-e

The weak system is:

	MASC.	FEM.	NEUTER	PLURAL
N	-e	-e	-e	-en
G	-en	-en	-en	-en
D	-en	-en	-en	-en
A	-en	-e	-e	-en

The mixed system is:

N	-er	-e	-es	-en
G	-en	-en	-en	-en
D	-en	-en	-en	-en
A	-en	-e	-es	-en

It is evident at a glance that the strong endings are, except for the genitive case of the masculine and neuter, identical with the endings of the **dieser**-words,* and there are only two weak endings, namely -e and -en, the first of which, -e, occurs only in five places: the nominative of all three genders and the accusative of the feminine and neuter. The mixed system, a combination of the other two, follows the strong declension in having -er in the masculine nominative and -es in the neuter nominative and accusative. In other respects it follows the weak system.

C. Whether an adjective takes a strong or weak ending depends upon what precedes it. Thus, the adjective takes a weak ending when it is preceded by a **der**- or **dieser**-word*: **das schönste Hellblau, dem benachbarten Gebirge, die seltsamsten Töne.** It takes strong endings when it is not preceded by an inflected modifier, that is, either when there is no preceding modifier at all, or when the preceding modifier has no case ending: **wilde Tiere, gutes Brot, dreißig fremdartige Gefäße.** The mixed declension shows weak endings after the **kein**-words* which have case endings: **einen peinigenden Hunger, eine schwarze Kappe, ihre munteren Tiere,** and the strong endings after the other forms of the **kein**-words,* namely the masculine nominative and the neuter nominative and accusative: **ein steiler Felsen, ein leises Husten.**

D. Certain irregularities in the declension of adjectives may well be noted here. (1) The words **all, manch, solch,** and **welch** need take no endings. In such an instance the following adjective has the strong endings: **welch furchtbare Felsen, solch brennendes Rot.** (2) After the plural indefinites **einige, andere, mehrere, viele, wenige,** the adjective is very frequently inflected as follows:

N	**einige seltsame Töne**	D	**einigen seltsamen Tönen**
G	**einiger seltsamen Töne**	A	**einige seltsame Töne**

* See the Ninth Unit, Grammatical Comment, II.

(3) The adjective **hoch** changes the **ch** to **h** whenever an ending is added: **die hohen Felsen.**

II. Uses of the Adjective

A.   The uninflected adjective stands in the predicate: **Ich war erschöpft.** *I was exhausted.* Almost any adjective in its uninflected form may be used as an adverb: **Die Alte hustete laut.** *The old woman coughed loudly.*

B.   The inflected adjective stands before a noun: **eine schwarze Kappe** *a black cap.* It is often used as a noun; it is then capitalized but it retains its adjective declension: **der Alte,** *the old man;* **die Alte** *the old woman;* **die Alten** *the old people, the Ancients;* **das Alte** *the old, that which is old.* The adjective with strong neuter endings stands in apposition to the words **etwas** and **nichts: etwas Seltsames** *something strange;* **nichts Außerordentliches** *nothing unusual.*

C.   The numerals are, of course, adjectives. The cardinal numerals with the exception of **ein, eine, ein** are, with rare exceptions, uninflected: **zwei Bäume** *two trees;* **drei Vögel** *three birds.* The ordinal numerals, however, are declined like any other adjective: **der zweite Baum** *the second tree;* **am fünften Tage** *on the fifth day.*

III. The Comparison of Adjectives

A.   Grammarians say that there are three degrees of any adjective: positive, comparative, and superlative. In English there are two regular ways of comparing an adjective: *cold, colder, coldest* and *beautiful, more beautiful, most beautiful.* All German adjectives follow the *cold, colder, coldest* pattern, some with umlaut in the comparative and superlative and some not: **klein, kleiner, kleinst-; bekannt, bekannter, bekanntest-; alt, älter, ältest-; stolz, stolzer, stolzest-.** Adjectives of more than one syllable do not umlaut. Some of the most common adjectives and adverbs have an irregular comparison: **gut** (*good*), **besser, best-; hoch** (*high*), **höher, höchst-; nah** (*near*), **näher, nächst-; viel** (*much*), **mehr, meist-; gern** (*gladly*), **lieber, liebst-; bald** (*soon*), **eher, ehest-.**

B. The regular case endings are added to the comparative and superlative degrees of an adjective when it stands before its noun: **ein seltsamerer Ton** *a more peculiar sound;* **das schönste Hellblau** *the most beautiful light blue.* The comparative degree of an adjective in German as in English is often used to indicate a rather high degree without expressing an actual comparison: **eine ältere Frau** is *an older woman,* but by no means *an old woman.* In the predicate, however, the comparative degree occurs without any ending, just as does the positive: **Alle Gegenstände umher wurden mir bekannter.** *All objects round about became more familiar to me.* The superlative degree, on the other hand, *never* appears without declensional endings. When used in the predicate, it may function as an attributive modifying a suppressed noun: **Dieser Vogel ist der prächtigste [Vogel].** *This bird is the most splendid.* Or else it may appear in a phrase with am: **Wenn der Vogel sich stolz aufblähte, war er am schönsten.** *The bird was most beautiful when he puffed up proudly.*

C. The comparative degree of an adjective is used without declensional endings as an adverb: **Der Vogel blähte sich stolz auf und sang noch schöner als zuvor.** *The bird puffed up proudly and sang still more beautifully than before.* The superlative degree of the adverb is expressed by means of the phrase with am, e.g. **am schönsten,** or aufs, e.g. **aufs schönste.** The phrase with am shows a real comparison: **Dieser Vogel singt am schönsten.** *This bird sings the most beautifully [of all].* The phrase with aufs indicates a high degree without comparison: **Der Vogel sang wirklich aufs schönste.** *The bird really sang very beautifully* or *most beautifully.*

EXERCISES

I. These exercises are at page 207.

II. These exercises are at page 208.

III. Write out the full declensions of the following (three additional forms each). Strong declension: schwarzer Kaffee, süße Milch, kaltes Wasser, frische Eier. *Weak declension:* der munterere Hund, jede ältere Frau, das brennendste Rot, die seltsamsten Töne. *Mixed declension:* ein glänzenderer Käfig, deine schwarze Kappe, ein kleines Tal, unsere kleinen Hunde.

IV. Arrange the following sentences according to their proper sequence in the story.

1. Als der Tag graute, weckte mich die Alte und sagte mir, ich müßte für den munteren Hund und den seltsamen Vogel sorgen.

2. In dem glänzenden Käfig sah ich einen Vogel mit fasanenartigen Federn am Halse.

3. Die Alte faßte mich ins Auge und sagte dann, ich möchte ihr folgen.

4. Als ich oben auf dem steilen Felsen stand, war rings um nichts zu sehen.

5. Da ich lange nichts gegessen hatte, stellte sich ein peinigender Hunger ein.

6. Lauter fremdartige Gefäße standen auf allen Tischen in der kleinen Hütte.

7. Ich war eine längere Zeit so fortgegangen, als die Nacht hereinbrach.

8. Mit dem Einschlafen aber hatte es einen Anstand, denn der Wind klagte durch die Felsen aufs furchtbarste.

9. Bald wünschte ich kaum noch zu leben, bald fürchtete ich mich vor dem Tode.

10. Ich hielt die schwarz gekleidete Alte mit dem Krückenstock für nicht ganz richtig im Kopf.

V. Select the untrue statement in each group.

GROUP 1

a. Das Seltsamste an dem Vogel war eigentlich sein außerordentlicher Gesang.

b. Am Morgen weckte mich der Vogel mit seinem munteren Gesang.

c. Als wir vom Hügel hinunter und auf die kleine Hütte zu gingen, war mir, als käme ein wunderbarer Gesang aus der Hütte.

d. Mit der Zeit wurden mir der Hund, der Vogel und all die seltsamen Gegenstände bekannter.

GROUP 2

a. Ich hätte nur zu gerne gewußt, wo die seltsame Alte den wunderbaren Vogel her hatte.

b. Indem ich die ihr Gesicht bewegende und mit dem Kopfe schüttelnde Alte betrachtete, überlief mich manch ein Schauer, und ich wäre am liebsten fortgelaufen.

c. Als wir vor der kleinen Hütte anlangten, sagte mir die Alte, ich möchte mit hineintreten.

d. Der Vogel war es, der das Waldeinsamkeitslied gesungen hatte.

GROUP 3

a. Ich mußte für die Tiere der Alten mein Möglichstes tun.

b. Ich mußte nun auf freiem Felde, wo es immer dunkler wurde, eine Moosstelle aussuchen, um dort zu ruhen.

c. Der Vogel, der in dem kleinen Käfig hing, war kein gewöhnlicher Vogel, wie sie in dem Walde herumfliegen.

d. Der Hund war aber einer der muntersten und freundlichsten, die ich je gesehen hatte.

VI. Correct the misinformation (in German).

1. Die Alte und ich stiegen einen Hügel hinan, von oben konnten wir keinen Baum, keine Wiese erspähen.

2. Als die Nacht hereinbrach, öffnete ich, fast ohne daß ich es wußte, die Tür unserer Hütte.

3. Ich mußte auf einer Moosstelle neben der Hütte der Alten schlafen.

4. Den Hund besah die Alte von allen Seiten.

5. Als ich erwachte, war mir plötzlich, als hörte ich einen seltsamen Gesang.

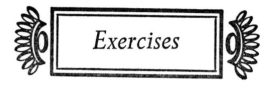

Exercises

At the discretion of the instructor, the exercises on pages 179-210 may be assigned to be completed outside of class, detached, and handed in for correction.

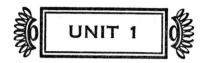

UNIT 1

STUDENT'S NAME

I. *Underline the English expression which best translates the word or words in bold face type in each sentence:*

1. Es **wird** meine Sorge sein, diesen edlen Schatten aufzuheben.

   a. will   b. becomes
   c. is being   d. was

2. Er **wird** wohl die Goldstücke schon **eingesteckt haben.** (See Note 7 to the German Text.)

   a. will have to pocket   b. will have been pocketed
   c. has probably pocketed   d. is going to pocket

3. Eine kurze Zeit **genoß** er das Glück sich in ihrer Nähe zu befinden.

   a. enjoys   b. will enjoy
   c. is delighted   d. enjoyed

4. Der Herr im grauen Rock **betrachtet** schöne Schatten **gern.**

   a. liked to look at   b. has observed with pleasure
   c. likes   d. enjoys looking at

5. Der Mann **wird** verlegen.

   a. will be   b. becomes
   c. is   d. has been

179

6. Nichts **entschuldigt** Ihre Zudringlichkeit.

   a. excused   b. excuse!
   c. excuse   d. excuses

7. Der Mann im grauen Rock **war** schnell auf mich zu gekommen.

   a. had come   b. was coming
   c. was to come   d. were coming

8. Ihr **unterbrecht** mich so oft während ich rede.

   a. interrupt   b. interrupts
   c. interrupted   d. breaks off

9. **Verziehen** habe ich ihm seine Zumutung nicht.

   a. pardoned   b. pardon
   c. to pardon   d. distort

10. Er **erbat** sich die Erlaubnis, den Schatten zu sich zu stecken.

    a. requests   b. forbids
    c. begs   d. asked

I. *Underline the English word or words which best translate the word or words in bold face type in each sentence.*

1. Heute in acht Tagen **sind** wir Mann und Weib.

   a. are   b. find
   c. may be   d. will be

2. Das schwarze Halstuch mit rotem Rand **hat** sie am Tage vor dem Hochzeittag **weggelegt**.

   a. put away   b. had laid away
   c. has to lay aside   d. had to lay away

3. Als die Bergleute den Jüngling aus der Grube zu Tag ausförderten, **trauerte** die alte Frau schon seit fünfzig Jahren um ihren Verlobten.

   a. mourns   b. has mourned
   c. had been mourning   d. will have mourned

4. Kurz nach dem **Einschlafen** ist der Jüngling gestorben.

   a. sleep   b. go to sleep
   c. sleeping on   d. going to sleep

5. Den auf das Fenster zu **kommenden** jungen Mann hat sie nicht erkannt.

   a. to come   b. come
   c. approached   d. approaching

181

6. Grau und zusammengeschrumpft kam sie an einer Krücke **gegangen** hinter den Bergleuten her.

    a. gone   b. had gone
    c. walked   d. walking

7. „Bergleute **geholt**," sagte dann der Offizier zu den Umstehenden.

    a. go and get   b. fetched
    c. held   d. hold

8. Er **klopft** jeden Morgen an ihrem Fenster.

    a. knock   b. knocks
    c. knocked   d. used to knock

9. „Lassen Sie ein Grab für ihn auf dem Kirchhof **rüsten**," sagte sie endlich.

    a. prepare   b. to prepare
    c. prepared   d. preparing

10. Die Franzosen und Spanier kehrten nach Hause zurück ohne Gibraltar **erobert zu haben.**

    a. having conquered   b. conquering to have
    c. have to conquer   d. having to conquer

UNIT 3

I. *Underline the English word or words which best translate the words in bold face type in the German sentence.*

1. Dieser strenger Selbstzucht und gesammelter Tatkraft bare Mensch **will** Künstler sein!

    a. will   b. wants to
    c. is going to   d. pretends to

2. Allmählich **ward** ihm auch das geduldige Sitzen lieb.

    a. becomes   b. was
    c. grew   d. waits

3. Der Arbeiter **wollte** eben Feierabend machen, da erschien aber sein Weib in dem Stüblein und sagte ihm, „Vollende das Werk, das du begonnen hast!"

    a. was about to   b. would
    c. wants to   d. will

4. Sind die Ferien **herum,** so haben wir nichts getan.

    a. round about   b. over
    c. hither   d. here about

5. Der reiche Mann **ließ** beim Künstler eine große Arbeit ausführen.

    a. had   b. lets
    c. left   d. permits

6. Im Augenblicke des ersten Wurfes sitzen wir gleichsam hoch zu Roß.

a. calmly   b. evenly
c. immediately   d. so to speak

7. Eine gestohlene Stunde gilt mehr als zwölf geschenkte.

a. yielded   b. gilds
c. paid   d. is worth

8. Hinter dem seine Reihen hoch zu Roß musternden und ordnenden Feldherrn her kam der Mann im grauen Rock.

a. along   b. here
c. up to   d. away

9. Es kommen hier Wanderer von hüben und drüben vorbei.

a. comes past   b. goes by
c. came past   d. pass by

10. Kein großes Werk wird ohne äußeren Zwang vollendet.

a. finishes   b. completes
c. completed   d. finish

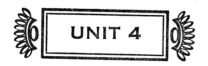

UNIT 4

STUDENT'S NAME

I. Underline the English word or words which best translate the words in bold face type in the German sentence.

1. Was **sollte** dann Mozart von dem Präsent des Barons sagen?

    a. should
    c. shall

    b. is supposed
    d. was supposed to

2. Mozart überhörte seine Sachen gleichsam wie ein schönes Bild im Geiste und nicht nacheinander, wie sie hernach kommen **mußten**.

    a. had to
    c. must

    b. would have to
    d. must have

3. Der Baron **wollte** auch etwas vom Contrapunkt verstehen.

    a. would
    c. wants to

    b. pretended to
    d. liked to

4. Das **darf** ein guter Musiker ja nicht tun.

    a. can
    c. will

    b. was allowed to
    d. must

5. Ich **möchte** nur immer fort arbeiten, **dürfte** ich nur immer solche Musik machen, wo ich mir selbst was daraus mache.

MÖCHTE

    a. would like to
    c. wanted to

    b. liked to
    d. like to

185

DÜRFTE

a. am allowed to   b. were allowed to
c. can   d. must

6. Der Baron **sollte** viel Geld haben; aber er war wirklich sehr arm.

    a. should   b. was said to
    c. ought to   d. must

7. Ich **könnte** mich nicht bei der Arbeit stören lassen.

    a. could   b. was able to
    c. might   d. were able to

8. Es **muß** ihm der Herrgott diese Gabe **geschenkt haben.**

    a. must have given   b. would have to give
    c. had to give   d. must give

9. Das **kann** nur Mozart **gespielt haben.**

    a. can have to play   b. can have played
    c. could have played   d. will have been able to play

10. Das **hat** nur Mozart **spielen können.**

    a. can have played   b. had been able to play
    c. was able to play   d. has to be able to play

11. Mozart **hätte** Hofmeister die drei Klavier-Quatuor nicht **anbieten sollen.**

    a. had been supposed to offer   b. should have offered
    c. was said to have offered   d. shall have offered

12. Manches **soll geschehen sein,** was nicht geschehen **sollte.**

    SOLL GESCHEHEN SEIN
    a. shall be happening   b. is said to have happened
    c. shall happen to be   d. has been supposed to happen

SOLLTE

    a. shall   b. was supposed to
    c. should have   d. must

13. Manches soll geschehen sein, was nicht **hätte geschehen sollen.**

    a. had been supposed to happen   b. ought to have happened
    c. is said to have happened   d. should have to happen

14. So ist es, und nicht wie Ihnen dumme oder böse Lumpen **mögen gesagt haben.**

    a. may have told   b. have enjoyed saying
    c. would have liked to say   d. like to have said

UNIT 5

I. Underline the best translation.

1. Hätte ein Affe in den Spiegel hineingeguckt, so **hätte** der Apostel nicht **heraussehen können.**

   a. can have looked out
   c. could have looked out

   b. has been able to look out
   d. will have been able to look out

2. Man **räume** den Alten keine Vorzüge **ein,** die sie nicht verdienen.

   a. concedes
   c. should concede

   b. would concede
   d. conceded

3. Hätte Homer gewußt, daß er gut schrieb, dann **hätte** er nicht mehr ganz so gut **geschrieben.**

   a. would have written
   c. has written

   b. had written
   d. would write

4. **Wir wollen** an dem arbeiten, was wir gerade vor uns haben.

   a. we let
   c. we wished

   b. we would want
   d. let us

5. Er **wäre** nicht krank **geworden,** wenn er sich nicht eingebildet hätte, krank zu sein.

   a. would have been
   c. had been

   b. would have become
   d. were becoming

189

6. Mancher **würde** jetzt glücklich **leben,** wenn er sich um anderer Leute Sachen so wenig bekümmert hätte als um seine eigenen.

a. could live b. would be living
c. were living d. would have lived

7. Auf dieser Insel **halte** der Reisende des Nachts beständig Wache.

a. holds b. let . . . keep
c. held d. would keep

8. Die Leute auf dieser Insel halten beständig Wache, als **wäre** die ganze Insel von Räubern bewohnt.

a. is b. was
c. had been d. were

9. Wenn manches Insekt mehr durch das Vergangene als das Künftige **geleitet würde, sähe** die Welt vielleicht anders **aus.**

GELEITET WÜRDE

a. was guided b. were guided
c. would guide d. would have been guided

SÄHE AUS

a. would look b. seen out
c. would have looked out d. seemed

10. Hätten die Tiere ebensoviel Erinnerung des Vergangenen als Vorgefühl vom Künftigen, so **wäre** uns manches Insekt überlegen.

a. would be b. were
c. was d. will be

11. **Könnten wir** nur die Welt so erkennen, wie sie wirklich ist!

a. let us be able b. we could
c. if we could d. if we had been able

12. Solche Menschen dürfte es nicht geben.

   a. Such people ought not to give it.
   b. Such people should not have the right to exist.
   c. It was not possible to give such people [anything].
   d. Such people would not be allowed to give it.

13. So was hätte ihm nur ein Engel erzählen können.

   a. Only an angel could have told him such a thing.
   b. Only an angel had been able to tell him such a thing.
   c. Only an angel can have told him such a thing.
   d. Only an angel will have been able to tell him such a thing.

14. Er hätte das nicht tun sollen.

   a. He ought not to have done that.
   b. He was not supposed to have done that.
   c. He would not be supposed to do that.
   d. It is supposed he would not do that.

15. Er müßte ins Tollhaus gebracht werden.

   a. He must have been taken to the madhouse.
   b. He would have had to be taken to the madhouse.
   c. He would have to be taken to the madhouse.
   d. He must be taken to the madhouse.

16. Er hätte ins Tollhaus gebracht werden müssen.

   a. He has had to be taken to the madhouse.
   b. He must have been taken to the madhouse.
   c. He would have had to be taken to the madhouse.
   d. He must be taken to the madhouse.

17. Das dürfte wahr sein.

   a. That was allowed to be true.
   b. That is certainly true.
   c. It is possible that it was true.
   d. That might be true.

18. Es ließe sich davon plaudern.

    a. It left [much] to be talked about.
    b. One could talk about that.
    c. We could have talked about that.
    d. It allowed itself to chat about it.

19. Es **sei** unsere Hypothese, daß sich etwas mit der Schnelligkeit des Lichts von dem einen Ende eines Sandkörnchens bis zum andern bewegt.

    a. would be   b. were
    c. was   d. let be

20. Es **wäre** unsere Hypothese, daß sich etwas mit der Schnelligkeit des Lichts von dem einen Ende eines Sandkörnchens bis zum anderen bewegt.

    a. would be   b. were
    c. was   d. let be

UNIT 6

I. In each of the following groups of sentences there is a direct statement in German followed by the skeleton, so to speak, of that statement as reported in indirect discourse. That is, the verbs are omitted. Underline the verb forms which should stand in the blank spaces. Always leave the report open to doubt.

1. Der König deutete auf eine aus dem flachen Boden aufsteigende Festung. *Indirect:* Der Fischer berichtete, daß der König auf eine aus dem flachen Boden aufsteigende Festung _____.

   a. deute
   c. werde gedeutet haben

   b. gedeutet habe
   d. deuten würde

2. Meine Arme werden die sehnende Braut sehr bald umfangen. *Indirect:* Der König sagte fröhlich, daß seine Arme die sehnende Braut sehr bald _____.

   a. umfingen
   c. umfangen werden

   b. umfangen
   d. umfangen würden

3. Der König sprang als erster aus dem anlandenden Schiffe. *Indirect:* Man hat mir gesagt, der König _____ als erster aus dem anlandenden Schiff _____.

   a. werde springen
   c. würde springen

   b. wäre gesprungen
   d. werde gesprungen sein

4. Man hört die Glocken nicht an dieser Stelle. *Indirect:* Der

193

Hirt hatte dem König gesagt, daß man die Glocken an dieser Stelle nicht _____.

a. gehört habe   b. höre
c. gehört hätte   d. gehört hat

5. Nachdem der König auf einem kurzen Streifritt Umschau gehalten hatte, kehrte er an den Strand zurück. *Indirect:* Es geht das Gerede, daß der König, nachdem er auf einem kurzen Streifritt Umschau __ [a,b,c,d] __, an den Strand __ [e,f,g,h] __.

a. hielt   b. hält
c. gehalten hätte   d. gehalten haben würde
e. zurückkehrte   f. zurückgekehrt wäre
g. zurückkehrt   h. zurückgekehrt sein würde

6. „Komm etwas näher heran!" sagte der König dem Hirten. *Indirect:* Der König sagte dem Hirten, daß er etwas näher _____.

a. herankommen werde   b. herankommen würde
c. herankommen sollte   d. herangekommen wäre

II. *Underline the English word or phrase which best translates the word or words in bold face type.*

1. Der Hirt sagte, **man höre die Glocken nicht** an dieser Stelle.

a. one did not hear the bells
b. one should not hear the bells
c. one had not heard the bells
d. one may not hear the bells

2. Der König **wollte** eben einen kurzen Streifritt den Strom entlang machen, als er das Läuten der Glocken hörte.

a. wants to   b. would want to
c. was about to   d. is about to

3. Vor Hunderten von Jahren, berichtete der Hirt, **habe** an dieser Stelle eine große, reiche Stadt **gestanden.**

a. stood   b. will have stood
c. had stood   d. has to stand

4. Der Hirt sagte, daß er es **nicht wisse** und daß er auch **nicht wünsche,** daß der König das Läuten gehört habe.

NICHT WISSE

a. does not know   b. had not known

c. will not know   d. did not know

NICHT WÜNSCHE

a. did not wish   b. does not wish

c. will not wish   d. has not wished

I. Underline the best translation.

1. Den Leuten, die auf das Entstehen warten, **wird** von allen Seiten **zugerufen:** „Seid doch keine Träumer!“

   a. will call
   b. are called
   c. will be admonished
   d. the admonition is addressed

2. Die Tiere und Pflanzen **wurden** nach und nach größer und vielfältiger.

   a. were
   b. would be
   c. became
   d. would become

3. **Gesorgt wird** dafür, daß nur ganz bestimmte auserlesene Reize bis zum Nervensystem eindringen.

   a. it will be difficult
   b. provision is made
   c. Gesorgt becomes
   d. if provision is made

4. Die kleine Berlinerin glaubte, die Bäume **müssten auch** irgendwo **gemacht worden sein.**

   a. must have been made
   b. would have to be made
   c. must be made
   d. will have to be made

5. Eine Zeitlang **wurde versucht,** auch in die Welt des Naturgeschehens den Fortschritt hineinzubringen.

   a. was attempted
   b. would try
   c. had been tried
   d. the attempt was made

197

6. Uexkülls Theorie nach **würde** es im Schnee Grönlands keine Tiere mit Springfüßen **geben können.**

    a. could be given   b. would be given
    c. could be   d. was able to give

7. Es sieht so aus, als **wäre** die Flosse durch das Wasser **geformt worden.**

    a. were being formed   b. was being formed
    c. is formed   d. had been formed

8. Nach und nach **werden** die biologischen Strukturen kompliziert.

    a. become   b. became
    c. will be   d. are

9. Das Zusammenklingen aller Einzelheiten zu einem großen Ganzen **muß erforscht werden.**

    a. must be investigated   b. must have been investigated
    c. will have to investigate   d. must be investigating

10. In der Umweltstheorie, die von Uexküll **aufgestellt worden ist,** gibt es keine Stufenleiter der Tiere.

    a. is to be proposed   b. has been proposed
    c. will have been set up   d. had been set up

UNIT 8

I. Underline the form (or forms) which correctly translates the English word and indicate its position in the complete sentence.

1. Die Nabelschweine und Tapirs, von dem Tiger *[pursued, raged through]* den Wald.

PURSUED

    a. verfolgte   b. verfolgt

    c. verfolgen   d. verfolgten

RAGED THROUGH

    a. durchtobt   b. durchtobten

    c. durchtoben   d. durchtobte

2. Der Kampf *[continued]* lange.

    a. setzte sich fort   b. fortgesetzt

    c. sich fortsetzten   d. setzte fort

3. Unser Hund bellte *[uninterruptedly]*.

    a. unterbrochen   b. unterbrach sich

    c. nicht unterbrechen   d. ununterbrochen

4. Die Lichtmasse, die auf den Strom *[poured forth]*, strahlte funkelnd zurück.

    a. ergossen   b. sich . . . ergoß

    c. ergießen   d. sich . . . ergießt

199

*II. Complete each sentence by inserting the correct form or forms
in the appropriate places. Underline the form and indicate where
it belongs. Do not change the relative order of the words in each
group.*

1. Die Eidechsen scheinen mit Wonne die heiße Luft.

   a. einatmen   b. atmen ein
   c. eingeatmet   d. einzuatmen

2. Die größeren Tiere in das Dickicht der Wälder.

   a. verbargen sich   b. sich verborgen
   c. sich verbergen   d. verbergen

3. Nach der Landessitte die Indianer jedes Bivouac mit Feuer
   der Angriffe des Jaguars wegen.

   a. geben um   b. sich umgeben
   c. umgeben   d. geben sich um

4. Der Anblick des Feuers die Krokodile.

   a. anlockte   b. lockte an
   c. anlockt   d. anlockend

5. Der Franziskanermönch, der uns begleitete, pflegte zu
   sagen: „Der Himmel den wilden Bestien des Waldes eine
   ruhige Nacht!"

   a. gewährt   b. gewähre
   c. gewähren   d. gewährte

6. In dem undurchdringlichen Wald viele Papageien und andere fasanenartige Vögel.

   a. es gibt   b. gaben es
   c. gab es   d. geben es

7. Der Hund vor dem Tiger und suchte heulend unter den
   Hangematten Schutz.

   a. sich gefürchtet   b. sich fürchtete
   c. sich fürchtend   d. fürchtete sich

8. Die Indianer _____ dem Lärm der Tiere.

    a. sich freute   b. sich freuen
    c. freute es   d. gefreut
    e. zuzuhören   f. zu hören
    g. zuhörend   h. zuhören

9. Die von dem Strom _____ Lichtmasse machte die nebelartige Röte noch bemerkbarer.

    a. zurückstrahlende   b. zurückstrahlt
    c. strahlt zurück   d. zurückstrahlte

10. Die Szene, die ich hier schildere, _____ jede Nacht.

    a. wieder holte   b. holte wieder
    c. wurde wiedergeholt   d. wurde wiederholt

UNIT 9

I. *Each sentence in the following exercise has one or more bracketed spaces. Following each sentence are groups of words corresponding to the bracketed spaces. Underline the appropriate form in each group. Translate the sentence.*

1. [a,b,c,d] vergleicht [e,f,g,h] andere gesagt haben und sucht so hinter [i,j,k,l] der Sachen zu kommen.

   a. Der Bücherphilosophen   b. Die Bücherphilosophen
   c. Den Bücherphilosophen   d. Der Bücherphilosoph

   e. wen   f. was
   g. wessen   h. wer

   i. die Wahrheit   j. der Wahrheit
   k. den Wahrheiten   l. die Wahrheiten

2. [a,b,c,d] die Sache selbst [e,f,g,h] fassen wollte, könnte durch ein wenig Selbstdenken bald zu [i,j,k,l] gelangen.

   a. Was   b. Wen
   c. Wer   d. Wem

   e. im Auge   f. in die Augen
   g. in den Augen   h. ins Auge

   i. die Ziele   j. das Ziel
   k. dem Ziele   l. der Ziele

3. Bei [a,b,c,d] Bücherphilosophen ist alles aus [e,f,g,h], lauter [i,j,k,l].

   a. der   b. die
   c. des   d. dem

203

204

e. zwei Händen	f. zweite Hand
g. zwei Hände	h. zweiter Hand
i. gangbare Modeworte	j. gangbaren Modeworten
k. gangbarer Modeworte	l. gangbarem Modewort

4. Der Selbstdenker [a,b,c,d] Ursprünglichkeit schon an [e,f,g,h] zu erkennen ist, sagt nur aus, [i,j,k,l] er objektiv aufgefaßt hat.

a. dessen	b. des
c. welches	d. deren
e. der Vortrag	f. den Vortrag
g. dem Vortrag	h. den Vorträgen
i. wessen	j. wem
k. was	l. wen

5. Man könnte sich über [a,b,c,d] des Ernstes wundern, [e,f,g,h] aus der Ursprünglichkeit [i,j,k,l] entspringt.

a. dem Gepräge	b. die Gepräge
c. der Gepräge	d. das Gepräge
e. die	f. welches
g. welche	h. denen
i. der Selbstdenker	j. die Selbstdenker
k. dem Selbstdenker	l. den Selbstdenkern

6. Man gewöhne sich nicht an [a,b,c,d] Gehen [e,f,g,h], damit man [i,j,k] nicht verlerne.

a. die	b. den
c. das	d. dem
e. ein fremder Gedankengang	f. einen fremden Gedankengang
g. einem fremden Gedankengang	h. eines fremden Gedankenganges
i. das Selbstdenken	j. des Selbstdenkens
k. dem Selbstdenken	

7. Selbst der größte Kopf bedarf [a,b,c,d] um zu [e,f,g,h] ursprünglichen Auffassung [i,j,k,l] zu gelangen.

a. die innere Stimmung	b. der inneren Stimmung
c. die inneren Stimmungen	d. den inneren Stimmungen
e. einem	f. einer
g. einen	h. eines
i. der Sachen	j. die Sachen
k. den Sachen	l. die Sache

8. Die großen [a,b,c,d] sind oft [e,f,g,h] fähig, daß man sie nicht verstehen kann.

a. Geist	b. Geiste
c. Geister	d. Geistes
e. eine so paradoxe Aussage	f. einer so paradoxen Aussage
g. so paradoxe Aussagen	h. so paradoxen Aussagen

- -

STUDENT'S NAME

UNIT 10

I. *Underline the form or forms appropriate to each bracketed space.*
Translate.

1. Die Alte war [a,b,c,d] gekleidet und in der [e,f,g,h] Hand
hielt sie einen [i,j,k,l] Krückenstock.

a. schwarz	b. schwarzer
c. schwarze	d. schwarzen
e. rechte	f. rechten
g. rechter	h. rechtem
i. seltsamer	j. seltsamem
k. seltsamen	l. seltsameres

2. Den [a,b,c,d] Wind hielt ich für das Geschrei [e,f,g,h]
Tiere.

a. klagend	b. klagenden
c. klagende	d. klagendes
e. wilde	f. wilderer
g. wilder	h. wilden

3. Das [a,b,c,d] am [e,f,g,h] Vogel war die [i,j,k,l] Farbe
seiner Federn.

a. Auffallendstes	b. Auffallendster
c. Auffallendste	d. Auffallendsten
e. kleiner	f. kleinen
g. kleines	h. kleinem

207

i. prächtige   j. prächtiger
k. prächtig   l. prächtigen

4. Vor der [a,b,c,d] war ein [e,f,g,h] Felsen; sie kletterte
   hinauf und ihr [i,j,k,l] Hund kletterte mit hinauf.

   a. Alte   b. Alten
   c. Alter   d. Alt
   e. steiler   f. steile
   g. steil   h. steilen
   i. klein   j. kleinere
   k. kleiner   l. kleines

5. Ich lernte mich [a,b,c,d] in meine Arbeit finden.

   a. schnellste   b. aufs schnellste
   c. am schnellsten d. die schnellste

*II. Select the proper grammatical label, i.e., case, number, degree of
comparison (e.g. nominative singular positive, accusative plural
comparative, etc.), for each of the following phrases. If there are
two possibilities underline them both.*

Example: ein leiseres Husten

   a. nom. sing. pos.   b. gen. sing. comp.
   c. <u>nom. sing. comp</u>   d. gen. sing. pos.
   e. <u>acc. sing. comp.</u>

1. prächtigere Federn

   a. nom. sing. pos.   b. gen. pl. pos.
   c. acc. pl. comp.   d. nom. pl. comp.
   e. gen. sing. pos.

2. furchtbarer Felsen

   a. nom. sing. pos.   b. nom. sing. comp.
   c. gen. pl. comp.   d. gen. pl. pos.
   e. dat. sing. pos.

3. muntererer Hunde

    a. nom. sing. pos.   b. gen. pl. pos.
    c. gen. pl. comp.   d. gen. sing. comp.
    e. dat. sing. comp.

4. möglichen Farben

    a. dat. pl. pos.   b. acc. sing. pos.
    c. dat. pl. comp.   d. acc. pl. comp.
    e. gen. pl. pos.

5. benachbarter Gebirge

    a. gen. pl. pos.   b. gen. sing. pos.
    c. dat. sing. pos.   d. nom. sing. comp.
    e. nom. pl. comp.

STUDENT'S NAME

Appendix

ALPHABETICAL LIST OF STRONG AND IRREGULAR VERBS[1]

INFINITIVE	SIMPLE PAST	PRESENT SUBJUNCTIVE II	PAST PARTICIPLE	PRESENT INDICATIVE	IMPERATIVE
backen *bake*	buk *or* backte	büke *or* backte	gebacken	bäckst / bäckt	back(e)
befehlen *command*	befahl	beföhle	befohlen	befiehlst / befiehlt	befiehl
befleißen (sich) *apply one's self*	befliß	beflisse	beflissen	befleiß(es)t / befleißt	
beginnen *begin*	begann	begönne *or* begänne	begonnen		
beißen *bite*	biß	bisse	gebissen	beiß(es)t / beißt	
bergen *hide*	barg	bärge	geborgen	birgst / birgt	birg
bersten *burst*	barst	börste	ist geborsten	birst / birst	birst
bewegen[2] *induce*	bewog	bewöge	bewogen		
biegen *bend*	bog	böge	gebogen		
bieten *offer*	bot	böte	geboten		
binden *bind*	band	bände	gebunden		
bitten *beg, request*	bat	bäte	gebeten		
blasen *blow*	blies	bliese	geblasen	bläst	blas(e)

	Preterite	Pret. Subjunctive	Past Participle	Present 2nd/3rd sing.	Imperative
bleiben *remain*	blieb	bliebe	ist geblieben		
bleichen³ *bleach*	blich	bliche	ist geblichen		
braten *roast*	briet	briete	gebraten	brätst brät	brat(e)
brechen *break*	brach	bräche	gebrochen	brichst bricht	brich
brennen *burn*	brannte	brennte	gebrannt		
bringen *bring*	brachte	brächte	gebracht		
denken *think*	dachte	dächte	gedacht		
dingen *engage*	dang *or* dingte	dingte	gedungen *or* gedingt		
dreschen *thresh*	drosch	drösche	gedroschen	drisch(es)t drischt	drisch
dringen *press*	drang	dränge	gedrungen		
dünken *seem*	deuchte *or* dünkte	deuchte *or* dünkte	gedeucht *or* gedünkt	es dünkt *or* deucht mich *or* mir	
dürfen *be allowed*	durfte	dürfte	gedurft *or* dürfen	ich darf, du darfst, er darf	

¹ The present tense second and third persons singular and the singular imperative are given only if these forms exhibit a change in the stem vowel or some other peculiarity.

² **Bewegen** *to put in motion* or *to affect*, is weak: **er bewegte den Arm** *he moved his arm*; **er war tief bewegt** *he was deeply moved.*

³ **Bleichen** when transitive is weak. **Erbleichen** *to turn pale* is weak. **Er erbleichte** *He turned pale.* It is strong when it means *to die, to pale.* **Das Licht der Sterne ist erblichen.** *The starlight has grown dim.*

STRONG AND IRREGULAR VERBS—(*Continued*)

INFINITIVE	SIMPLE PAST	PRESENT SUBJUNCTIVE II	PAST PARTICIPLE	PRESENT INDICATIVE	IMPERATIVE
empfehlen *recommend*	empfahl	empföhle	empfohlen	empfiehlst empfiehlt	empfiehl
erlöschen[4] *go out* (*of a flame*)	erlosch	erlösche	ist erloschen	erlisch(es)t erlischt	erlisch
erschrecken[5] *become frightened*	erschrak	erschräke	ist erschrocken	erschrickst erschrickt	erschrick
essen *eat*	aß	äße	gegessen	issest (ißt) ißt	iß
fahren *drive*	fuhr	führe	ist gefahren	fährst fährt	fahr(e)
fallen *fall*	fiel	fiele	ist gefallen	fällst fällt	fall(e)
fangen *catch*	fing	finge	gefangen	fängst fängt	fang(e)
fechten *fight*	focht	föchte	gefochten	fichtst ficht	ficht
finden *find*	fand	fände	gefunden		
flechten *twine*	flocht	flöchte	geflochten	flichtst flicht	flicht
fliegen *fly*	flog	flöge	ist geflogen		

	Preterite	Subjunctive	Perfect	Present	Imperative
fliehen *flee*	floh	flöhe	ist geflohen		
fließen *flow*	floß	flösse	ist geflossen	fließ(es)t fließt	
fressen *devour*	fraß	fräße	gefressen	frißt frißt	friß
frieren *freeze*	fror	fröre	gefroren		
gären[6] *ferment*	gor	göre	gegoren		
gebären *bear*	gebar	gebäre	geboren	gebierst gebiert	gebier
geben *give*	gab	gäbe	gegeben	gibst gibt	gib
gedeihen *thrive*	gedieh	gediehe	ist gediehen		
gehen *go*	ging	ginge	ist gegangen		
gelingen *succeed*	gelang	gelänge	ist gelungen		
gelten *be worth*	galt	gölte	gegolten	giltst gilt	gilt
genesen *recover*	genas	genäse	ist genesen		
genießen *enjoy*	genoß	genösse	genossen	genieß(es)t genießt	
geschehen *happen*	geschah	geschähe	ist geschehen	es geschieht	

[4] Das Feuer ist erloschen. *The fire has gone out.* Löschen is a weak verb. **Das Feuer wurde gelöscht.** *The fire was extinguished.*

[5] The transitive erschrecken *to frighten* is weak. **Er hat mich erschreckt.** *He has frightened me.*

[6] Gären is weak when used figuratively. **Es gärte im Lande.** *The country was in a state of agitation.*

215

216

STRONG AND IRREGULAR VERBS—(Continued)

INFINITIVE	SIMPLE PAST	PRESENT SUBJUNCTIVE II	PAST PARTICIPLE	PRESENT INDICATIVE	IMPERATIVE
gewinnen *gain*	gewann	gewönne *or* gewänne	gewonnen		
gießen *pour*	goß	gösse	gegossen	gieß(es)t gießt	
gleichen *resemble*	glich	gliche	geglichen		
gleiten *glide*	glitt	glitte	ist geglitten		
glimmen *gleam*	glomm *or* glimmte	glömme *or* glimmte	geglommen *or* geglimmt		
graben *dig*	grub	grübe	gegraben	gräbst gräbt	grab(e)
greifen *seize*	griff	griffe	gegriffen		
haben *have*	hatte	hätte	gehabt	hast hat	habe
halten *hold*	hielt	hielte	gehalten	hältst hält	halt(e)
hangen⁷ *hang*	hing	hinge	gehangen	hängst hängt	häng(e)
hauen *hew*	hieb	hiebe	gehauen		
heben *lift*	hob	höbe	gehoben		

heißen *bid, be called*	hieß	hieße	geheißen	heiß(es)t heißt	
helfen *help*	half	hülfe	geholfen	hilfst hilft	hilf
kennen *know*	kannte	kennte	gekannt		
klimmen *climb*	klomm *or* klimmte	klömme *or* klimmte	ist geklommen *or* geklimmt		
klingen *sound*	klang	klänge	geklungen		
kneifen *pinch*	kniff	kniffe	gekniffen		
kommen *come*	kam	käme	ist gekommen		
können *can*	konnte	könnte	gekonnt *or* können	ich kann, du kannst, er kann	
kriechen *creep*	kroch	kröche	ist gekrochen		
küren *choose*	kor	köre	gekoren		
laden *load, invite*	lud	lüde	geladen	lädst (ladest) lädt (ladet)	lad(e)
lassen *let*	ließ	ließe	gelassen	lässest (läßt) läßt	laß
laufen *run*	lief	liefe	ist gelaufen	läufst läuft	lauf(e)
leiden *suffer*	litt	litte	gelitten		
leihen *lend*	lieh	liehe	geliehen		

[7] Instead of the present tense of **hangen** the forms of the weak verb **hängen** are usually employed. **Die Hüte hängen an der Wand.**

217

STRONG AND IRREGULAR VERBS—(*Continued*)

INFINITIVE	SIMPLE PAST	PRESENT SUBJUNCTIVE II	PAST PARTICIPLE	PRESENT INDICATIVE	IMPERATIVE
lesen *read*	las	läse	gelesen	lies(es)t liest	lies
liegen *lie*	lag	läge	gelegen		
lügen *lie*	log	löge	gelogen		
meiden *shun*	mied	miede	gemieden		
melken *milk*	molk *or* melkte	mölke *or* melkte	gemolken *or* gemelkt		
messen *measure*	maß	mäße	gemessen	missest (mißt) mißt	miß
mögen *like, may*	mochte	möchte	gemocht *or* mögen	ich mag, du magst, er mag	
müssen *must*	mußte	müßte	gemußt *or* müssen	ich muß, du mußt, er muß	
nehmen *take*	nahm	nähme	genommen	nimmst nimmt	nimm
nennen *name*	nannte	nennte	genannt		
pfeifen *whistle*	pfiff	pfiffe	gepfiffen		
pflegen[8] *attend to*	pflog	pflöge	gepflogen	pflegst pflegt	
preisen *praise*	pries	priese	gepriesen	preis(e)st preist	

Infinitive	Preterite	Subjunctive	Past Participle	Present	Imperative
quellen *gush*	quoll	quölle	ist gequollen	quillst / quillt	quill
raten *advise*	riet	riete	geraten	rätst / rät	rat(e)
reiben *rub*	rieb	riebe	gerieben		
reißen *tear*	riß	risse	gerissen	reiß(es)t / reißt	
reiten *ride (on horseback)*	ritt	ritte	ist geritten		
rennen *run*	rannte	rennte	ist gerannt		
riechen *smell*	roch	röche	gerochen		
ringen *wring, wrestle*	rang	ränge	gerungen		
rinnen *run*	rann	rönne *or* ränne	ist geronnen		
rufen *call*	rief	riefe	gerufen		
saufen *drink*	soff	söffe	gesoffen	säufst / säuft	sauf(e)
saugen *suck*	sog	söge	gesogen		
schaffen[9] *create*	schuf	schüfe	geschaffen		

[8] **Pflegen** is weak in the sense of *to nurse, to be accustomed.* It is strong only in a few expressions, as: **Rat pflegen** *to hold counsel;* **Umgang pflegen** *to associate with,* etc.

[9] **Im Anfang schuf Gott Himmel und Erde.** *In the beginning God created heaven and earth.* **Schaffen** is weak in phrases such as: **an einen Ort schaffen** *to convey to a place;* **Rat schaffen** *to find an expedient.* It is also weak in the compounds **abschaffen** *to abolish;* **fortschaffen** *to remove;* **herbeischaffen** *to procure;* etc.

STRONG AND IRREGULAR VERBS—(*Continued*)

INFINITIVE	SIMPLE PAST	PRESENT SUBJUNCTIVE II	PAST PARTICIPLE	PRESENT INDICATIVE	IMPERATIVE
scheiden *part*	schied	schiede	geschieden		
scheinen *appear*	schien	schiene	geschienen		
schelten *scold*	schalt	schölte	gescholten	schiltst schilt	schilt
scheren[10] *shear*	schor	schöre	geschoren	schierst (scherst) schiert (schert)	schier (scher(e))
schieben *shove*	schob	schöbe	geschoben		
schießen *shoot*	schoß	schösse	geschossen	schieß(es)t schießt	
schinden *flay*	schund	schünde	geschunden		
schlafen *sleep*	schlief	schliefe	geschlafen	schläfst schläft	schlaf(e)
schlagen *strike*	schlug	schlüge	geschlagen	schlägst schlägt	schlag(e)
schleichen *sneak*	schlich	schliche	ist geschlichen		
schleifen[11] *whet*	schliff	schliffe	geschliffen		
schließen *shut*	schloß	schlösse	geschlossen	schließ(es)t schließt	
schlingen *sling*	schlang	schlänge	geschlungen		
schmeißen *fling*	schmiß	schmisse	geschmissen	schmeiß(es)t schmeißt	

schmelzen melt	schmolz	schmölze	geschmolzen	schmilz(es)t schmilzt	schmilz
schnauben snort	schnob or schnaubte	schnöbe or schnaubte	geschnoben or geschnaubt		
schneiden cut	schnitt	schnitte	geschnitten		
schreiben write	schrieb	schriebe	geschrieben		
schreien cry	schrie	schriee	geschrien		
schreiten stride	schritt	schritte	ist geschritten		
schweigen be silent	schwieg	schwiege	geschwiegen		
schwellen[12] swell	schwoll	schwölle	ist geschwollen	schwillst schwillt	schwill
schwimmen swim	schwamm	schwömme or schwämme	ist geschwommen		
schwinden vanish	schwand	schwände or schwünde	ist geschwunden		
schwingen swing	schwang	schwänge	geschwungen		
schwören swear	schwur	schwüre	geschworen		
sehen see	sah	sähe	gesehen	siehst sieht	sieh
sein be	war	wäre	ist gewesen	ich bin, du bist, er ist	sei

[10] Scheren (= kümmern) to concern, to bother, is weak. Das scherte mich sehr wenig. That bothered me very little.

[11] Schleifen is weak when it means to drag, to raze: er schleifte den Sack mit sich he dragged the sack along with him; die Wälle wurden geschleift the walls were razed.

[12] The transitive schwellen is weak. Der Wind hat die Segel geschwellt. The wind has swelled the sails.

STRONG AND IRREGULAR VERBS—(Continued)

INFINITIVE	SIMPLE PAST	PRESENT SUBJUNCTIVE II	PAST PARTICIPLE	PRESENT INDICATIVE	IMPERATIVE
senden *send*	sandte *or* sendete	sendete	gesandt *or* gesendet		
sieden[13] *boil*	sott	sötte	gesotten		
singen *sing*	sang	sänge	gesungen		
sinken *sink*	sank	sänke	ist gesunken		
sinnen *think*	sann	sönne *or* sänne	gesonnen		
sitzen *sit*	saß	säße	gesessen	sitz(es)t / sitzt	
sollen *shall*	sollte	sollte	gesollt *or* sollen	ich soll, du sollst, er soll	
speien *spit*	spie	spiee	gespieen	spei(e)st / speit	spei
spinnen *spin*	spann	spönne *or* spänne	gesponnen		
spleißen *split*	spliß	splisse	gesplissen	spleiß(es)t / spleißt	
sprechen *speak*	sprach	spräche	gesprochen	sprichst / spricht	sprich

sprießen *sprout*	**sproß**	sprösse	ist gesprossen	sprieß(es)t / sprießt	
springen *spring*	**sprang**	spränge	ist gesprungen		
stechen *prick*	**stach**	stäche	gestochen	stichst / sticht	stich
stecken[14] *stick, be inserted*	**stak**	stäke	gesteckt		
stehen *stand*	**stand**	stände *or* stünde	gestanden		
stehlen *steal*	**stahl**	stöhle *or* stähle	gestohlen	stiehlst / stiehlt	stiehl
steigen *ascend*	**stieg**	stiege	ist gestiegen		
sterben *die*	**starb**	stürbe	ist gestorben	stirbst / stirbt	stirb
stieben *scatter*	**stob**	stöbe	ist gestoben		
stinken *stink*	**stank**	stänke	gestunken		
stoßen *push*	**stieß**	stieße	gestoßen	stöß(es)t / stößt	stoß(e)
streichen *stroke*	**strich**	striche	gestrichen		
streiten *contend*	**stritt**	stritte	gestritten		

[13] **Sieden** is weak when used intransitively. **Das Wasser siedete im Topfe.** *The water boiled in the pot.*
[14] The strong form **stak** is used only to mean *was inserted.* **Der Schlüssel stak noch im Schlüsselloch.** *The key was still in the keyhole.* The weak forms are transitive. **Er steckte den Schlüssel ins Schlüsselloch.** *He put the key in the keyhole.*

STRONG AND IRREGULAR VERBS—(Continued)

INFINITIVE	SIMPLE PAST	PRESENT SUBJUNCTIVE II	PAST PARTICIPLE	PRESENT INDICATIVE	IMPERATIVE
tragen *carry*	trug	trüge	getragen	trägst trägt	trag(e)
treffen *hit*	traf	träfe	getroffen	triffst trifft	triff
treiben *drive*	trieb	triebe	getrieben		
treten *step*	trat	träte	ist getreten	trittst tritt	tritt
triefen *drip*	troff *or* triefte	tröffe *or* triefte	ist getroffen *or* getrieft		
trinken *drink*	trank	tränke	getrunken		
trügen *deceive*	trog	tröge	getrogen		
tun *do*	tat	täte	getan	ich tu(e), du tust, er tut, wir tun, ihr tut, sie tun	tu(e)
verderben *spoil*	verdarb	verdürbe	verdorben	verdirbst verdirbt	verdirb
verdrießen *vex*	verdroß	verdrösse	verdrossen	verdrieß(es)t verdrießt	
vergessen *forget*	vergaß	vergäße	vergessen	vergissest (vergißt) vergißt	vergiß
verlieren *lose*	verlor	verlöre	verloren		

224

Infinitive	Preterite	Subjunctive	Past participle	Present (2nd/3rd sing.)	Imperative
wachsen *grow*	wuchs	wüchse	ist gewachsen	wächs(es)t / wächst	wachs(e)
waschen *wash*	wusch	wüsche	gewaschen	wäsch(e)st / wäscht	wasch(e)
weben[15] *weave*	wob *or* webte	wöbe *or* webte	gewoben *or* gewebt		
weichen *yield*	wich	wiche	ist gewichen		
weisen *show*	wies	wiese	gewiesen	weis(es)t / weist	
wenden *turn*	wandte *or* wendete	wendete	gewandt *or* gewendet		
werben *sue* (e.g. for someone's hand)	warb	würbe	geworben	wirbst / wirbt	wirb
werden *become*	wurde *or* ward	würde	geworden	wirst / wird	werde
werfen *throw*	warf	würfe	geworfen	wirfst / wirft	wirf
wiegen *or* wägen[16] *weigh*	wog	wöge	gewogen		
winden *wind*	wand	wände	gewunden		

[15] Strong only in elevated style. Usually weak.

[16] **Wägen** is used mainly in a figurative sense: **er wägt alle seine Worte** *he weighs all his words.* But: **der Kaufmann wiegt die Waren** *the merchant weighs the goods.* **Wiegen** is weak when it means *to rock, to cradle:* **sie wiegte das Kind in Schlaf** *she rocked the child to sleep.*

STRONG AND IRREGULAR VERBS—(Continued)

INFINITIVE	SIMPLE PAST	PRESENT SUBJUNCTIVE II	PAST PARTICIPLE	PRESENT INDICATIVE	IMPERATIVE
wissen *know*	wußte	wüßte	gewußt	ich weiß, du weißt, er weiß	wisse
wollen *will*	wollte	wollte	gewollt *or* wollen	ich will, du willst, er will	
zeihen *accuse*	zieh	ziehe	geziehen		
ziehen *draw*	zog	zöge	gezogen		
zwingen *force*	zwang	zwänge	gezwungen		

CONJUNCTIONS

CO-ORDINATING CONJUNCTIONS (take subject-verb order):

1. aber *however, but*
2. allein *however, nonetheless*
3. sondern *but rather*
4. und *and*
5. oder *or*
6. denn *for*
7. entweder . . . oder *either . . . or*
8. weder . . . noch *neither . . . nor*
9. sowohl . . . als auch *both . . . and*

SUBORDINATING CONJUNCTIONS (take transposed order):

1. als *when*
2. bevor *before*
3. bis *until*
4. da *as, since* (in a causal sense)
5. damit *in order that*
6. daß *so that, that*
7. ehe *before*
8. indem *while*
9. nachdem *after*
10. ob *whether*
11. obgleich *although*
12. obwohl *although*
13. seitdem *since* (in a temporal sense)
14. sobald *as soon as*
15. trotzdem (daß) *although, in spite of the fact that*
16. während *while*
17. wann *when* (interrogative)
18. weil *because, since*
19. wenn *if, when, whenever*
20. wie *how, as*
21. wo *where*

PREPOSITIONS

WITH ACCUSATIVE ONLY:

1. bis *until*
2. durch *through, by means of*
3. für *for, in behalf of*

4. gegen *against*
5. ohne *without*
6. um *about, around*
7. wider *against*

WITH DATIVE ONLY:

1. aus *out of*
2. außer *besides*
3. bei *near, with, at*
4. mit *with*
5. nach *after, towards*
6. nebst *together with*
7. samt *together with, including*
8. seit *since*
9. von *from, of*
10. zu *to*

WITH DATIVE OR ACCUSATIVE:

1. an *at, to*
2. auf *on, upon, to*
3. hinter *behind*
4. in *in, within*
5. neben *near, next to*
6. über *over, above*
7. unter *under, below*
8. vor *before*
9. zwischen *between*

WITH GENITIVE:

1. anstatt (statt) *instead of*
2. halber *in behalf of* (with preceding genitive)
3. kraft *by virtue of*
4. mittels *by means of*
5. trotz *in spite of*
6. um . . . willen *for the sake of*
7. ungeachtet *notwithstanding*
8. unweit *not far from*
9. vermöge *by virtue of*
10. während *during*
11. wegen *on account of*

12. außerhalb *outside of*
13. innerhalb *inside of*
14. oberhalb *above*
15. unterhalb *below*
16. diesseits *on this side of*
17. jenseits *on the other side of*

VERBS WITH DATIVE OBJECT

1. antworten *answer*
2. begegnen *encounter*
3. danken *thank*
4. drohen *threaten*
5. entfallen *drop*
6. entfliehen *escape*
7. entspringen *escape*
8. entwischen *escape*
9. erwidern *answer*
10. folgen *follow*
11. gefallen *please*
12. gehorchen *obey*
13. gehören *belong to*
14. helfen *help*
15. nachlaufen *run after*
16. nützen *benefit*
17. schaden *injure*
18. scheinen *seem*
19. schmeicheln *flatter*
20. trauen *trust*
21. zuhören *listen to*
22. zusehen *watch*

Vocabulary

Personal and possessive pronouns, numerals, and a few obvious cognates have been omitted. The numerals in parentheses indicate in which Unit the word is first used.

ab·brechen a o i (*s.* or *h.*) (4)
   break off, cease
der Abdruck –s ⸚e (9)   printed
   impression, copy, impression
der Abend –s –e (2)   evening
das Abendessen –s – (10)   evening meal
sich ab·geben a e i (7)   concern
   oneself, be busy
abgeneigt (1)   disinclined, un-
   willing
abgesetzt (8)   set off, interrupted,
   at intervals
ab·hängen i a (9)   depend
ab·kaufen (1)   buy from, pur-
   chase
ab·nehmen a o i (1)   take off,
   doff
ab·schließen o o (3)   bring to an
   end, close off
ab·schneiden i i (5)   cut off, am-
   putate
abseits (6)   to one side
ab·wägen o o (*also weak*) (9)
   weigh, estimate
ab·warten (9)   wait (for something to happen)
ab·wenden, wandte . . . ab, abge-
   wandt (6)   turn away, avert
ab·ziehen, zog . . . ab, abgezogen
   (*s.* or *h.*) (6)   depart, withdraw, remove
der Ackermann –s, die Ackerleute
   (2)   farmer
der Affe –n –n (5)   monkey
ähnlich (9)   similar
allein (3)   alone; however, but
allemal (3)   always
allenfalls (4)   in any case, at all
   events
allerschwerst (4)   most difficult
   of all
allgemein (7)   general, common,
   universal
allmählich (3)   gradual
alsdann (2)   then
also (1)   thus

alt (5)   old; die Alten (5)   the
   Ancients
das Alter –s – (2)   age
der Aluate –n –n (8)   aluate,
   howler monkey
die Amöbe –n (7)   amoeba
an·bieten o o (4)   offer
der Anblick –s –e (8)   the sight,
   view
ander (2)   other, second, following (*This word always appears
   in some inflected form*)
ändern (9)   change, make a difference
anders (4)   different, otherwise
aneinandergedrängt (8)   crowded
   up to one another
der Anfang –s ⸚e (3)   beginning
an·fangen i a ä (2)   begin, com-
   mence
an·gehen ging . . . an, angegangen
   (6)   affect, concern, interest
an·gehören (2)   belong to, be
   kin to
angewurzelt (1)   rooted to the
   spot
der Angriff –s –e (8)   attack
die Angst ⸚e (1)   fear, dread
an·haben, hatte . . . an, angehabt
   (2)   have on, wear
an·halten ie a ä (8)   persist, continue
an·landen (*s.*) (6)   land, go
   aground
an·langen (*s.*) (3)   arrive at
der Anlaß –es ⸚e (9)   occasion
an·legen (4)   aim
an·locken (8)   attract, entice
an·nehmen a o i (4)   take on,
   assume
an·passen (7)   accommodate, adjust
an·reden (1)   address
anschaulich (9)   immediately perceptible, directly visible, vivid
an·sehen a e ie (1)   look at
die Ansicht –en (8)   view, aspect
an·springen a u (10)   jump up
   against

der **Anstand** –s ̈e (9) dignity, decency, delay, objection

an·steigen ie ie (s.) (3) begin the ascent

der **Antrag** –s ̈e (1) proposition

an·treffen a o i (5) encounter, come upon

antworten (6) answer

an·weisen ie ie (10) instruct, direct, show

an·zeigen (2) indicate, report

an·zünden (8) light, kindle

der **Apfel** –s ̈ (7) apple

der **Aphorismus** – –ismen (5) aphorism

der **Apostel** –s – (5) apostle

die **Arbeit** –en (2) work, task

arbeiten (4) work

arm (4) poor

der **Arm** –s –e (6) arm

die **Art** –en (4) manner, fashion, way

auf·bauen (7) build up, construct

sich **auf·blähen** (10) puff up

aufeinander·folgen (s.) (8) follow one upon the other

auf·fallen i a ä (s.) (10) strike the attention, amaze

auf·fassen (9) grasp, comprehend

die **Auffassung** –en (9) conception, grasp

auf·heben o o (1) pick up

auf·hören (3) cease, stop

auf·lockern (8) loosen

die **Aufregung** –en (8) excitement

aufrichtig (5) upright, honest

auf·rufen ie u (2) summon, call the banns

auf·schließen o o (2) open, unlock

auf·spielen (5) strike up a tune, play

auf·steigen ie ie (s.) (6) rise up

auf·stehen, stand . . . auf, aufgestanden (s.) (10) arise

auf·stellen (7) set up, propose

auf·suchen (1) seek out

das **Auge** –s –n (1) eye

der **Augenblick** –s –e (3) moment

der **Augenzeuge** –n –n (9) eyewitness

aus·arbeiten (4) work out

aus·breiten (4) spread out, extend

die **Ausdauer** (3) perseverance, endurance

der **Ausdruck** –s ̈e (4) expression

aus·erlesen a e ie (7) select (This verb occurs almost exclusively in the past participle form.)

aus·fördern (2) take out, remove

aus·führen (3) carry out, perform

die **Ausführung** –en (3) execution, performance

der **Ausgang** –es ̈e (10) way out, exit

ausgetreten (9) well-trodden, well-worn

aus·lassen ie a ä (4) let off, let out

aus·sagen (9) assert, state

aus·sehen a e ie (4) look, appear, seem

das **Aussehen** –s (4) appearance

außen (4) outside

die **Außenwelt** –en (7) external world

äußer (3) outer, external (This word always appears in some inflected form)

äußerlich (7) external, on the outside

außerordentlich (10) unusual, extraordinary

aus·sprechen a o i (9) pronounce, enunciate

aus·suchen (10) seek out, choose

aus·wählen (7) pick out, select

autoptisch (9) autoptic, based on personal observation

bahnen (8) smoothe or prepare a way

234

banal (9) banal
bannen (1) charm, petrify
bar (3) bare, bereft, lacking
bauen (2) build
der Bauernbursch –en –en (7)
peasant lad
das Bauernmädel –s – or –s (7)
peasant girl
der Baum –s ∸e (7) tree
baumartig (8) treelike
bedecken (8) cover
bedeuten (5) mean, signify
bedingen (7) be the necessary
condition for, limit
die Bedingung –en (7) condition
die Beerdigung –en (2) burial
der Befehl –s –e (10) command,
order
befestigen (8) fasten, secure
die Befestigung –en (6) fortification
sich befinden a u (1) be, be
located, be found
begabt (3) gifted
sich begeben a e i (6) betake
oneself, go, turn to
beginnen a o (3) begin
begleiten (2) accompany
begrenzen (8) limit, bound, re-
strict
der Begriff –s –e (9) concept,
idea
behalten ie a ä (4) keep
behängen i a (also weak) (5) be-
deck, hang
die Behauptung –en (7) assertion
behindern (8) impede, hinder
beide (3) both
bei·kommen a o (s.) (4) occur to
beinahe (3) almost
bekannt (2) acquainted, known,
familiar
bekommen a o (1) receive, get
sich bekümmern (5) concern
oneself, trouble
belieben (1) deign, be so good
as to

das Belieben –s (9) the pleasure,
will, desire
beliebig (1) suitable
bellen (8) bark
das Bellen –s (10) the barking
bemerkbar (8) observable,
noticeable
bemerken (8) notice, observe
benachbart (10) neighboring,
nearby
benutzen (9) use, employ
beobachten (8) observe
berechnen (6) calculate
der Berg –s –e (3) hill, mountain
bergauf (3) uphill
bergen a o i (7) conceal, harbor
der Bergmann –s, Bergleute (2)
miner
die Bergmannskleidung –en (2)
miner's garb
das Bergwerk –s –e (2) mine
berichten (6) report, relate
beschreiben ie ie (4) describe
besehen a e ie (10) look at, examine
besichtigen (1) inspect, review
besitzen, besaß, besessen (7)
possess
besonder (3) especial, particular,
peculiar (This word always appears in an inflected form.)
die Besonderheit –en (4) peculiarity, uniqueness
beständig (5) constant
bestehen, bestand, bestanden (9)
consist of
die Bestie –n (8) beast
bestimmt (7) definite, certain
betrachten (1) contemplate, observe, watch
die Betrachtung –en (9) consideration
das Bett –es –en (10) bed
betteln (1) beg
der Bettelnde –n –n (1) beggar
der Beutel –s – (1) bag
bewegen (5) move
die Bewegung –en (2) motion,
movement

das **Bewegungswerkzeug** –s –e (7) instrument of movement
der **Beweis** –es –e (1) proof
bewohnen (5) inhabit
der **Bewohner** –s – (6) inhabitant
bewundernswürdig (1) admirable
die **Bewunderung** (1) admiration
biegen o o (6) bend
das **Bild** –s –er (4) picture
bilden (7) form, construct
die **Bildung** –en (7) formation
bisweilen (8) at times
die **Bitte** –n (1) request
bitten a e (4) request
bleiben ie ie (s.) (3) remain;
  stehen bleiben (3) stop;
  stecken bleiben (3) be stuck
der **Blick** –s –e (1) glance
blicken (6) gaze, look
der **Blitz** –es –e (5) lightning, flash
bloß (1) mere, simple, bare
die **Blume** –n (4) flower
die **Blütezeit** –en (3) time of blossoming
der **Boden** –s ⁼ (2) ground, surface, floor, bottom
bombardieren (2) bombard
böse (4) bad, wicked, evil
brauchen (4) use
die **Braut** ⁼e (2) fiancée, bride-to-be
der **Bräutigam** –s –e (2) fiancé, husband-to-be
breit (6) broad
die **Breite** –n (8) breadth, width
brennen, brannte, gebrannt (3) burn
der **Brief** –s –e (4) letter
bringen, brachte, gebracht (5) take
der **Brocken** –s – (4) fragment, scrap
das **Brot** –s –e (10) bread
der **Bruder** –s ⁼ (7) brother
der **Brüllaffe** –n –n (8) howler monkey
die **Brust** ⁼e (2) breast
das **Buch** –s ⁼er (5) book

der **Bücherphilosoph** –en –en (9) book philosopher
buntgefleckt (8) gaily spotted

das **Dach** –s ⁼er (6) roof
dagegen (3) on the other hand, on the contrary, against it
daher (3) for this reason
die **Dämmerung** –en (10) dusk, twilight
die **Dampfmaschine** –n (7) steam engine
danken (6) thank
das **Dasein** –s (7) existence
darum (3) for that reason, therefore
dauernd (7) constant, continuous
dazwischen (3) in between, at intervals
decken (6) cover
die **Demut** (1) humility, obsequiousness
denken, dachte, gedacht (1) think
dennoch (3) nonetheless
derb (4) substantial, solid, rude
dergleichen (4) the like
deucht (3rd sg. pres.) (3) seems;
  mir deucht thinks, as in methinks; or seems, as in meseems
deuten (6) point to, indicate
dicht (8) dense, close
dick (3) thick
das **Dickicht** –s –e (8) thicket
dickschuppig (8) thick-scaled
das **Dienstmädchen** –s – (7) servant-girl
dieserhalb (9) for this reason, on account of this
das **Ding** –s –e (4) thing; **guter Dinge** (4) in good spirits
der **Donner** –s – (8) thunder
doppelt (1) double
dringen a u (s.) (7) penetrate, press forward, press
drinnen (4) in it, inside
drüben (3) yonder
drucken (5) print

der **Duft** –s ⸚e (10)   haze, vapor
der **Dukaten** –s – (1)   ducat
dumm (4)   stupid
dumpf (8)   hollow, dull
dunkel (4)   dark, obscure
dünken, deuchte, gedeucht, dünkt
   or **deucht** (3)   seem, appear;
   mich dünkt (5)   methinks, meseems
dünn (3)   thin
die **Durchbildung** –en (7)   development
durchbrechen a o i (8)   break
   through
durchdringen a u (2)   penetrate,
   impregnate
durcheinander (7)   mixed up,
   pell-mell
durch·gehen, ging durch, durch-
   gegangen *(s.)* (3)   run away
durch·graben u a ä (2)   dig
   through
durchtoben (8)   rage through
dürr (8)   dry

eben (4)   precisely, just
ebensogut (3)   just as well
ebensoviel (7)   just as much
ebensowenig (7)   just as little
echt (1)   genuine
edel (1)   noble
ehelich (2)   matrimonial, in wed-
   lock
ehemalig (2)   former
eher (4)   sooner
das **Ei** –s –er (7)   egg
eigen (1)   one's own, peculiar
eigentlich (4)   actual, real
eigentümlich (8)   peculiar, indig-
   enous
ein·atmen (8)   breathe in
sich **ein·bilden** (5)   imagine, fancy
die **Einbildung** (4)   imagination
ein·brechen a o i (8)   break in
ein·dringen a u *(s.)* (7)   penetrate,
   enter into
einfach (7)   simple

sich **ein·finden a u** (9)   turn up,
   appear, occur
der **Einfluß** –es ⸚e (5)   influence
einförmig (8)   monotonous
ein·händigen (1)   hand in, turn in
einigemal (1)   a few times
ein·passen (7)   fit in, accommodate
ein·räumen (5)   concede, grant
ein·reißen i i (5)   tear down, wreck
ein·schlafen ie a ä *(s.)* (2)   go to
   sleep
ein·schlagen u a ä (1)   grasp hands
ein·stecken (1)   put in one's
   pocket
sich **ein·stellen** (9)   put in an appearance, arrive
ein·trocknen *(s.)* (3)   dry up,
   wither
ein·wenden, wandte ein, einge-
   wandt *(also weak)* (9)   object,
   protest
die **Einzelheit** –en (7)   individual
   thing, unit
einzeln (7)   single, alone, by itself
einzig (2)   only, single, unique
einzigartig (4)   unique, unpar-
   alleled
der **Eisbär** –en –en (7)   polar bear
der **Eisenvitriol** –s –e (2)   iron
   vitriol
die **Elle** –n (2)   ell, yard
empfangen i a ä (3)   receive, conceive
empfänglich (8)   receptive, sen-
   sitive
das **Ende** –s –n (2)   end
endlich (2)   finally
eng (10)   narrow
der **Engel** –s – (5)   angel
die **Entbehrung** –en (3)   depriva-
   tion, renunciation, self-denial
entdecken (10)   discover
entfernt (5)   distant, removed
entfremden (9)   estrange
sich **entgegen·biegen o o** (6)
   bend towards
entgegen·kommen a o *(s.)* (10)
   come towards

entgehen, entging, entgangen *(s.)*
(8) escape
enthalten ie a ä (7) contain
entlehnen (8) borrow from, take
from
entschuldigen (1) excuse
entspringen a u *(s.)* (9) arise,
spring from
entstehen, entstand, entstanden *(s.)*
(7) arise, originate
entwerfen a o i (3) plan
sich entwickeln (8) develop
der Entwurf –s ⸚e (3) plan,
sketch
sich entziehen, entzog, entzogen
(9) withdraw, retire
das Entzücken –s (2) delight,
rapture
erbitten a e (1) request
das Erdbeben –s– (2) earthquake
der Erdboden –s (7) surface of
the earth, soil
die Erde –n (7) earth
die Erdepoche –n (7) period in
the earth's history
erfahren u a ä (7) find out, experience, learn
die Erfahrung –en (8) experience
erfinden a u (5) discover, invent
erforschen (7) investigate scien-
tifically
erfreuen (10) make happy
ergeben a e i (6) yield, give as a
result
ergießen o o (8) pour out
ergreifen i i (2) seize, overpower
die Erhaltung (7) preservation,
maintenance
erheben o o (8) raise, elevate
erhitzen (4) heat, stimulate, excite
sich erholen (2) recover
die Erinnerung –en (5) recollection, reminiscence, memory
erkämpfen (3) gain by means of
a struggle
erkennen, erkannte, erkannt (2)
recognize

die Erkenntlichkeit (1) gratitude,
appreciation
erlauben (1) allow
die Erlaubnis (1) permission
erleben (7) experience, live
through
das Erlebnis, –ses, –se (7) experience
erleuchten (8) illuminate, en-
lighten
der Ernst –s (9) seriousness
erobern (2) conquer
erproben (1) try out
erraten ie a ä (5) guess correctly,
divine
erregen (9) excite, stimulate
der Ersatz –es (3) substitute, re-
placement
erscheinen ie ie *(s.)* (3) appear
erschöpfen (10) exhaust
erschrecken a o i *(s.)* (1) be
startled
erschrecken (8) startle, frighten
erspähen (1) spy out, catch
sight of
erst (2) first, only, not until
das Erstaunen –s (9) amazement
sich erstrecken (7) extend
ertönen (8) ring out, resound
erwachen *(s.)* (2) awake
erwecken (8) arouse, awaken
erwidern (1) reply
erzählen (5) tell, narrate
erzeugen (7) produce
ewig (3) eternal

fähig (9) capable, able
die Fähigkeit –en (7) capacity,
ability
die Fahrt –en (6) journey, trip
fallen ie a ä *(s.)* (1) fall, seem,
be; fallen lassen (4) let fall,
drop
falsch (5) false, incorrect
falten (1) fold
fangen i a ä (1) capture
die Farbe –n (10) color

fasanenartig (8) pheasantlike
der Faselhans – or –ens ⸚e (7)
    babbler, fool
fassen (9) seize, grasp
fast (4) almost
fatal (5) annoying, unfortunate
faul (4) lazy
das Faultier –s –e (8) sloth (ani-
    mal)
die Feder –n (4) pen, feather
der Fehler –s – (5) fault, failing
der Feierabend –s –e (3) evening
    rest, cessation of work, time off
feiern (8) celebrate
fein (8) fine, delicate
das Feld –s –er (10) field
der Feldherr –n –en (3) general
das Fell –s –e (7) fur
der Fels –ens –en (8) rock, cliff
der Felsblock –s ⸚e (8) rock,
    boulder
der Felsen –s – (10) cliff, boulder
das Fenster –s – (2) window
die Ferien (pl. only) (3) vacation
die Ferienarbeit –en (3) vacation
    work
fern (8) distant
die Ferne –n (8) distance, far-
    away place
fertig (4) ready, finished
fest·halten ie a ä (4) hold fast,
    hold firm
fest·nähen (1) sew fast, sew firm
die Feuchte (8) dampness, hu-
    midity
das Feuer –s – (8) fire
fieberkrank (8) ill with fever
finden a u (1) find
der Fischer –s – (6) fisherman
flach (6) flat, level
die Flamme –n (2) flame
der Fleck –s –e (6) spot
fließen o o (s.) (6) flow
flimmern (1) glimmer, flicker
die Flosse –n (7) fin
flöten (8) flute
die Flucht –en (8) flight, escape

der Flug –s ⸚e (3) flight (e.g. of
    a bird)
der Flügel –s – (7) wing
der Fluß –es ⸚e (6) river, brook
die Flußenge –en (8) narrow
    part of a river
das Flußnetz –es –e (8) river
    network
die Flut –en (6) stream, tide
die Folge –n (8) consequence,
    result
folgen (s.) (8) follow
die Forelle –n (7) trout
der Forscher –s – (7) scientific
    investigator, researcher
die Forst –en (8) forest
fort·schreiten i i (s.) (7) advance,
    move ahead
der Fortschritt –s –e (7) progress
fort·setzen (8) continue
fragen (6) ask
das Fragment –s –e (3) fragment
der Franziskanermönch –s –e (8)
    Franciscan monk
französisch (2) French
die Frau –en (6) woman, wife
frei (2) free, untrammeled
freilich (1) to be sure, indeed
fremd (9) foreign, unknown
fremdartig (10) odd, strange
die Freude –n (4) joy
freudig (2) joyful
freuen (10) make happy; sich
    freuen (8) rejoice
der Freund –s –e (1) friend
der Friede –ns (2) peace
frisch (10) fresh
fröhlich (3) joyous, happy
fromm (8) religious, upright,
    reverent
fühlen (10) feel
führen (1) lead, carry, guide,
    conduct, carry on
funkeln (8) sparkle
die Furcht (1) fear
furchtbar (10) terrible, awful
fürchten (8) fear; sich fürchten
    (8) be afraid
der Fuß –es ⸚e (1) foot

die **Gabe** –n (4) gift
gangbar (9) "going," popular
die **Gans** ⁓e (4) goose
ganz (1) complete, quite, very
das **Ganze** –n (7) whole, total
gar (3) at all; **gar nichts** (3) nothing at all; **wohl gar** (3) actually
der **Garten** –s ⁓ (7) garden
das **Gebäude** –s – (5) building, structure
geben a e i (4) give
das **Gebirge** –s – (8) mountain range
der **Gebirgspass** –es ⁓e (3) mountain pass
die **Gecko-Eidechse** –n (8) gecko lizard
der **Gedanke** –ns –n (4) thought, idea
der **Gedankengang** –s ⁓e (9) line of thought
geduldig (3) patient
gefallen ie a ä (4) please
das **Gefäß** –es –e (10) vessel, jar
das **Gefreunde** –s –e (2) friends of both sexes (an archaic collective)
die **Gegend** –en (3) area, region
der **Gegensatz** –es ⁓e (7) contrast, opposite
gegenseitig (7) reciprocal
der **Gegenstand** –s ⁓e (5) object, subject
das **Gegenteil** –s –e (7) opposite, contrary
gehen, ging, gegangen (s.) (1) go, walk; **es geht mir** (1) I feel
das **Geheul** –s (8) howling
das **Gehirn** –s –e (4) brain
gehören (7) belong
der **Geist** –s –er (3) mind, spirit, intellect
die **Geistesarbeit** –en (3) mental work
der **Geistesarbeiter** –s – (3) mental worker
geistig (3) intellectual, mental, spiritual

gelangen (s.) (9) arrive at, attain to
das **Geld** –es –er (4) money
das **Geldstück** –es –e (1) piece of money, coin
gelten a o i (1) be valid, be worth, be of avail, be meant for, pertain to
die **Gemäldeausstellung** –en (7) exhibition of paintings
gemein (5) common, ordinary
gemeinsam (7) together, in common
das **Gemüt** –s (2) mind, soul, feelings, personality, disposition
genießen o o (1) enjoy
genug (1) enough
der **Genuß** –es ⁓e (3) pleasure, gratification
das **Gepräge** –s – (9) stamp, mark
gerade (5) straight, precisely, just
das **Geräusch** –es –e (8) noise
das **Gerede** –s – (6) talking, gossip
das **Gesamterlebnis** –ses –se (7) total experience
das **Gesamtwerden** –s (7) total becoming, total process
der **Gesang** –s ⁓e (10) song
geschehen a e ie (s.) (4) happen
das **Geschehnis** –ses –se (7) event, happening
die **Geschichte** –n (1) story, history
der **Geschichtsforscher** –s – (9) research historian, researcher in history
der **Geschichtsschreiber** –s – (9) history writer, historian
die **Geschicklichkeit** (1) skill, deftness
das **Geschrei** –s –e (8) call, cry
gesellig (8) social, sociable
das **Gesetz** –es –e (5) law
das **Gesicht** –s –er (5) face

der **Gesichtszug** –s ⁝e (2) facial
feature
gespalten (8) split, cracked
die **Gestalt** –en (2) shape, figure
gestreift (8) striped
gewahr (10) aware
gewähren (8) grant
das **Gewehr** –s –e (5) gun
gewinnen a o (3) win, obtain
gewiß (1) certain
das **Gewitter** –s – (8) (thunder)
storm
sich **gewöhnen** (9) grow accustomed
gewöhnlich (3) usual, ordinary
der **Gipfel** –s – (8) top, peak
glänzen (10) gleam, shine
glatt (6) smooth
der **Glaube** –ens (6) belief, faith
glauben (4) believe
gleich (4) immediately right
away, directly; like, similar,
equal, same
gleichen i i (9) resemble
gleichsam (1) so to speak
gleichzeitig (8) simultaneous
das **Glied** –s –er (5) limb
die **Glocke** –n (6) bell
das **Glück** –s (1) happiness, good
fortune
glücklich (5) happy, fortunate
der **Glückssäckel** –s – (1) purse
of plenty
glühen (6) glow
die **Gnade** (6) grace, mercy
gnädig (1) gracious
das **Goldstück** –s –e (1) gold coin
der **Gott** –es ⁝er (2) god
das **Grab** –s ⁝er (2) grave
graben u a ä (2) dig
der **Grad** –s –e (8) degree
die **Granitmasse** –n (8) granite
mass
das **Gras** –es ⁝er (1) grass
grau (1) gray
graublau (6) grayish blue
grauen (10) grow gray

grimmig (4) furious, enraged
grob (1) coarse, rude
(das) **Grönland** –s (7) Greenland
groß (1) great, large, tall
die **Grube** –n (2) mine, pit
der **Grund** –s ⁝e (9) bottom,
ground
gutmütig (8) good natured

das **Haar** –s –e (6) hair
der **Hai** –s –e (7) shark
der **Hals** –es ⁝e (10) neck, throat
das **Halstuch** –s ⁝er (2) scarf,
neckerchief
halt (4) simply, just
haltbar (1) durable
halten ie a ä (5) hold, consider,
take for
hämmern (2) hammer
die **Hand** ⁝e (1) hand
der **Handarbeiter** –s – (3) manual
laborer
der **Handel** –s (1) deal, business,
trade
handeln (7) deal with, act, be
about
die **Hangematte** –n (8) hammock
hängen i a (1) hang
harmonieren (9) harmonize
harren (6) wait in expectation
häufig (3) often
das **Haupt** –s ⁝er (1) head
das **Hauptproblem** –s –e (7)
chief problem
das **Haus** –es ⁝er (2) house
die **Hausfrau** –en (7) mistress of
the house
heftig (2) violent, severe
heilen (5) heal, cure
heiß (7) hot
heißen ie ei (3) be called, be the
same as
helfen a o i (3) help
hell (4) bright
das **Hellblau** (10) light blue
die **Henne** –n (7) hen
herab·kommen a o (s.) (8) come
down

heran·kommen a o *(s.)* (6)   come
up to
herausgebogen (4)   hooked,
beaked, curved outward
heraus·graben u a ä (2)   dig out
heraus·sehen a e ie (5)   look out
herausziehen, zog heraus, heraus-
gezogen (1)   draw out
der Herbst –es –e (4)   autumn,
fall
die Herde –n (6)   herd
herein·brechen a o i *(s.)* (10)
break in
hernach (4)   afterwards
der Herr –n –en (1)   lord, gentleman, Sir
der Herrgott –s (4)   Good Lord,
Lord God
herrlich (1)   glorious
herrschen (8)   reign, prevail
herumgehen, ging . . . herum,
herumgegangen *(s.)* (1)   go
around
herzlich (4)   cordial, sincere
hessisch (7)   Hessian
heulen (8)   howl
heutig (5)   of today
die Hilfe (10)   aid, assistance
der Himmel –s – (5)   sky, heaven
hin und her (6)   back and forth
hinan·steigen ie ie *(s.)* (10)   ascend, go up
das Hindernis –ses –se (2)   hin-
drance, obstacle
hinein·blicken (6)   look into
hineinbringen, brachte hinein, hineingebracht (7)   bring into
hineingehen, ging hinein, hineingegangen *(s.)* (7)   go into
hinein·greifen i i (1)   put one's
hand into
hinein·gucken (5)   peer in, look
in
hingegen (9)   on the other hand
hin·halten ie a ä (1)   hold out,
extend
hin·schauen (6)   look over at
sich hin·setzen (9)   sit down
hinuntergehen, ging hinunter, hin-

untergegangen *(s.)* (10)   walk
down
hinunter·steigen ie ie *(s.)* (3)
climb down
hin·welken *(s.)* (2)   fade away,
wither
der Hirt –en –en (6)   herdsman
hoch (3)   high
die Hochzeit –en (2)   wedding
der Hochzeittag –s –e (2)   wedding day
die Hoffnung –en (10)   hope
die Höhe –n (8)   height
hold (2)   sweet, charming, lovely,
good, gentle, lovable
holen (2)   fetch, go and get
das Holz –es –er (7)   wood
hörbar (8)   audible
horchen (6)   listen
hören (4)   hear
horsten (8)   roost, nest
hüben (3)   from this side (*con-
trasted with* drüben from that
side *or* over there)
hübsch (2)   pretty
der Hügel –s – (10)   hill
das Huhn –s –er (4)   hen, chicken
der Hund –s –e (6)   dog
das Hundert –s –e (6)   hundred
husten (10)   cough
der Hut –s –e (1)   hat
die Hütte –n (6)   hut, shack
die Hymenoptera *(pl.)* (8)   hymenoptera (*order of insects*)

die Idee –n (3)   idea
immer (2)   always
innen (4)   inside
das Innere (8)   interior
die Insel –n (5)   island

das Jahr –s –e (2)   year
die Jahrmillion –en (7)   million
of years
jammern (8)   complain
jederzeit (9)   at any time, at
every time

jemand (2) somebody, anybody
jetzt (5) now
jugendlich (2) youthful
jung (2) young
der Jüngling -s -e (2) youth, young man

kaiserlich (6) imperial
der Kaffee -s (10) coffee
der Käfig -s -e (10) cage
kalt (7) cold
die Kammer -n (10) room, chamber
der Kampf -s ̈e (7) struggle
das Känguruh -s -s (7) kangaroo
die Kappe -n (10) cap, hood
das Kästlein -s - (2) little box
keck (3) bold, audacious
keineswegs (8) by no means
kennen, kannte, gekannt (2) know
keuchen (10) pant
die Kimmung -en (8) mirage
das Kind -s -er (5) child
die Kirche -n (2) church
der Kirchhof -s ̈e (2) churchyard
klagen (8) complain, lament, wail
der Klang -s ̈e (4) sound, timbre
das Klavier-Quatuor -s -s (4) piano quartet, i.e. music for three instruments plus piano
kleiden (10) dress
klein (5) small
das Kleinod -s -ien (1) jewel, gem, treasure
klettern (s.) (10) climb, clamber
klimatisch (7) climatic
klingen a u (5) sound
klopfen (2) knock
die Kluft ̈e (8) cleft, crack, gorge
klug (3) clever, intelligent, sensible
kommen a o (s.) (1) come
kompliziert (7) complicated
der König -s -e (6) king

können, konnte, gekonnt, kann (1) be able
der Kontrapunkt -s (4) counterpoint
kontrastieren (8) contrast
konventionell (9) conventional
der Kopf -s ̈e (1) head
der Körper -s - (5) body
kosten (3) cost
köstlich (3) precious, delicious
krachen (8) crash
die Kraft ̈e (8) power, strength, force
kräftig (7) powerful, strong
kraftlos (2) powerless, weak
der Kram -s (9) rubbish, trash
die Krankheit -en (3) illness, disease
der Krebs -es -e (8) crayfish
die Kreidezeit (7) Cretaceous Period
der Kreuzer -s - (4) Kreuzer (small coin)
der Krieg -s -e (2) war
kriegen (4) get, obtain
kritisch (9) critical
kritisieren (9) criticize
das Krokodil -s -e (8) crocodile
die Krücke -n (2) crutch
der Krückenstock -s ̈e (10) crooked walking stick
der Kuguar -s - (8) cougar, puma
kühn (1) bold, audacious
künftig (5) future, coming
die Kunst ̈e (5) art
der Künstler -s - (3) artist
kurz (1) short
kürzlich (6) recently
küssen (2) kiss
die Küste -n (6) coast

lächeln (2) smile
lachen (4) laugh
lächerlich (7) ridiculous
die Landessitte -n (8) custom of the country
die Landung -en (6) landing

lang, lange (3) long, for a long time
der Lärmen –s, *now usually* der Lärm –s (8) noise, din, uproar
lassen ie a ä (2) let, allow, have (something done)
das Laub –s (8) foliage
die Laubkrone –n (6) crown of foliage, tree-top
lauschen (8) listen
laut (8) loud
läuten (6) ring, toll
lauter (9) only, nothing but, pure
leben (5) live
das Leben –s (4) life
lebendig (3) living, vital
der Lebensgenuß –es ͏͏ͤe (3) joy of living
die Lebenssubstanz (7) life material, vital substance
das Lebewesen –s – (7) organism
das Leder –s (1) leather
ledern (1) of leather, leathern, leathery
die Lehre –n (7) teaching, theory
lehren (8) teach, instruct
der Leib –s –er (10) body
die Leiche –n (2) corpse
der Leichnam –s –e (2) corpse
leicht (4) easy, light
leiden, litt, gelitten (5) suffer, endure
leihen ie ie (5) lend, contribute
leise (1) soft, not loud
leiten (5) guide
lernen (5) learn
lesen a e ie (4) read
letzt (3) last; die letzteren (5) the latter
die Leute (*pl. only*) (3) people
das Licht –s –er (5) light
die Lichtmasse –n (8) mass of light
lieb (4) dear
die Liebe (2) love
lieben (2) love
lieb·gewinnen a o (3) become fond of

liebhaben, hatte lieb, liebgehabt (4) be fond of, love
das Lied –s –er (10) song
liegen a e (3) lie, be situated
die Linke –n (6) left hand
loben (4) praise
lösen (1) loosen, pry loose, dissolve
der Löwe –n –n (8) lion
die Lücke –n (3) gap
die Luft ͏͏ͤe (6) air
das Lüftchen –s – (8) breeze
der Luftkreis –es –e (8) atmosphere
der Lump –en –en (4) scoundrel, rogue

machen (1) make, do
die Macht ͏͏ͤe (2) might, power
mager (6) thin
der Magister –s – (5) master (of arts)
mahlen, mahlte, gemahlen (2) grind, mill
die Mahlzeit –en (4) meal
das Mal –s –e (1) time, occasion
der Malariaparasit –en –en (7) malaria parasite
mancherlei (4) many kinds of things
manchmal (4) often, sometimes
die Manier –en (4) manner, style
der Mann –s ͏͏ͤer (1) man, husband
das Manuskript –s –e (4) manuscript
das Märchen –s – (6) fairy tale
die Maschine –n (3) machine
mäßig (1) moderate, medium
matt (9) faint, feeble
das Meer –s –e (6) ocean, sea
mehr (2) more, further, again; nicht mehr (3) no longer
mehrere (8) several
meinen (9) think, mean
die Meinung –en (1) thought, opinion, intention, meaning

meist (3) most

sich melden (2) report, announce oneself

der Mensch –en –en (2) person, human being, man

menschlich (7) human

merken (1) notice

merkwürdig (8) remarkable

die Metallader –n (2) vein of metal

die Milch (10) milk

mischen (8) mingle

der Mißgriff –s –e (7) failure, mistake

die Mittagsstunde –en (8) noon hour

die Mitte –n (3) middle, midpoint

das Modewort –s ⸚er (9) popular word

mögen, mochte, gemocht, mag (1) like to; be able to (rare and archaic)

möglich (5) possible

die Möglichkeit –en (7) possibility

der Monat –s –e (8) month

mondhell (8) moonlit

die Mondhelle –n (8) brilliance of the moon

die Moosstelle –n (10) mossy spot

der Morgen –s – (2) morning

morgend (4) dawning, coming; die morgende Post (4) tomorrow's mail

müde (10) tired

die Mühe –n (3) toil, trouble, exertion

das Mühlrad –s ⸚er (1) millwheel

die Mühsal –e (3) toil, distress, affliction

der Müller –s – (2) miller

der Mund –s –e or ⸚er (8) mouth

munter (10) cheerful, awake, alert

die Münzsorte –n (9) kind of coins

murren (8) growl

müssen, mußte, gemußt, muß (1) have to

mustern (3) muster, inspect

die Mutter ⸚ (3) mother

das Nabelschwein –s –e (8) peccary

nach und nach (8) gradually

nacheinander (4) in sequence, one thing after the other

der Nachen –s – (8) boat, skiff

nachmals (9) afterward

die Nachstellung –en (8) pursuit

die Nacht ⸚e (4) night

der Nachtaffe –n –n (8) nocturnal monkey

nackt (8) naked

der Nagel –s ⸚ (3) nail

nah (1) near, close

die Nähe –n (1) vicinity

nähern (8) bring close; sich nähern (8) draw near, approach

namenlos (6) nameless

nämlich (4) that is, you see, to wit

die Nase –n (4) nose

die Natur –en (3) nature, personality, individual

das Naturgeschehen –s – (7) natural happening, process of nature

natürlich (4) natural

die Naturszene –n (8) scene of nature

die Naturwissenschaft –en (7) natural science

nebelartig (8) foglike

nebeneinander (7) side by side

neblig (10) foggy

nehmen a o i (4) take

nennen (3) name, call

das Nestlein –s – (2) little nest

neu (1) new; die Neuren (5) the Moderns

die Neugierde (6) curiosity, in-
  quisitiveness
die Neuzeit (7) modern era
nie (2) never
nieder·knieen (1) kneel down
nieder·schlagen u a ä (5) strike
  down, depress; sich nieder-
  schlagen (3) settle down
nieder·sinken a u (s.) (2) sink
  down, collapse
niemand (1) nobody
nimmer (2) never again
noch (2) still, yet; noch einmal
  (2) again
die Not ᵕe (3) distress, toil,
  trouble, tribulation
nur (1) only

die Oberfläche –n (6) surface
öffnen (8) open
die Öffnung –en (2) opening
das Ohr –s –en (6) ear
ordnen (3) order, arrange
die Ordnung –en (5) order, system
der Ort –s –e (2) place

das Paar –s –e (4) pair, couple;
  ein paar (4) a few, two or
  three
der Papagei –s –en (8) parrot
das Papier –s –e (4) paper
passen (1) suit, be fitting
die Pastete –n (4) pasty, pie
der Pecari –s –s (8) peccary
peinigen (10) torment
die Phantasie –n (3) fancy,
  power of imagination
der Pfad –s –e (9) path
der Pfarrer –s – (2) clergyman
der Pfeifenton –s ᵕe (8) piping
  sound
die Pflanze –n (7) plant
pflegen (6) be accustomed to
sich placken (4) torment oneself,
  pinch; sich placken und schinden (4) pinch and scrape
der Platz –es ᵕe (2) place, square
plaudern (4) chat, talk

plötzlich (10) suddenly
die Post (4) mail
prächtig (10) magnificent,
  splendid
prägen (9) mint, stamp, coin
das Präsent –s –e (4) gift,
  present
predigen (3) preach
der Preis –es –e (1) price, prize
der Priester –s – (2) priest,
  clergyman
der Punkt –s –e (4) point

der Rand –s ᵕer (2) edge
rasch (6) swift
der Räuber –s – (5) robber
der Raum –s ᵕe (7) space
recht (3) real, right, proper, correct
das Recht –s –e (2) right, law
die Rede –n (1) speech
reden (5) speak
die Regel –n (3) rule
sich regen (8) move, budge
der Regenguß –es ᵕe (8) shower
  of rain
reich (3) rich, abundant, full
das Reich –s –e (5) realm, nation
reichen (3) reach, go, extend
reif (3) mature, ripe
die Reihe (3) row, line
rein (3) pure, clean
die Reise –n (4) trip, journey
reisen (s.) (5) travel
der Reiz –es –e (7) stimulus
die Reizanzahl –en (7) number
  of stimuli
das Reptil –s –ien (7) reptile
restaurieren (1) repair, refurbish
das Resultat –s –e (3) result
richtig (7) right, correct
riesig (7) gigantic
die Rinde –n (8) bark
rings (6) round about
der Rock –s ᵕe (1) jacket, coat,
  skirt
das Roß –es –e (3) steed

rot (2) red; das Rot (10) the red; die Röte (8) the redness
das Ruder –s – (8) oar
rufen ie u (9) call
die Ruhe (8) rest, quiet
ruhen (5) rest
ruhig (8) quiet
rüsten (2) prepare

die Sache –n (4) thing, affair
der Säckel –s – (1) purse
säen (2) sow
sagen (1) say
der Salamander –s – (8) salamander, lizard
sammeln (3) collect, concentrate
der Sand –s (8) sand
die Sandfläche –n (8) sandy surface, level stretch of sand
das Sandkörnchen –s – (5) little grain of sand
sanft (6) soft, gentle
der Satz –es ⁻e (5) sentence, statement, proposition
sauer (3) sour, difficult, toilsome
das Säugetier –s –e (7) mammal
säumen (2) edge, hem, put a border on
die Schacht –en (2) shaft
das Schaf –s –e (6) sheep
schaffen u a (3) create, produce
die Schanze –n (6) breastwork, entrenchment
die Schar –en (8) crowd, large number
scharfgeladen (5) loaded with shot, i.e. not a blank
der Schatten –s – (1) shadow
schattenhaft (6) shadowlike
der Schauer –s – (10) shudder
scheinbar (8) apparent, seeming
scheinen ie ie (1) seem, appear, shine
der Scheitelpunkt –s –e (3) summit, dividing line
schenken (3) give, present
scherzen (6) jest, joke

die Schicht –en (2) layer, stratum, shift, day's work
das Schiff –s –e (6) ship
schildern (8) describe
schimmern (6) shimmer
schinden u u (4) flay; sich placken und schinden (4) pinch and scrape
der Schlaf –s (3) sleep
schlafen ie a ä (2) sleep
die Schlange –n (1) serpent
schlecht (5) bad, poor
schließlich (7) finally
der Schmaus –es ⁻e (4) feast, banquet
der Schmerz –es –en (2) grief, pain
der Schmied –s –e (2) smith
schmücken (6) adorn
schnarchen (8) snore, snort
schnarren (8) rasp, rattle
der Schnee –s (7) snow
schneiden, schnitt, geschnitten (2) cut, harvest
schnell (1) quick, rapid
die Schnelligkeit –en (5) speed
die Schnellkraft (3) elasticity
die Schnur ⁻e (1) cord
schön (1) beautiful, fine
die Schöne (2) beauty
die Schönheit –en (10) beauty
schöpferisch (3) creative, productive
schreiben ie ie (4) write, compose
der Schriftsteller –s – (5) writer
der Schritt –s –e (3) step, pace
die Schule –n (3) school, training
der Schutt –s (2) rubble
schütteln (6) shake
der Schutz –es (8) protection
schützen (6) protect
schwach (8) weak
die Schwäche –n (5) weakness
schwarz (2) black
schwarzseiden (2) of black silk
der Schwede –n –n (6) Swede
(das) Schweden (6) Sweden
schweigen ie ie (1) be silent

der Schweiß –es (3) sweat
schwer (2) difficult, heavy; **schwer fallen** (3) be difficult, cause trouble
schwierig (6) difficult
der Schwindel –s (1) the (fit of) dizziness
schwinden a u (s.) (7) vanish
schwirren (8) buzz
die See –n (6) sea
die Seele –n (4) soul, mind, feelings
segnen (2) bless, consecrate
sehen a e ie (1) see
sehnen (6) yearn, long
die Seite –n (7) side
selber (1) self
selbig (2) same
selbst (4) self *(intensive)*
das Selbstdenken –s (9) self-thinking, independent thinking
der Selbstdenker –s – (9) self-thinker, independent thinker
die Selbsterkenntnis (3) knowledge of self
die Selbstzucht (3) self-discipline
selig (3) blissful, blessed, dead
selten (3) rare, seldom
seltsam (1) odd, strange, unusual
senken (8) sink, bury
siebenjährig (2) seven-year
singen a u (10) sing
sinken a u (s.) (6) sink, set
der Sinn –s –e (1) sense, mind, meaning
das Sinnesorgan –s –e (7) sense organ
das Sinneswerkzeug –s –e (7) instrument of perception
sitzen, saß, gesessen (3) sit, be located
sogar (5) even, actually
sogleich (1) immediately
der Soldat –en –en (6) soldier
sollen, sollte, gesollt, soll (1) be supposed to, shall
das Sommergras –es ̈er (6) summer grass

die Sonne –n (1) sun
sonst (2) otherwise, in other respects
das Sonntagsgewand –s ̈er (2) the Sunday raiment, Sunday garment
die Sorge –n (1) care, worry
sorgen (7) care for, worry, provide
sorgfältig (8) careful
spanisch (2) Spanish
die Spannung –en (9) tension
spät (10) late
spazieren (s.) (4) stroll
der Spiegel –s – (5) mirror
die Spiegelung –en (8) reflection
das Spiel –s –e (3) game, play
spielen (4) play
spinnen a o (10) spin
sprechen a o i (4) speak
springen a u (s.) (6) spring, jump, leap
der Springfuß –es ̈e (7) leaping leg
die Spur –en (6) trace, track, spoor
der Staat –s –en (9) state, country
die Stadt ̈e (2) city
das Stadtmädchen –s – (7) city girl
der Standpunkt –s –e (9) point of view, standpoint
stark (1) strong, stout, powerful
die Stärke (5) strength, force
statt·finden a u (6) take place
staubartig (8) dustlike
stecken (1) stick, put, place
stecken, stak (or steckte), gesteckt (3) inhere, be present in, stick, be stuck or inserted
stehen, stand, gestanden (1) stand
stehlen a o ie (3) steal
steigen ie ie (s.) (6) ascend, rise
steigern (8) increase, intensify
steil (3) steep

das **Steingeröll** –s –e (8) stone, rubble, scree
die **Stelle** –n (1) place
sterben a o i (s.) (2) die
der **Stern** –s –e (4) star
stetig (6) constant
stets (8) always
stier (1) staring, rigid
der **Stil** –s –e (9) style
die **Stille** –n (8) stillness, silence
stillstehen, stand still, stillgestanden (6) stand still
die **Stimme** –n (1) voice
die **Stimmung** –en (9) mood, feeling
der **Stoff** –s –e (3) material, substance
stolz (10) proud
stören (4) disturb
der **Strauch** –s ⁼er (8) bush, shrub
das **Strauchwerk** –s (8) brush, undergrowth
streicheln (10) stroke
der **Streifen** –s – (2) strip
der **Streifritt** –s –e (6) scouting ride
streng (3) severe, strict
der **Strom** –s ⁼e (6) stream
strömen (6) stream, flow
stromweis (4) streaming, in torrents
das **Stüblein** –s – (2) little room
die **Stufenleiter** –n (7) graduated scale
stumpf (9) dull
die **Stunde** –n (2) hour
stürzen (6) rush, plunge
das **Subjekt** –s –e (5) subject, individual mind
suchen (8) seek, try
der **Sumpf** –s ⁼e (7) swamp, bog
sumsen (4) hum
das **Surrogat** –s –e (9) surrogate, substitute
süß (10) sweet

der **Süßwasserdelphin** –s –e (8) freshwater dolphin
der **Tag** –s –e (2) day, daylight
das **Tagebuch** –s ⁼er (8) diary
das **Tagewerk** –s (3) daily labor
das **Tal** –s ⁼er (10) valley
tanzen (5) dance
die **Tasche** –n (1) pocket, bag
die **Tat** –en (7) deed, act
tätig (8) active
die **Tatkraft** (3) energy
tausend (3) thousand
der **Teil** –s –e (3) part
teilen (2) divide, share
tief (1) deep, profound
das **Tier** –s –e (3) animal
die **Tierart** –en (7) animal species
das **Tiergeschrei** –s –e (8) animal scream
der **Tierkampf** –s ⁼e (8) struggle of animals
die **Tierwelt** –en (8) world of animals
der **Tisch** –es –e (10) table
der **Tod** –es (2) death
das **Tollhaus** –es ⁼er (5) madhouse
der **Ton** –s ⁼e (1) tone, sound, shade
topp (1) agreed, shake on it
tot (2) dead
das **Totenkleid** –s –er (2) burial costume
tragen u a ä (2) bear, carry
die **Träne** –n (2) tear
trauern (2) mourn
der **Traum** –s ⁼e (4) dream
träumen (3) dream
der **Träumer** –s – (7) dreamer
traurig (4) sad
treiben ie ie (6) drive
treten a e i (s.) (1) step
der **Trieb** –s –e (5) urge, drive
die **Tropen** (pl.) (8) tropics
das **Tropenaquarium** –s Tropenaquarien (7) tropical aquarium

tüchtig (1) strong, durable, excellent
tun, tat, getan (1) do
die Tür –en (10) door
turmartig (8) like a tower
der Turmknopf –s ⁼e (6) knob on a steeple

überall (3) everywhere
überein·stimmen (9) agree
überhaupt (4) in general, at all, generally speaking, as a class
überhören (4) hear over, grasp by hearing
überkommen (9) transferred, handed down
überlassen (1) turn over, surrender
überlaufen (10) run over, run through
überlegen (5) superior
der Übermut –s (6) arrogance, excessive pride
übersehen a e ie (4) survey, take in at a glance
überzeugen (5) convince
überzogen (10) covered
übrig (5) remaining
das Ufer –s – (8) shore, bank
umfangen i a ä (6) surround, embrace
umgeben a e i (8) surround, encircle
die Umgebung –en (7) surroundings
umgekehrt (3) reversed, on the contrary
umhüllen (8) envelop, wrap, veil
um·kehren (5) turn around, reverse
um·legen (2) put around (someone's neck)
der Umriß, Umrisses, Umrisse (8) outline
die Umschau (6) survey
umstehen, umstand, umstanden (2) stand about, surround
die Umwelt –en (7) surrounding world, environment

unaussprechlich (1) ineffable
unbedeutend (7) insignificant
unbegrenzt (3) unlimited
unbekannt (1) unknown
unbequem (5) uncomfortable
die Unbequemlichkeit –en (5) discomfort, inconvenience
unbeweglich (8) motionless
undurchdringlich (8) impenetrable
die Unendlichkeit (6) infinitude
unerforschlich (7) inscrutable, impenetrable
ungeahnt (3) unsuspected
ungefähr (1) approximately
ungemähnt (8) without a mane
ungewöhnlich (8) unusual
ungewohnt (8) unaccustomed
ungleich (9) unequal, very
das Unglück –s (2) misfortune
unglücklich (7) unhappy
unheimlich (7) uncanny, mysterious
das Universitätsstudium –s Universitätsstudien (3) university study
unlösbar (7) indissoluble, inextricable
unmittelbar (9) immediate, direct
die Unmittelbarkeit (9) immediacy, directness
unsicher (1) unsure
unterbrechen a o i (1) interrupt
unterdessen (2) meanwhile
unterirdisch (2) subterranean
die Untersuchung –en (6) investigation, examination
ununterbrochen (8) uninterrupted
unverändert (2) unchanged
unverhofft (2) unexpected
unverwest (2) undecayed, preserved
unwahrscheinlich (6) improbable
die Unzahl (8) excessively large number, very great number

der **Urgrund** –s (7) primal cause, original basis, first substance
die **Ursache** –n (4) cause
die **Ursprünglichkeit** (9) original force, primitiveness

die **Vakanz** –en (3) holiday, vacation
der **Vater** –s ⸚ (2) father
die **Vegetationsbedingung** –en (7) condition of vegetation
die **Verachtung** (1) contempt
verändern (1) change
verbergen a o i (8) conceal
die **Verbesserung** –en (5) improvement
sich **verbeugen** (1) bow
verbürgen (7) guarantee
verderblich (7) harmful, destructive
verdienen (5) deserve, merit
sich **verdoppeln** (3) be doubled
vereinigen (2) unite
verfolgen (8) pursue
der **Verfolger** –s – (7) pursuer
verfolgt (7) pursued
vergeblich (2) in vain, fruitless
vergehen, verging, vergangen (s.) (5) pass away
vergessen a e i (2) forget
vergleichen i i (9) compare
vergönnen (3) grant, accord
sich **verhalten** ie a ä (9) behave, be related
das **Verhältnis** –ses –se (5) relationship
verknüpfen (7) unite, tie together
verkündigen (8) proclaim
verlassen ie a ä (6) leave, abandon
verlegen (1) embarrassed
verlernen (9) unlearn, forget
verlieren o o (6) lose
verlobt (2) engaged, betrothed
vermeiden ie ie (1) avoid

vermögen, vermochte, vermocht, vermag (7) be able
vernehmbar (8) audible, perceptible
vernehmen a o i (6) perceive, hear
sich **verneigen** (1) bow
verrückt (1) crazy, touched
die **Verschanzungsarbeit** –en (6) work of fortification
verschieden (1) various, several, different
die **Verschiedenheit** –en (9) difference
verschlingen a u (6) devour, swallow up
verschwinden a u (s.) (7) disappear
versetzen (4) deal (said of blows)
versinken a u (s.) (6) sink down, submerge
versprechen a o i (3) promise
verstehen, verstand, verstanden (1) understand
verstümmeln (5) mutilate, cripple
versuchen (4) try
verzeihen ie ie (1) pardon
verzichten (8) renounce, forego
viel (3) much, many
vielfältig (7) complex, manifold
vielgestaltig (7) many-shaped, multiform
vielleicht (4) perhaps
vielmal (4) many times, often
vielseitig (7) many-sided
das **Vitriolwasser** (2) vitriolated water
der **Vogel** –s ⸚ (1) bird
das **Vogelgeschlecht** –s –er (8) race, family, or tribe of birds
das **Volk** –s ⸚er (5) people, nation
vollenden (3) complete
voller (1) full of
vollführen (3) complete, perform, execute
völlig (2) fully, completely
vollkommen (7) perfect, complete

der **Vollmond** –s –e (8) full moon
vorbei (2) past, over
das **Vorgefühl** –s –e (5) premonition
vorgehen, ging vor, vorgegangen (s.) (4) occur, go on, happen
vorhaben, hatte vor, vorgehabt, hat vor (5) be engaged upon
vorhanden (7) on hand, in existence, present
vorher (4) previously
vor·kommen a o (s.) (5) seem, appear, occur
die **Vorrichtung** –en (7) the arrangement, device, contrivance
vor·schreiten i i (s.) (3) advance, progress
sich **vor·stellen** (5) imagine, picture, represent, present
der **Vortrag** –s ⁼e (9) lecture, method of delivery
vorübergehen, ging vorüber, vorübergegangen (s.) (2) pass by
vorwärts (10) forward
die **Vorzeit** (7) prehistoric time
der **Vorzug** –s ⁼e (5) advantage, merit

die **Wache** –n (5) sentry, guard, watch
wachsen u a ä (s.) (7) grow
die **Wage** –n (5) scales, balance
wagen (1) venture, dare
wägen o o (or weak) (5) weigh
der **Wagen** –s – (4) carriage, coach
die **Wahl** –en (1) choice
wählen (7) choose, select
wahr (5) true, truthful
währen (6) last
die **Wahrheit** –en (6) the truth
wahrlich (4) truly
der **Wald** –s ⁼er (7) woods, forest
die **Waldeinsamkeit** (10) forest solitude
der **Wanderer** –s – (3) the traveler, hiker, wanderer

warten (7) wait
der **Waschbottich** –s –e (7) the washtub
das **Wasser** –s – (6) water
das **Wasserbecken** –s – (8) basin of water
das **Wassertier** –s –e (8) water animal
der **Wassertropfen** –s – (7) drop of water
die **Watsche** –n (4) blow, cuff
wechseln (6) change, alternate
die **Wechselwirkung** –en (7) interaction
wechselvoll (7) changing, alternating
wecken (10) waken, rouse
wedeln (10) wag
weder . . . noch (7) neither . . . nor
der **Weg** –s –e (8) road, path
weg·legen (2) put away
die **Wehmut** (2) sadness
das **Weib** –s –er (2) woman, wife
weich (6) soft, yielding
die **Weile** –n (6) while, lapse of time
der **Weinbecher** –s – (6) wine goblet, wine cup
weinen (2) weep
weise (5) wise
die **Weise** –n (1) the manner, way; **unbekannter Weise** (1) in an unknown way, i.e. without being introduced
die **Weisheit** (5) wisdom
weiß (6) white
weit (4) far, distant
weiter (3) on, further; **weiter nichts** (4) nothing more
weiter·geben a e i (7) transmit, pass on
weiter·träumen (3) dream on, continue to dream
die **Wellenbewegung** –en (8) wave motion

wellenförmig (8) wavelike, wavy, undulating
die **Welt** –en (5) world
das **Weltgebäude** –s (5) structure of the world, cosmos
wenig (5) little; **wenige** (6) few; **wenigstens** (5) at least
werfen a o i (1) throw, cast
das **Werk** –s –e (3) work
die **Werkstatt** ·· en (2) workshop
wert (4) worthy, worth
der **Wert** –s –e (5) worth, value
das **Wesen** –s – (5) being, creature
wesentlich (7) essential, chief, most important
wichtig (7) important
wiederholen (8) repeat
das **Wiedersehen** (2) the reunion
die **Wiese** –n (10) the meadow
wiewohl (9) although
die **Wildnis** –se (10) wilderness
wildwachsend (6) growing wild
der **Wille** –ns (4) will
die **Willenskraft** (3) strength of will
winken (6) beckon, gesture
winseln (8) whimper
wirklich (3) real, actual
die **Wirkung** –en (7) effect
der **Wirt** –s –e (7) host
die **Wirtschaft** –en (10) household
wissen, wußte, gewußt, weiß (2) know
das **Wissen** –s (3) knowledge
die **Woche** –n (4) week
wogen (8) billow
wohl (3) no doubt, probably, well
wohnen (2) dwell
wollen, wollte, gewollt, will (1) want to, profess, intend
die **Wonne** –n (3) bliss, ecstasy, delight
das **Wort** –s –e *or* ·· er (1) word; **Wörter** disconnected words

das **Wunder** –s – (3) miracle, wonder
wunderbar (7) wonderful
wundern (9) amaze; **sich wundern** (9) be amazed
wundersam (1) wondrous, marvelous
wünschen (6) wish
das **Wünschhütlein** –s – (1) wishing cap
der **Wurf** –s ·· e (3) cast, throw, projection

zaghaft (6) timid
zahllos (7) innumerable
zaudern (9) hesitate
das **Zeichen** –s – (6) sign, token
zeigen (10) show
die **Zeit** –en (1) time, age
die **Zeitlang** (7) span of time
zerstören (2) destroy
ziehen, zog, gezogen (s. and h.) (1) move, draw, pull
das **Ziel** –s –e (9) goal
ziemlich (4) fairly, rather
die **Zirkulation** (9) circulation, money, currency
der **Zoll** –s –e (8) inch
zubringen, brachte zu, zugebracht (8) spend, pass
die **Zudringlichkeit** (1) importunity, urgency
zufällig (8) accidental
zu·führen (9) take to
der **Zug** –s ·· e (8) train, procession
zugehen, ging zu, zugegangen (s.) (4) happen, take place
zugleich (5) at the same time
zu·greifen i i (7) grab, seize hold, pitch in
zugrunde·liegen a e (7) be at the basis of, underlie
zu·hören (8) listen to
zu·kommen a o (s.) (8) reach, come up to
zukünftig (5) future
zuletzt (1) finally

die **Zumutung** –en (1) presumption, expectation, imputation
zünden (3) kindle, spark, inflame, stir
zurück·kehren *(s.)* (2) return
zurück·kommen a o *(s.)* (2) come back
zurück·strahlen (8) shine back, be reflected
zu·rufen ie u (7) call to
zusammen (2) together
zusammen·fallen ie a ä *(s.)* (3) fall together, coincide
zusammengeschrumpft (2) shriveled, withered
der **Zusammenhang** –s ⸚e (7) connection
das **Zusammenklingen** –s (7) harmony, sounding together

zusammen·passen (7) fit together, be suited
zusammen·rollen (1) roll up
das **Zusammentreffen** –s (9) meeting, coincidence
zusammen·trödeln (9) accumulate *or* gather by begging, bargaining, and rummaging
zu·sehen a e ie (6) look on
zuweilen (6) at times
der **Zwang** –s (3) compulsion
zwar (2) to be sure
der **Zweifel** –s – (1) doubt
zweifeln (5) doubt
der **Zweig** –s –e (7) branch
zwingen a u (7) compel
zwischendurch (4) at intervals

Index

forms appear in all ten units of the book. Elements that cause less impediment to reading are considered only in the later units. This program of systematic review has a cumulative impact, as the student is constantly called on to examine new aspects of material that he has encountered in previous units.

The exercises stress comprehension of the reading passages as well as complete understanding of the material in the Grammatical Comments. At least one set of exercises in each unit can be detached from the book and handed to the instructor after it has been completed. A full vocabulary at the end of the book and brief biographical sketches that precede each reading passage add to the usefulness of *A Review of German.*

About the author

Sten G. Flygt received his B.A. and M.A. degrees from Wesleyan University and his Ph.D. from Northwestern University. Prior to his present position as Associate Professor of German at Vanderbilt University, he taught at Wesleyan, Northwestern, and Princeton universities and Reed and Muhlenberg colleges. Professor Flygt served for two years as University Specialist for the Office of Military Government in Bavaria. He has been the recipient of an American Council of Learned Societies Scholar's Award (1951-1952) and a John Simon Guggenheim Memorial Fellowship (1958-1959). Author and co-author of several books including a study of Friedrich Hebbel and *A Modern Course in German,* Professor Flygt is a frequent contributor of articles and reviews to professional journals. He holds memberships in the Modern Language Association of America, the American Association of Teachers of German, the Society for the Advancement of Scandinavian Studies, and the American Association of University Professors.